T. M Hopkins

Spots on the Sun

The plumb-line papers. Being a series of essays, or critical examinations of difficult passages of Scripture - together with a careful inquiry into certain dogmas of the church

T. M Hopkins

Spots on the Sun

The plumb-line papers. Being a series of essays, or critical examinations of difficult passages of Scripture - together with a careful inquiry into certain dogmas of the church

ISBN/EAN: 9783337815431

Printed in Europe, USA, Canada, Australia, Japan

Cover: Foto ©Lupo / pixelio.de

More available books at **www.hansebooks.com**

THIRD EDITION.

SPOTS

ON THE SUN;

OR,

THE PLUMB-LINE PAPERS.

BEING

A SERIES OF ESSAYS, OR CRITICAL EXAMINATIONS OF DIFFICULT PASSAGES OF SCRIPTURE; TOGETHER WITH A CAREFUL INQUIRY INTO CERTAIN DOGMAS OF THE CHURCH.

"And there appeared a great wonder in Heaven; a woman clothed with the sun, and the moon under her feet."—Rev. xii. 1.

"Thus he showed me; and behold, the Lord stood upon a wall, made by a plumb line; with a plumb-line in his hand."—Amos vii. 7-8.

BY REV. T. M. HOPKINS, A.M.,
GENEVA, N. Y.

AUBURN:
WILLIAM J. MOSES.
1862.

WM. J. MOSES, STEREOTYPER AND PRINTER, AUBURN, N. Y.

INDEX.

CONTENTS.

CHAPTER I.—SAMSON AND HIS FOXES.

(1) Preliminary, (2) Calmet's Hypothesis, (3) The Argument from שׁוּעָל shoo āl, (4) Mr. Calmet's Theory again, (5) Object in Presenting these Difficulties, (6) Belonging to the Interpolation, (7) Additional Absurdities, (8) Derivation of שׁוּעָל shoo-āl Considered, (9) Absurdities Again, (10) Derivation of שׁוּעָל shoo-āl again, (11) Argument from Examples, (12) The Absurdity too glaring, (13) Absurdities of the Translation, (1) Words are used in Different Senses, (15) An Appropriate Inquiry, (16) Argument from its Use Elsewhere, (17) Closing Considerations, (18) Closing the Argument.

CHAPTER II.—DIAL OF AHAZ.

(1) Preliminary considerations. (2) Barns' views, and that of Josephus, (3) Names of things, coeval with the things tney represent, (4) No term in the Hebrew for sun-dial, (5) The day could not have been prolonged, (6) Tradition of Herodotus considered, (7) The term *hour*, its import at that time, (8) Application to the matter in hand, (9) Question of a new version, (0) The law of speech, [11] Application of the argument, [2] No tradition or knowledge of a longer day, [13] The Admonition of the Prophet, [14] Harmony of Science with Revelation, [15] Another view possible [16] Final Hypothesis.

CHAPTER III.—THE RESURRECTION OF THE BODY.

[1] "Death destroys the Identity of the Body," [2] There is not Room for the Dead to stand on the Earth, if They should be raised.

CHAPTER IV.—THE GOD-LIKENESS IN MAN.

[1] Christ never once referred to the fall of man! [2] Difficulties of the Common Theory. [3] The Recitation, [4] The Law from Existing Relations, [5] The Law of Moral Influence, [6] Man a Spiritual Being. [7] Results of Moral Actions. [8] Influence of Moral Actions. [9] Man can foretell Moral Results, [10] Man's Capacity for Knowledge. [11] Sir Isaac Newton. [12] Man a Creator, [13] God, not the Author of Sin, [14] Recapitulation and Conclusion

CHAPTER V.—THE INEXORABLE ELEMENT IN LAW.

[1] Man cannot believe what he *knows* to be untrue, [2] "That which is not of Faith is Sin." [3] Illustration ; 4th power of 5, [4] Paul's Conscience Examined. [5] The Drop of Water upon the Hill, [6] Starts for the Ocean in a wrong Direction, [7] Influence of Adam's Sin upon his Posterity, [8] Sin the Act or Deed of a Sinner [9] This certainty a Moral One. [10] The *cause* of Sin not necessarily sinful, [11] Relation Determines the Character of Works.

(v)

CHAPTER VI.—DID CHRIST PREACH THE WHOLE GOSPEL?

[1] Importance of the Question, [2] The Author's Conversation with a Romish Priest, [3] Is it a Doctrine found in the Scriptures? [4] "All sinned in Adam," [5] The Manichean Theory, [6] The Old Testament knows nothing of this Doctrine, (7) One Sense, and only One, in which it was true, that Adam was our Federal Head and Representative, (8) That Man to be pitied whose Creed contains Doctrines not found in the Bible.

CHAPTER VII.—STOPPING OF THE SUN AND MOON.—PART I.

[1] Statement of the Question, [2] Indefensible Points to be Surrendered, [3] Theories in Defense of the Common Opinion, [4] Hypothesis ; the Rays of Light bent from their Natural Direction, [5] An Example of Poetic License, [6] Passage in Dispute a Quotation or Extract, [7] Notice of the Book of Jasher 2d Samuel, Chap. i. 18, (8) The whole passage is Hebrew Poetry, (9) Never to be another day like it! (10) And in what respect? (11) No Tradition of any such day in any part of the Earth, (12) Tradition of the Egyptian Priests, as noticed by Herodotus, (13) Relative Position of the Places named, irreconcilable with the Statements made, (14) Habakkuk iii. 11, Origin of the Passage in Jasher, (15) Further consideration of verse 15, "And Joshua returned," etc., (16) History of the Campaign, (17) Plain Statement of the Case, (18) "Book of Jasher" found, and in the Hands of the Writer.

CHAPTER VIII.—STOPPING OF THE SUN AND MOON.—PART II.

(1) Preliminary Remarks, (2) Methodist Quarterly, (3) Book of Jasher found ! (4) Passage including the disputed One, quoted in Extenso, (5) Choice between two Evils, (6) Character of the Book of Jasher inquired into, (7) Difficulties " Seen in the Distance," (8) Professor John's Kindness, (9) He graciously condescends to Argue both sides of the Question ! (10) " The Passage is Poetry," duly considered. (11) Professor J.'s Annihilation of Argument vi (12) The Writer is " in at the Death," (12) The *Professor's* Hypothesis, (13) This Passage not once mentioned in the Bible, unless Hab. iii. 11, be that Reference, (13) But this Passage must be Explained as the rest of the Chap., (14) Prof. J.'s Hypothesis Again, (15) Clinching and Closing the Argument.

INTRODUCTION.

THE subjects discussed in the following papers are among those which, in the course of some twenty or thirty years, have accumulated upon the author's study-table. They have been gathered in consequence, or as the fruit of his endeavor to obey the injunction, " prove all things ; hold fast that which is good."

The course adopted was essentially the following :—We aimed to have some one or more of those difficult questions or passages of scripture, which we occasionally found, where we could call it up in a moment, investigate it as far as possible, for the time, then lay it aside. Considerations for, and against, we carefully weighed and faithfully marked, till the question was regarded as effectually settled.

Our labors of this description, as any one may see, would be likely to be regarded by some as attacks upon Revelation. But if so, they are and have been for the purpose of exposing error, and if possible, expelling it from the word of God. This is a labor which we think none but the sincere friends of truth will attempt to perform. They who are its enemies, will select those passages, which they suppose are capable of being turned against the Bible, and will make the most of them for that purpose. The friends of truth may possibly fix upon the same ; but it will be to show, either that those passages can be so explained as to harmonize with the other portions of the word ; or, that they form no part of the Bible, and should consequently be cast out.

(vii)

And yet, as we are obliged to confess, both these classes are viewed with suspicion and distrust. The great mass of even those who receive the word with joy, are steadfastly and conscienciously opposed to any inquiry into a difficult passage ; they discover a restive, uneasy state of feeling, whenever an attempt is made, by either friend or foe, to inquire into any thing, or move any question which threatens to involve the truth of any part of the sacred record. We often hear them exclaim with a sigh,—'' when shall we be permitted to see these questions settled?'' In fact, if any difference may be seen, in the degree of unkind feeling with which these two classes are viewed, it has seemed to us,—*that* difference was in favor of those who were known as the enemies of the Bible. They appear to incur less displeasure, excite less suspicion, than they who meddle only with those passages which are obviously stumbling blocks in the way of anxious inquirers after truth ; and are sources of great perplexity to those who aim to understand what they read, that they may reduce it to practice.

This fact, unquestionably, is at the bottom of that reluctance which is felt by almost every intelligent friend of the Bible, to an investigation of those passages which seem to involve a difficulty. An individual may regard himself perfectly qualified for a most thorough investigation,—and as having all the requisite means for arriving at a safe result ; yet, when he looks forward to the probability, that he shall succeed only in awaking suspicion, in minds that were before at ease, and be compelled to reap for his reward no very kind feeling from them, he will most certainly pause.

Perhaps, his inquiries, in respect to a particular passage have been such as to lead him, not only to suspect, but to *know*—that it is spurious ; what shall he do ? He has before him the certainty, that if he shall breathe his suspicions aloud, he will be marked as a heretic and as such shunned if not despised. Men, that ought to know better, will attribute his labors to a desire to distinguish himself in some other way, rather than to that which is laudable and right   They will sssign almost any motive but the right one ; and he will be ranked among the enemies of religion, for the very reasons which should place him among its faithful and warm friends.

Suppose, for example, the famous passage, 1st John v. 7 is under consideration. He looks at it, at first, as *all* do, who have professed to believe in the Bible, with every requisite degree of allowance ; yet he thinks it may be well to examine it, as there are some suspicious marks about it and much is said against it. The great doctrine, which it seems to teach, is evidently found elsewhere in the Bible, if not in the very next verse ; which would seem to be a mark in its favor : yet as he is obliged to confess, the weight of authority, from MSS. is decidedly against it ; so much so, that if he should receive it, with all this weight in opposition, he would feel compelled to receive huge masses of similar productions, that are not only known to be spurious, but are obviously worthless, even if they were not. Many will call him by a very bad name, if he rejects it ; and others will laugh at his credulity, if he should receive it. Further investigations convince him that there is not one word to be said in its defense ; he must dismiss it from his mind, as being any portion of the word of God, let the con-sequences be what they will.

Forth step a thousand anxious inquirers and desire him to say, what would be the injury to any man, even if the passage were demonstrated to be spurious, and he should believe it ? " Is it not a less evil, a far less evil," they inquire, " to believe even what you cannot prove, than to unsettle the faith of thou-sands, by stating openly that you do not think it any part of the word of God ?"

These considerations apply with equal force to several *doc-trines* which are examined in the volume before us. In fact it will be said by many, that—one and the same course of argument—would bear upon both. That Plumb-line, which discloses the inaccuracies and errors of certain passages, will reveal most vital defects in some of the so-called doctrines of Revelation. The question now is, "what shall be done with them? *Can* it be any advantage to anybody, in any circum stances whatsoever, to believe what is false? to receive for truth, that which is undoubtedly error?"

We answer all these inquiries and reply to all these objections, by affirming, that the great majority of them originate in a radical want of faith, with those who bring them forward. The man that truly believes will not *care* how often the Plumb-line, even in the hand of an angel, is suspended by his "word or doctrine;" it will be matter of indifference with him, how often or how thoroughly you inquire into the foundation upon which he is building; knowing, that if he is on the sand, it will be discovered, and, that, being so, it cannot be known too soon : and if upon the rock, *that* will also be revealed. Truth, as everybody knows, never shrinks from investigation; has nothing to fear from it; but ardently desires, and honestly invites it.

"The more excellent way," therefore, would seem to be, to deal with error, when combined with truth, just as we would with poison if found in our food : let it be cast out; it is an element wholly evil by itself and can in no way subserve the purposes of truth. The plea for the sparing of the tares, was valid, because it was known, they were so combined with the wheat, or their roots so entwined with those of the good grain, that they could not *be* removed without destroying it. All which was true of that to which the parable was to be applied; but cannot be, in respect to the word of God.

There is, however, as we are obliged, in candor, to admit, some ground to fear, that the pruning-knife, once admitted, will not be satisfied with the removal of dead and worthless branches only*; but that a zeal to cleanse the word of God, except when guided by the wisdom which is from above, may result in the removal of a part which is truth, and which cannot well be spared.

To this we have only to reply. The preservation of the words of life is a matter which God has committed wholly to man ; he will work no *miracle* to do it. It was so before the flood ; it was so—to the days of Christ; it was so for centuries subsequent to that period. Men pretended to have seen visions, to have dreamed dreams, which were of God ; to have had revealed to them that which could only be learned from heaven ; they made a record of these things ; and during the first three or four centuries of the Christian period they labored to get them acknowledged as inspiration ; they sought to weave them in with the obvious and manifest oracles of God, so as to have them pass for such without scruple. And God employed his people in earnest and patient endeavors to weed them out : he gave them no inspiration to prepare them for that purpose : they needed none : they were only required to use that reason with which he had endowed them, in the way in which reasonable beings should always act, and the desired object was attained.

And then, when the scriptures were to be translated from their original languages into those of living men and living nations, the same reasoning powers were to be employed in this work, which were demanded in the other. It is a fact well known, that several successive translations from their original language, were made into the Latin, before a copy could be obtained which was sufficiently perfect to justify its being used as the word of God ; notwithstanding each separate translation was pronounced by an infallible Pope to be perfect! But the garnered wisdom of the church, despite its corruptions and ignorance, was sufficient to expose the errors and inconsistencies of each separate translation, and reject them with decisive firmness, till that same Pope, who had pronounced one perfect, would be obliged to review and correct his infallible decisions, suppress the whole, and order another!

That which seems to us, however, as the severest struggle in this direction, was nearer to our own day. When the scriptures were to be translated into the English language, the Adversary appeared to awake as from a dream, and gird himself for his last and most vigorous struggle. He seemed to have had no objections to their being translated into the Latin, or the Greek; but reserved all his hostility to oppose their translation into English. There was no *order* to the madness of those who felt and acted with him; they were opposed to a new translation, and they were in *favor* of it! Kings ordained that one should be made; then imprisoned and burnt their subjects for reading it! In every conceivable way, this bewilderment contributed to awaken an interest in the sacred writings till men had learned more of *revealed truth* than had been known before: and had become qualified to examine each separate translation, compare it with the original scriptures, amend and correct, till the appearance of our present authorized translation. In nothing is the hand of God more clearly seen, than in the existence of a work so worthy of acceptation, as in the case before us; yet, in the nature of things, it was not to be expected that every error should be avoided, every imperfection left out. Ther remain certain passages, which are as clearly spurious as is the silly story of "Bell and the Dragon." Nothing is more natural than such a result. A translation is the work of man; an uninspired man; it is but the decision of his judgment, as to the import of certain passages in another, and perhaps, long since *dead* language. Other men, in great numbers, are capable of reviewing his work, and of correcting it, long ages after he is dead. The translators of our present Bible, evidently regarded the term which they translate *day*, in the history of the creation, as expressive of the common period of 24 hours; but a generation has arisen to demonstrate that that cannot *be* its meaning, and they have used the original Hebrew itself, as the principal argument in the demonstration. No man, at the present day, who makes the slightest pretension to a knowledge of the Bible, will attempt to defend that which, a few years since, was regarded as the *only* correct one.

These are the facts in the case, whatever may be said, or felt in the way of complaint against those who aim at a more correct version of the scriptures. I know not that the evil will be in any measure diminished by this complaint, or by the summary process of *ignoring* difficult passages of scripture; a plan which seems to be rather the most popular at the present day. God evidently intends, that men shall be wise enough, and sufficiently pious too, before the millennium, to reject everything of error, and receive and practice all that is truth.

The day is doubtless at hand, when a struggle more vigorous and appalling than has been witnessed in the church since the days of Wickliffe, or Luther, will be found in that church again. It will not be upon the question of what are, or what are not, canonical books, or that of " the real presence ;" but it will be upon that which involves all others, which are of vital interest in our holy religion ; *the inspiration of those who wrote the Bible.* " Apostolic succession," the polity of the church, the doctrines of grace, and even that of the supremacy of the Pope, will be left undisturbed for the more vital and important ones, " what is inspiration ? who were inspired ? and are the scriptures their writings ?"

For such a period, it is wise for us to prepare ; as come it will, whether we are prepared for it or not ; and one important part of that preparation will evidently be, to ascertain those portions of the scriptures, if any, whose inspiration cannot be defended, that we may leave them to their fate. Many a hard battle has been fought over the passage we have named, (1 John, v. 7,) always resulting disastrously to the friends of truth, because they had undertaken to defend an error, with arguments that would support only truth The late discovery of the Sinaitic Codex, we think should be regarded as among the most marked providences of God ; since this, of itself, will settle many grave questions, in respect 'to revelation, which could not otherwise be adjusted.   Our aim, therefore, is, and has been only to remove the *cob-webs*, which monkish superstition and bigotry have suffered to accumulate in the windows of Revealed Truth ; and thus demonstrate that " the word of the Lord is right."   THE AUTHOR.

GENEVA, N. Y., MAY, 1861.

PLUMB-LINE.

CHAPTER I.

SAMSON AND HIS FOXES.

JUDGES XV. 4, 5.

" The crooked shall be made straight." Isaiah xl. 4.

WE are by no means sure, that we should regard it as anything more than a kind of justifiable sensitiveness, that some, who undoubtedly receive the scriptures as the word of God, feel uneasy and perhaps unkind, whenever an honest endeavor is put forth in a most careful manner, to reconcile apparent difficulties, remove objections, or set forth, in a given case, the evident impropriety of a particular translation. Assured that it is only a jealousy for the honor of God, and that jealousy a scriptural one, a zeal for the truth, or an unwillingness that the sacred record should be trifled with, we should not feel at liberty to complain; but in many cases this uneasiness arises from a far more objectionable trait of character. It is often the evidence of a consciousness, on the part of its possessor, that he has himself both seen and felt the difficulties in the case before him, but for reasons best known to himself, has not thought best to attempt their removal. Perhaps this sensitiveness, of which we are speaking, is only the development of a belief, that we are to receive everything, "doubting nothing," which has for a long time been received and stoutly defended by those who have been generally regarded as wise and great men. Possibly it may appear to us the offspring of an idea, that the translators of our present version were in some sense inspired, or were furnished with facilities for understanding the word which the men of the present generation, however learned, do not possess; in which case we should certainly feel justified in wholly dissenting, as well as in attempting to set forth "a more excellent way."

Some few years since, a writer in "The Biblical Repository" came out with the astounding assertion, that Joshua x. 12–15 was evidently *an interpolation;* and that, consequently, the so-called miracle of "the standing still of the sun and moon," at the command of Joshua, never took place.* His arguments in support of his position, as all were obliged to confess, were somewhat troublesome things;—but then, the thing had so long been believed, so long been regarded as a fact, such a multitude of astute and learned commentators had not only endeavored to explain and defend it, but it had become inwrought into many of our psalms and hymns, by those who were regarded as our very best writers of sacred poetry; it would not do at all to overthrow it, whatever might be the arguments against it. A man,

---

* See Biblical Repository for January 1845 and 1846.

to rise up at this late hour of the world and call it in question, was thought to be not only unsound in the faith, "but a setter forth of most pernicious heresy." The author was at once denominated "a young Neologist, a veritable disciple of the school of Strauss," or of some other errorist. By some he was desired to cease tinkering with the Bible. Others inquired as to the benefit, the probable good that would result from the discovery, even if it were so. Said one of the most moderate, "Suppose it is as you say, and as you seem to have proved, there certainly was no harm in believing it just as it reads; and the only result which we can see, as likely to arise from what you have done, is—to unsettle the faith of many an honest believer, strengthen the hands and encourage the hearts of those who do not believe, and who are waiting, with longing expectation, the appearance of something of that nature to subvert the faith of all who do believe."

Very similar, we fear, will be the reception which the following argument will meet with : Men have so long regarded the story of Samson and his foxes as the veritable record of an event that actually occurred, all understood and explained according to the letter in English, we have little reason to suppose they will feel greatly obliged, should we prove, as we probably shall, that the whole story is without even the shadow of a foundation, and that nothing remains to the friends of truth, but to submit as best we can to a revision of the record, a rejection of the translation, with all its dependencies. We are too well aware of the consequences in every similar case: those efforts which are put forth, however honestly or successfully, to undermine what has long been believed, by well-meaning and confiding people, are always regarded with distrust if not disfavor. Many will cling to a position which they have been induced to take, (though aware of serious difficulties,) whether that position regard religion or science, with a tenacity that would seem to make up for all deficiencies of proof, from a dread of the painful and unpleasant reflections which they will feel compelled to cast upon themselves, for having consented, though unwittingly, to say "therefore," without knowing wherefore: so that, whatever else may be assigned as our motive in sending forth the considerations which follow, it evidently is not, that we expect "the loaves and fishes" of human approbation in return.

The result, which we have reached, may not be as satisfactory to any as it is conclusive. Yet we have no apologies to make, and of course no steps to retrace. More than thirty years ago, on entering the ministry of Christ, we determined upon a single aim, one which we would pursue to the end, which was, to the full extent of our ability, whether natural or what we might acquire, to aim at *the overthrow of error*. And it affords us no little degree of satisfaction to reflect on what has been accomplished in the case before us. The sacred Record, *to us*, has been purged of a most pernicious and silly story, one that has no more existence in the original Hebrew than the Pontifical occupant of the so-called chair of St. Peter has in the New Testament. The day will come, and we believe it is not far distant, when they who read the Bible will know nothing of the story of Samson and his Foxes; except as they may learn it from the record of those things that have been cast out.

We seek not the smile of any one that is not in search
of truth ; we ask the companionship of those only who
are willing to go where truth leads.   In pursuit of this,
we endeavor to govern ourselves by the single principle
that as we pass along the line of narrative we carefully
weigh the statements that are made, the circumstances
that are introduced, comparing them one with another,
and all of them with the principles which are obviously
involved, till we become perfectly satisfied—either that
the statement is true, or that it is utterly false—whatever
may happen to long established and fondly cherished
notions; and it is scarcely necessary for us to add, we
can never be perfectly satisfied of either, so long as there
are statements made, the relevancy of which does not
appear, or whose relation to the main point we cannot
see.   Under such circumstances, he that would secure
a specific result, or come out with a foregone favorite
conclusion, has no alternative, but to push his way
through accumulating evidence that a vital error has
found its way into the very citadel of his subject, and
that the prospect of arriving at a conclusion which shall
harmonize with the truth, retires instead of approaches ;
an alternative we shall never knowingly adopt.

The passage which we propose to examine, as it stands
in the common version, is as follows :   " And Samson
went and caught three hundred foxes, and took fire brands,
and turned tail to tail, and put a fire-brand in the midst
between two tails.   And when he had set the brands on
fire, he let (them) go into the standing corn of the Philistines, and burned up both the shocks, and also the
standing corn, with the vineyards (and) olives." Judges
xv. 4-5.

The translation which we propose as the true one, and which at once relieves the passage from every embar-rassment, is the following: "And Samson went out and took three hundred bundles of grain, and took torches, and turning the sheaves tail to tail, applied his torches between the tails ; and having set the bundles on fire, he let it, (the fire,) go into the standing grain of the Philistines, and burned up both the shocks and the standing grain, together with their vineyards and olive yards."

We shall first consider the difficulties which are unde-niably inseparable from the common translation, just as they occur, on reading the passage, accompanying our thoughts with all needful suggestions in respect to " the more excellent way." They who have read it as it stands in our common Bibles, without being conscious of feeling any difficulty, either in respect to understand-ing it, or in fact believing it, will find no great difficulty, we think, in convicting themselves of having read it without much care or interest. A single glance at it would seem to be sufficient to convince any one, that a thorough knowledge of it would scarcely be required in order to lead to the discovery of several difficulties in the way of understanding it as it reads. Calmet, for exam-ple, is obliged to suppose, in the first place, that the animals employed by Samson were not foxes but jack-als. Next, that " the burners," as he calls them, or fire-brands, as they are called in the text, instead of being placed as they are said to have been between the tails of these animals, were fastened by a cord at a sufficient dis-tance from them, not to burn them. Again, he informs us, these burners were of a nature to hold fire long, so that the flames which were imparted to the standing grain of the Philistines, were, in his opinion, communicated by these burners, instead of the burning foxes, as would seem to be required by the version before us, and as was evidently supposed by the translators. He further supposes, these were a kind of *dead* burner, a contrivance to set fire to any material that will burn, but without giving light. It would seem, therefore, that Mr. Calmet supposes Samson must have carried his plans into execution during the night, in order to avoid giving alarm till the evil which he sought to do to the Philistines should be so far advanced as to render it impossible for them to prevent it.

The reader should allow himself to pause here for a single moment to contemplate the insurmountable difficulties which have already gathered around Mr. Calmet, in his attempt to explain or defend the common view of this subject. He has found it necessary at the very outset, to throw his foxes aside, and in their stead to introduce jackals. Why not say jackasses? wolves? lions? or, what would be somewhat nearer the borders of common sense, horses? There would be some approximation to reason or consistency in saying that he went and took that number of horses, and harnessed them for such an enterprise; but horses, wolves or jackals, are out of the question, since the Hebrew, as we shall soon see, allows of no such translation. And should the reader become dissatisfied with Mr. Calmet's hypothesis or theory, let him try his own. Let him sit down to the task of catching three hundred foxes either in Palestine or any where else, in the days of Samson or at any other period; and let him exercise his own ingenuity to the full extent of his power, in harnessing them up and getting them ready to execute his designs, and he will find difficulties multiplying upon him quite as fast as he will be able to take care of them.

Mr. C. evidently felt these, on reading the passage; and presuming that the translation was all right, he calmly and seriously endeavors to remove them before he can receive it. They are those which occur to him apparently, without an effort, or in spite of himself, *after* he has surmounted that which to us is the most serious one of all, viz.: where he got so many of these animals, and how were they obtained. Next, we come upon the awkward position in which he is said to have placed them, especially for running, for the common version evidently represents *the foxes* as being sent off into the grain which he would destroy; and it is the foxes which are set on fire, whether they may be made to burn or not. The Hebrew text as we shall see, relieves us in respect to this last difficulty: a consideration, however, which is not to be placed to the benefit of the present translation. Then we are followed by the absolute knowledge of the fact, that these animals, whether foxes or jackals, or indeed any other, if set on fire, are not likely to burn long nor communicate fire to standing grain if they should happen to run through it. The absolute impossibility of lodging a firebrand between the caudal extremities of two, as they are made to stand together, to say nothing of their running, is another fact which obviously would have troubled Samson quite as much as it has Mr. Calmet.

These, and a host like unto them, all of which are difficulties that to us are insurmountable without a miracle, have led us to search diligently for a solution which shall not only be a reasonable one, but one which shall in no sense or degree impeach the credibility of the sacred Record. But a miracle, in the case before us, is wholly out of the question. It is not in any sense, or by any one claimed. It is simply the record of gigantic, or almost superhuman efforts of one whose physical energies are made the subject of remark; and that too, without the slightest pretensions to anything like being aided by miraculous power. "Time was," says the Psalmist, "when a man was counted famous, accordingly as he had lifted up the axe against the thick trees;" the very period of which we are speaking, beyond all reasonable doubt. A time, when the single consideration of bodily strength was altogether the most important, inasmuch as it was by this that a man's influence, or importance among his fellow-men was determined more than by either his wisdom or his piety. "Goliath of Gath," was evidently regarded by his nation as more than the whole army of the Philistines besides. So Samson, who indeed seemed to possess almost superhuman strength, is regarded with deepest interest by his people, solely on account of his mighty physical powers. His deeds are all carefully recorded, at least, those which are of such a mighty character, while not a word is said of his piety or virtue in the sight of the Lord, any more than of his color or knowledge. In order to set forth his strength, it is recorded of him, that he suffered himself to be bound several times in a manner that would have been satisfactory to his deadliest enemies, but at each time, on being warned of approaching danger, his bonds are snapped asunder, as flax that parts at the touch of fire. When confined within the walls of his enemy's city, he finds no difficulty in removing with his own unaided arm, its gates, and thus making his escape. At another time he slays his thousands with the jaw-bone of an ass, and so manages when at the last his enemies have him in their power, as to avenge himself for the loss of his eyes; an evil which they had cruelly inflicted upon him.

But it may possibly be said, there are several instances in the record of his exploits, in which it is affirmed that "the spirit of the Lord was upon him;" and that, therefore, we are to regard the instance under consideration as the performance of a miracle. Not by any means, we reply, unless we are authorized to change the whole character of the record: the fact that it is *not* so affirmed in the case before us, should be regarded, we think, as an intimation on the part of God himself—that in the case of Samson's arrangements for setting fire to his enemies' fields he was *not* in any sense, under the superintendence or control of the Spirit of God. His plan from first to last is just that which an ordinary man would have chosen, whose object it was to destroy the hopes of his enemies by burning up their standing harvests; and the means which he employs must, of course, be like the general plan, those that would suggest themselves to an individual who was conscious that he must rely on his own unaided agency, rendered effective by the concealment of his purpose till his work was done. The sacred historian is careful to keep the man Samson before you, in the character of a most powerful man— powerful—in the natural strength of his corporeal energies; enough, at any time, for a thousand of the Philistines, who were his deadliest enemies. A great and irreparable injury he does them, but it is not by bringing fire from heaven to fall upon them and their harvests; it is by the subtlety of his contrivances, the secrecy of his plans, to destroy their supplies in a way and at a time which they could not prevent. The means which he employs, therefore, when properly understood, are such as need no special agency from God; no, not even in their procurement. All which we think will be made to appear in the considerations that follow.

Before we mention our central position, it is proper for us to inform the reader that, since the result must depend very much on the development of insurmountable difficulties, as seen in connection with the common translation, we purpose to return to a more extended and particular consideration of them, after such announcement; and, that in stating our position at this stage of the argument, we only yield to the consciousness or fear that the reader may have become impatient to know what foundation we propose to provide for him, after having removed that on which he he had previously rested. We bespeak, then, particular attention to the following considerations.

The word שׁוּעָל Shoo-ál, which is translated *fox*, in the passage under examination, is a regular and proper derivative of שָׁעַל Shâ-al, which signifies "to compress, squeeze together, bind;" and sustains to it, as its root, precisely the same relations that the word bundle, in English, does to the verb *bind*, from which it is derived. This point fairly made out, will of course settle the main question beyond dispute. יִלְכֹּד yil-chod, which is the word rendered "caught," where Samson is said to have "caught three hundred foxes," is properly translated "to seize, to take in haste, or by violence." לכד Lâ-châd, its root, signifies—"he caught, seized, laid hold of." But צדת Tzâ-dah, should have been used, as it signifies—"he purposed to kill, *he hunted*, or he *took*, as in hunting."

The difference between these two words, as will be readily seen, is precisely the same as that which is found between the words *take*, and *hunt:* and it would be just as proper to say, that Samson took three hundred wild-geese, without first having *caught* them, as to speak of it in the manner in which our translation does. The idea of hunting, or pursuing as in the chase, is not found in the verb לכד Lâ-chad, nor in any of its derivatives. It is proper to speak of a man's taking his horses and going about an enterprise, because, as is well-known, they are already in his possession. But, if these same animals were running wild in the desert, we should feel the necessity of saying something of his going out to hunt or catch them, as we do the fallow deer or the buffalo, upon our western prairies, before we spoke of his taking them with a view to harness them to his carriage.

These terms, thus defined, (and we challenge any man to produce another definition,) not only admit of, but actually demand the following paraphrase or translation, as the only one that will fully express the idea, or statement found in the Hebrew text: "Then went Samson and took three hundred bundles of grain, and turning each two of them tail to tail, he applied a lighted torch between them, thus setting them on fire: the fire he let go into the standing grain of the Philistines and burned it up, together with their vines and olive yards."

The italicized "*them*," which is found in our common English version only indicates what our translators *supposed* was the meaning of the passage. The idea was undoubtedly in their mind, that *the foxes*, all wrapped in flames, ran off into the grain. But there is no foundation whatever for it. The Hebrew, as I have before said, conveys the idea that it was *the fire* which ran off among the harvests of the Philistines and destroyed them: the three hundred bundles of grain, (or foxes, as the translation has it,) remain stationary: a consideration not to be lost sight of in determining the meaning of the passage. Our translators, of course, must be held responsible for the introduction of that word, as there is not the shadow of its existence in the original. Would that the type had never been set, to print it where it is!

It is, perhaps, sufficient for us to say, at this stage of the discussion, the above rendering is not only natural and easy, but evidently just what is required. It is one which instantly and effectually relieves the mind of the reader, as it makes the whole story consistent with itself. If his feelings are, or have been, like our own, when we have read the passage as it is in the authorized version, he will not fail to find great relief in the proposed translation.

We appeal to every honest, candid reader, if there is not something exceedingly repulsive and forbidding in the idea, that God's miraculous power or agency is called into requisition to furnish Samson with foxes, to enable him to destroy his enemies' grain? Especially is this so, when, as we shall see, the means thus furnished would require a greater miracle to make them effectual or successful, than it did at first to provide them. No man in his senses will suppose that Samson could have taken the number here designated *without* the miraculous assistance of God. The mildest term we can use, therefore, in respect to the supposition, that a special agency from God was furnished, is, that it is wholly unworthy of God, if not actually derogatory. Heathenism has suggested the propriety of attributing to the Deity only that which is worthy of him: and shall we allow ourselves in that which would shock heathenism?

But it may not be entirely proper or lawful for us to have those feelings of which we have spoken. Besides, there may be those who have them not; and they have as good right to their apathy on this subject, as we have to that which is opposed to it, call it what we may. "There is no disputing about taste;" and many may think it is only a matter of taste, that we are so shocked at the idea, that God's miraculous power should be represented as being sent on a mission of fox-hunting for any object whatsoever.

For the purpose, now, of showing the reader, that we are not alone in respect to the feelings which we have described, we will present the theory of a no less dispassionate critic than the one to whom we have already referred, Mr. Calmet; and it is a theory by which he endeavors to account for everything connected with the story, as well as remove the difficulties that are undeniably, if not universally felt. He does not seem to have thought of looking into the question of the correctness, or incorrectness, of the translation; but appears to take it for granted, that it is correct, very much as many others do. His endeavors to explain the passage, bring us, of course in sight of the difficulties which he obviously felt, as connected with the common understanding of it.

After administering a most fearful rebuke to all infidels in advance, for having made the passage (Judges xv. 4, 5), "the butt of ridicule," thus to prepare the way, as it would seem, for a more favorable reception of it and also his defence, he says, "The species of animals of which I have spoken, and which, as I suppose, was the kind employed by Samson, was very numerous in the east." In confirmation of this he gives us the testimony of Mr. Volney; who assures us, that "the wolf and the real fox are very rare: yet," he adds, "there is a prodigious quantity of the middle species, named shackal, (jackal) which, in Syria, is called 'waunwee,' from its howl. They go in droves, says Mr. Volney, and are concealed by hundreds in the gardens, among ruins, and in the tombs." — "We ask now," says Mr. Calmet, "where was the difficulty for Mr. Samson to procure three hundred of these animals; especially, *as the time* during which he had to provide them for his purpose, is not limited to a week or a month? Besides this," he adds—"it should be recollected, that Samson, at that time, sustained the highest office in the commonwealth, and, consequently, could be at no loss for persons to assist him in this singular enterprise."

This, we frankly confess, is getting over several most formidable difficulties in a very easy manner; since there is not the shadow of authority, either in the Bible or out of it, for changing fox into jackal, any more than for changing jackal into jackass. Our translators had just as good authority for translating שׁוּעָל shoo-âl —a lion, or a tiger, as for translating it as they did; and Mr. Calmet has just as much authority for substituting jackal for fox as he would have had for saying, that Samson went out and took three hundred *eagles*, and tying them tail to tail, lodged a fire-brand between and sent them forth on their errand of mischief. What would have become of this famous story, or rather *translation*, had not Mr. Calmet been favored with Mr. Volney's assurance of the "prodigious quantities of shackals" in Palestine? The difficulty attending the procuring so many foxes was so formidable—it seems—as to lead Mr. Calmet to inquire somewhat cautiously for a more feasible way. And here, Mr. Volney comes to his aid: suppose now this latter gentleman had said nothing about shackals, but instead—had mentioned, incidentally, that hyenas abounded there, (as in fact they do) why was not Mr. C. authorized to substitute these for his foxes? Or—to lay the blame where it belongs—why did not "our translators" affirm, that Samson caught that number of these animals instead of so many foxes? After dropping the rein upon the neck of imagination, it was as well, and would have been as wise to have elected an hypothesis which would have been somewhere within call of consistency.

But Mr. Calmet seems to think, that Samson has actually caught his "three hundred jackals, with which he designs to ruin the property of the oppressors of his country." He next proceeds to speak of the method by which he effected his purpose. Let us look at this.

"In considering the circumstances of this nature," he says, "there is some attention due to the nature and uses of the torches, or flambeaus, or lamps, employed by Samson in this procedure. And, perhaps, could we identify the nature or form of these, the story might be relieved from some of its uncouthness!" A somewhat remarkable concession, we should think, for a man to make while endeavoring to *defend* the story, (" uncouth" as it is) and make it appear that it is a portion of revealed truth! But let us hear him through. "They, i. e. these torches, flambeaus, lamps, or whatever else they were, are called לפִּידים Lâ-pa-dim, or more correctly, *lampadim;* as the Chaldee and Syriac write it: Whence the Greek Λαμπας—the English lamp. These lamps or burners," says Mr. Calmet, " were placed between two jackals, *whose tails were tied together!*" Where he obtains this information, he neither sees fit to inform us, nor does he tell us how these animals are going to *run* in this position—a circumstance we somewhat regret, as the Hebrew original evidently knows nothing about it. " Or, at least, there was a connection formed between them, *by a cord*," as he thinks, " since the reading of the LXX, in the Complutensian is to this effect." But, we reply, this Complutensian version, is only a translation, like our own, or like that of the French, or the Vulgate, and of no more authority. " Probably this cord was of a moderate length; and this burner, being tied in the middle of it, had something of the effect which we have seen among ourselves, when wanton malice has tied to the tail of a dog crackers, squibs, etc., which, being fired, wearied the poor animal to his den, where, supposing them still to burn, they might set all around them on fire."

But how is it, that Mr. Calmet has forgotten—it is " the standing grain of the Philistines," that Samson is said to have destroyed? not the dens of foxes or jackals,

nor anything around them : he adds, by way of explanation, as we suppose, "we know it is the nature of the
jackal to roam about dwellings and out-houses; this
would lead them to where the corn of the Philistines
was stored—which, being ignited, would communicate
conflagration in every direction. Besides, the fire, giving them pain, they would naturally fight each one his
associate, to which he was tied; this would keep them
among the corn longer than usual, and few pairs, thus
coupled, would agree to return to the same den as that
which they had formerly occupied among the mountains: so that nothing could be better adapted to produce a general conflagration, than this expedient of com-
bustion, communicated by these animals !"

We must therefore suppose, first, that these burners were
at some distance from the animals, so as not to burn
them; secondly, that they were of a nature to hold fire
long without being consumed; thirdly, that they were
either *dim*, in the manner of their burning, and in
respect to their light, or, perhaps, were not to be alarm-
ingly distinguished by their illumination. They might
burn *dead*, as we say ; so that their effect might be produced too late for the mischief to be prevented." (See
Calmet's Dictionary. Art. Fox. pp. 441 and 442.)

We cannot say that we admire anything in this extract,
save the evidence it furnishes us of untiring patience in
its author. It has not even the poor merit of what the
English would call *clever*. Still, all things considered,
and remembering, that *among* these, we place first and
foremost, the huge absurdity which it seeks to remove,
we ought, perhaps, to say something in its praise. In
his endeavors to remove the objections which Mr. O.

clearly saw would be made to it, his perseverance is worthy of a far better cause, if not our imitation. Our main object, however, in citing it at this tedious length, has been only to furnish the reader with an instructive view of the difficulties that will inevitably be felt by any man that reads it with attention, and, at the same time, regards it as the correct view of the passage.

That these difficulties may be seen in their true light, and that each may have its proper weight, so that every one who reads the passage may be led to appreciate the "more excellent way," whenever such way shall be found, we will briefly recapitulate them. They are such as every reader may see, as well as feel.

Its author finds it necessary, at the very outset, to multiply those animals, whether foxes or jackals, which Samson is said to have used on this occasion, beyond all credible example. No land, known to history, whether sacred or profane, could ever furnish them in sufficient abundance to meet the wants of the case before us, if we must understand this passage as it is translated. It is not enough for us to say that Mr. Calmet has drawn largely upon our forbearance or charity. Who can seriously entertain the belief, that any part of Palestine, either at that time or before, was sufficiently fruitful in these animals, to furnish such a gathering as is here represented? And what if it should be admitted, could a whole generation of men, though ever so well skilled in the chase, be supposed capable of securing the number which is given, in the time which must be reasonably allowed? Without a miracle, even beyond that which filled the net when cast on "the right side of the ship," it could not have been done ; and, as to a miracle in the case, that is out of the question.

Our next difficulty is that which regards *the time* for securing these animals. Mr. C. supposes, that Samson was not limited to even a week or a month. Is this the case ? How long .does the season of harvest, in Palestine or anywhere else, usually continue ? And, on the supposition that Samson with an army, or even a score of men, were engaged a month or a week in entrapping these foxes, where were the Philistines all this time, whose fields, ' already white for the harvest,' were standing and awaiting, not the reaper's sickle, but the irruption of those three hundred caged animals, their caudal extremities united by a cord, bearing - fire and devastation among their harvest-fields and vineyards ? Would they not be likely to make some inquiry as to the motive of those staunch hunters, as they were catching, caging and harnessing the foxes of the land ? Would they not desire to look into this matter ?

Is it not useless to multiply words here ? Is it not perfectly apparent, that whatever was Samson's device for destroying his enemies' corn, he is represented, by the sacred penman, as getting it in readiness with the utmost despatch ? His arrangements, like those of any other man, must not only be in secret, but must be made and executed in an hour. The word rendered ' *caught*,' as we have seen, implies ' to seize with haste, to lay hold of,' as if what is to be done must be performed with despatch, or never. This stands upon the very face of the record.

It was not our purpose to review Mr. Calmet, so much as it was to employ his pen—together with his device for removing difficulties here, to set forth that cloud of them, with which the question before us is beset, on the ground that the passage under examination be translated as in our authorized version. In doing this, we are persuaded we do but reiterate those which every man has felt who has read the passage with care; especially, if he be one who receives the Bible as the word of God, and sincerely desires that others should do so too. We shall, therefore, conclude what we have to say on this branch of our subject, by just noticing *the contrivances*, as we must call them, which Mr. C. is obliged to introduce to make Samson carry out his plan. Let not the reader's patience fail; we are almost through with this *chapter on difficulties*.

Mr. Calmet is compelled, (after consenting to call the " shoo-a-lim," foxes, or jackals,) in obedience both to the Hebrew and the translation, to place them as therein stated, *tail to tail*, with a brand of fire between the tails of each two; all for the purpose of enabling them to run and spread their mischief far and wide. However, it is not meant that we should hold the Hebrew original responsible for any thing but *the position* which is named; at this juncture it occurs to him, that they must be *fastened* there, or they will do little towards conveying fire or water anywhere. To meet this difficulty, as we have seen, it is proposed to fasten them there with a cord. Accordingly, he proceeds to complete his arrangement by proposing to fasten the caudal extremities of his extemporized team; allowing the cord—as a kind of traces—to drag at a considerable length behind, that he may fasten thereto, his torch of fire.

This is absolutely too bad. We cannot believe that an

intelligent reader will allow himself to waste his time, and wear out his patience in perusing such grave folly as· this; especially when assured that the Hebrew original knows nothing of either Mr. Calmet's contrivance or his difficulties. All this machinery of team, and gear, and tackle,—is rendered useless by the single consideration, that no coupling, or fastening of the materials, (whatever these were) which were employed—is found necessary, in the scriptures as they were written by the finger of God. Nothing of any cord to confine each two together, so that they may either run or burn;—not a word of their *being* confined there, in any way or for any purpose; nothing of their running, at all,—either to scatter fire or to get back to their dens, when the mischief for which they had been caught and harnessed had been accomplished! No; all is calm and easy with the descendant of Abraham, who reads this passage in his mother tongue. Troubles there are and difficulties—without number; but all are to be credited to the translation of the single term שׁוּעָל Shoo-âl. Let this be rendered as it evidently should be, *bundle*, or sheaf,—and the way is at once clear, the meaning of the whole passage easy and perfectly natural. But retain the translation, " fox or jackal," and you may have as many theories or contrivances as men have time to invent;—yet none will help you to escape from trouble.

If then *we* should be convicted of a little impatience here, we are ready to plead guilty to the charge. It is no very easy task, nor agreeable—to meet those entanglements, one after another, and feel at the same time, that they are the legitimate deductions of a position which we have been obliged to assume, and which we of course must now defend, right or wrong. The conviction gains as we proceed, that *the theory* is wrong; the great central term, that on whose meaning every thing depends, has evidently been perverted, and we feel bound to look into it. We cannot but admire the patience, the manliness of him who honestly seeks to remove these difficulties; especially, since we are to view him as laboring to establish a theory which he evidently regards as the correct one. We may yield him all due credit for honesty of intention and purity of purpose; though compelled to say, we think his labors worse than lost to the cause which he sincerely desires to sustain,— simply because he supposes it to be true.

Let no man, therefore, accuse us of having created these difficulties, with a view to make out a case, as it is said, and thus provide for ourselves a man of straw, that we may enjoy the luxury of demolishing it; nor in fact, for any other purpose, but the defence of truth. We could have compelled ourselves to read this passage all our days, as others have done, without pausing to inquire into it, or ascertain whether its apparent absurdities could be removed. This would have been a very easy and a very agreeable course, perhaps; (as many are able to testify;) but the propriety and wisdom of it we very much question. Not till we had read it a great many times, and each time with increasing dissatisfaction or pain, did we return, seriously to inquire into the cause of that uneasiness which we were conscious of feeling. It continued to force itself upon us till we felt bound to know its origin. We claim no merit, whatever, for having concluded to turn and see if these absurdities could be removed, for we were compelled to do it.

They forced themselves upon us, whenever we attempted to read the passage ; and more especially, when we were engaged in reflecting upon it; till we were obliged to admit that, as it stands before us, in our authorized version, they cannot be denied, neither concealed.

Nor does it serve to diminish their number or their magnitude for us patiently to reflect upon them, or seriously to aim at their removal. On the contrary, they are every way increased, by even the most honest effort to dispose of them. For confirmation of this, we refer the reader to his own experience in this matter. Is it not a fact, that while he has been engaged in contemplating them, many, very many, that he never before thought of, have made their appearance, rising into notice, in vastly greater numbers than those that have been satisfactorily disposed of? Now, let him set himself to account for it as he will, he will find them still gathering in dark masses along his path-way, however far or carefully he may push his investigations. In fact, let him dispose of them as he will, the conviction that they are the legitimate offspring of the translation which he is endeavoring to defend, will gather strength, till he will utterly refuse to regard it as worthy of his confidence, and will resolutely set himself to find one which is not subversive of the truth of God.

But, as our present argument is confessedly auxiliary to that which we regard as unanswerable, and as this last will be more sure to be thus regarded after that which consists in a faithful exhibition of the absurdities involved, has been fully presented, we shall proceed still further to speak of them. On the part of Samson, there is not the shadow of a higher agency than that which he can and does put forth, even thought of. As he is represented in the passage before us, he goes about the business of catching his " three hundred foxes," just as if it were one of the easiest things in nature. In *this* respect, the translation is fortunately faithful to the original. There, all is easy and natural. Samson does not seem to *dream* of any need of assistance from either God or man, any more than if he were going to take so many pieces of wood to set on fire. Not so when he leaned against the pillars, in the temple of his enemies, for the purpose of tasting a last revenge: though, with returning hair, his great strength had fully returned, he felt the need of special assistance from God, in the undertaking before him; and he accordingly asked that assistance. The Prophet, also, when he had erected the altar of the Lord, prepared the wood and made ready the sacrifice, knowing, as he did, that he must now rely on special aid from above, lifts his soul to God in search of it. But nothing of the kind in the case before us. Nothing but the bold assertion, that he went and caught the vast number which we have so many times named, and made a disposal of them that he would have been scarcely able to have done had they been so many domestic fowls! His aim is sufficiently obvious from the first; it is to destroy the unreaped grain of the Philistines. What more natural, now, than for us to look at the means which he proposes to employ? These, as they are represented in the translation before us, in spite of long and fondly cherished regard for the volume of Inspiration where they are found, we are obliged to say, with Mr. Calmet, are most uncouth and absurd. The thing to be done is perfectly feasible, provided the appropriate *means* be used ; but when these, of themselves, are altogether unnatural and inappropriate, there is an absolute *refusal*, or that which approaches it, in the mind of every intelligent reader, at least it is so with us, to receive it as truth. We cannot believe it, whatever may be said in its defence. No animal, like either of those named, can be easily set on fire; and if once made to burn, it would not continue to do so longer than a man might hold his hand in the fire. This is so evident to every intelligent reader, that it will not require argument. Neither will it help the matter in the least, to place two of the animals together, especially, in the position in which they are said to have been placed, should you wish them to run or even stand still. One will burn as freely and as long as a dozen, and no number of them more than ten seconds. In fact, it looks to us as if God had suffered the translator to involve himself, and his work in this manner, on purpose to jar open the eyes of the reader, to see the absurdity of the translation.

No, we cannot believe it, as we have several times affirmed ; nor can we help this, our unbelief. Our inability results from the very nature and constitution of the mind. We cannot believe a thing by simply determining to believe it. The Romanist cannot believe that he eats the body or drinks the blood of the Lord Jesus Christ, when he takes the Eucharist, though he may have sworn to it on every altar in Christendom. He knows that he does not believe it, and, that he cannot. His mind is so constituted by Him who made all minds, that though heaven or hell be suspended on it, (as indeed they are, in his creed,) yet, he cannot believe it; he knows better. Every man, whatever be his qualifications, in other respects, if he is sufficiently intelligent to be a responsible being, *knows better.*

Precisely so with respect to the passage before us. As it stands in our common Bibles we cannot believe it, whatever be the consequences. We receive the history of the ten plagues; the passage of the Red Sea; the giving of the law; the supply of Israel with food and water in the wilderness; together with all the well-authenticated miracles recorded in the scriptures. But we come to that which is under review, and we involuntarily pause. Men may pity us for our inability in this matter, as we presume many do; but we should most deeply and sincerely pity ourselves, were we *able* to receive as truth, the translation of Judges xv. 4, 5, which is found in our common Bibles.

Possibly, however, we have indulged in this train of remark quite as long as is profitable. That there are difficulties in and about the passage, others have felt as well as we. The question now "comes up in order," *can they be removed?* Can any man meet them fairly, sustaining his positions so as to make it certain that conviction shall close the argument! This, of course, can be better determined by what may follow.

It is, perhaps, well enough for us to remark in passing, that had we not found what we regard 'the more excellent way,' and one with which every reader who is blessed with a moderate share of common sense, we think, will be satisfied, we should not have felt at liberty to make even a suggestion, unfavorable to the reputation of the present translation. Since the inspiration of the Sacred Record has been established by such sound and cogent reasons, and that too, for so long a period; and since, from the nature of the case, this record has so long been made a subject of deepest study, and of most careful investigation; and, moreover, since the combined intelligence of the world, as well as its piety and virtue, have so long regarded the Bible with profoundest veneration and esteem, no man is justified in calling a passage in question, unless he is ready with soundest reasons, to set forth the better way; and not only to set it forth, but to sustain it with the most satisfactory and irrefragable proofs.

We are confident every candid reader, as well as every friend of truth, will not only desire to see the solution of the difficulty before us, but will be glad to find, that the sanctity and integrity of the sacred volume have remained untouched. Such have undoubtedly felt a degree of relief already, at the suggestions which have been made, in respect to the true import of the word upon which the whole meaning of the passage turns. That relief will be greatly increased, when it shall be made to appear, that the remaining terms as well as statements, fall naturally and easily into their appropriate place; conveying a clear and accurate meaning, without extravagance or anything at which the mind of the most intelligent reader will revolt. No drafts will be made upon his common sense; no subtile or even apparent invitation addressed to him, asking that he should enlarge the measure of his credulity, or move one foot in the way which is not plainly the way of truth.

The difficulties connected with the understanding of the passage, as we have already remarked, all vanish as soon as the meaning of the single term, שׁוּעָל shoo-al, be changed from that which designates a beast, whether fox or jackal, to that of a bundle or sheaf of grain. The passage, in all its remaining parts, is not only harmonious, but perfectly consistent with itself. It will then represent Samson as taking his three hundred bundles of grain, turning them, in accordance with the statements of the Bible, both Hebrew and English, "*tail to tail*," or as the husbandmen would express it, "turning the butt ends of the sheaves together," *so that the fire may kindle as speedily as possible*, he applies his torch, firebrand, or whatever he used to set the sheaves on fire; the fire spreads among the standing grain of the Philistines, burns up their harvests, as well as their vineyards and olive-trees.

On the supposition that these "three hundred" incendiaries are, as they are called, "foxes, or jackals," and Samson be permitted, as Mr. Calmet suggests, to harness them up, two and two, side by side, instead of tail to tail, "as *the law* directs," with a lamp or burner duly trimmed and lighted, it is beyond all controversy, that he is furnished with a great many more than he actually stands in need of for doing all the mischief in the way of setting fire to his enemies' harvests that his heart can desire; i. e. *if it be possible, in any sense, or to any extent, to set fire in this way*—a single couple, or a dozen of them, are as good as three hundred. But, *I* have yet to see the first element of adaptedness in this arrangement to anything like the purpose for which it is said to have been contrived. As we have already said, neither of the animals named can be made to burn, more than a sheep; or, were it possible to *kindle* the fire, it would not—could not be made to continue so long as it requires to write the word. Then again, what sane man, undertaking such a matter as this, will think of placing his animals in that position, whether to run or burn? From first to last of this examination, therefore, I have been tortured with the feeling, that I have been examining, as Mr. Calmet himself has called it, a most uncouth and awkward contrivance; one which nothing but insanity could have devised, or the miraculous power of God make efficacious: for, if a miracle be allowed, in the procuring of these animals, there must be another and a far more powerful one to carry it into effect. Nay; to the very consummation of it, it must be a work entirely out of—or one side of—the ordinary course of nature.

But, suppose you succeed in getting a couple of these animals, call them what you please—you get them together, harnessed, as the hypothesis requires; you start them on their errand of mischief. They will set fires enough, in running a mile, (if they will set any) to consume a whole plantation. What use will you have for the one hundred and forty-nine span, standing harnessed and idle? The fires are set, the flames are spreading in every direction; the work is done. At the extent, ten such contrivances are sufficient to set fire to the whole country of the Philistines, provided it be at a time when the harvests are in a situation to ignite—and when they are not, three are as good as three hundred.

"But," exclaims the reader, "let us have something like order or consistency in the argument. Just now, our attention was called, for the second time, to the consideration of that term, on the true import of which the whole argument turns—and now we are upon the old topic of 'difficulties' again." Yes, truly; and this is to be properly *the* topic, in some form or other, to the end: our object is to set forth, whether in order or not, some of the numerous difficulties or absurdities with which the translation is beset; and we promise to observe quite as much order in exhibiting them, as they did in intro. ducing themselves to our notice. Many a time, when reading the scriptures, whether before the family, or "in the great congregation," have we felt mortified and ashamed of such a profoundly silly story, for us to "read, mark and inwardly digest," with a view to our obtaining spiritual instruction from it! Wherefore we determined long ago, to set forth, in all their true ugliness, the absurdities with which this matter is surrounded.

To do this, we beg the reader to observe how readily these difficulties are disposed of, by the single change which we have recommended: call these "three hundred" agencies, which Samson employed, so many bundles of grain, and they are all needed, every one of them: he may start on his enterprise at as early an hour as the circumstances will permit—may seize the first two that come to his hand, turning them "tail to tail," as the word of truth directs; let him by all means apply his torch just where the same record prescribes, between these sheaves which are now turned butt ends together; (for it will be useless to attempt to set them on fire when the *heads* are in juxtaposition :) and let it be understood, that *the fire*, not the sheaves, runs off into the standing grain of the Philistines and consumes it.

It will be idle to maintain that the translators took essentially the same view of this subject. They evidently supposed, that it was these שׁוּעָלִים shoo-a-lim, "foxes," as they called them, that immediately, upon being set on fire, ran off into the grain and among the vineyards. Hence, the word "*them*," in italics, found in their translation. It is scarcely necessary to say, that this word is not found in the Hebrew scriptures. But to this fact we shall refer again.

Samson, having set fire to the first two bundles, hurries forward and seizes two more, turning them in like manner, that they may be made to burn as rapidly as possible; which he continues to repeat till he has used the whole number specified. In fact, every intelligent reader, who is at all acquainted with the subject under consideration, or—if he will bestow one moment of cool and deliberate reflection upon it, will see the necessity of Samson's doing just as he is represented to have done, *on the supposition that his agencies for kindling fire among his enemies' grain*, BE SHEAVES OF WHEAT, *instead of animals;* he must turn them "tail to tail," or as the husbandman would say, 'he must place *the butt ends* of the sheaves together if he would have them burn;' for it is well known, as we have already said, that a sheaf of wheat cannot be set on fire, at the end which contains "the full corn in the ear." At any rate, bundles placed in this position cannot be made to burn with despatch. They must be placed as described both in Hebrew and in English, but let them be *animals,* placed in that position, and let Mr. Calmet come forward with his cord and fasten them together, and we will wait to see them either run or burn.

It would seem, then, that dire necessity compels us to dismiss the common translation, notwithstanding its elaborate defence by Mr. C. And were we at all inclined to *favor* it, instead of endeavoring to disprove it, we should perhaps regret this necessity, inasmuch as his is the only attempt with which we are acquainted, for its defence. Strange as it may seem, it is nevertheless true, among all our commentators, writers in theology, or essayists, endeavoring to defend the Bible, there is not another serious and elaborate attempt to remove the absurdities that gather around the passage—as it stands in our common Bibles.

We must be permitted, therefore, to remind the reader of the ease and naturalness with which the different statements that are made, fall into place, when the translation proposed is adopted. The moment this single term is rendered sheaves, or bundles, all difficulties disappear from the record, the statements that are made are perfectly consistent, one with another, that which is affirmed of one part of the transaction harmonizes fully with the rest; the meaning of each word is natural and easy,—and nothing of which it may be said, as has been several times affirmed of the whole, nothing is either awkward or uncouth.

"All which is very well and very agreeable," says the reader, "provided the word which *is*, in fact, the central term of the translation, may be plainly and legitimately rendered as proposed. If it can be in a satisfactory manner shown, that its proper rendering is " bundles or sheaves "—the work is done.

It will go but a little way, as we suppose, towards convincing the reader, or satisfying any one, for us to affirm, at this point of the discussion, any way, either that it will, or that it will not, as the thing can be proved. It is matter of more than surprise to us, that it was ever translated in any other way. Is not the translator expected to exercise his judgment as to the meaning of a term? When the common and literal import of a word would subvert the whole chain of narative, what shall he do but inquire of every member of the sentence, and at the door of every circumstance connected with it, for a meaning which will harmonize the whole? What other course is left for him?

But the case before us happens to be plainer than even this; שׁוּעָל Shoo-ál is undeniably derived from שָׁעַל Shaw-ál, as its root. This proved, and every intelligent reader will admit, that we have abundant reasons for our surprise, especially, if the import or meaning of the root shall evidently be found in its derivative. Mark! we do not deny, that the word in question is several times translated in the Bible to mean fox, as in the case under examination, and probably correctly translated too. But that by no means proves, that it should be so translated in the case before us, as we shall see. In fact, this admission enables us to give the only reason we can think of for the rendering it has in the passage under debate. The translators, finding it in the text, and knowing it was the word which elsewhere was rendered *fox*, without pausing to look at its derivation, or even at the confusion it would introduce if thus rendered here, translated "fox," and passed on to the herculean task of rendering the other terms of the sentence so as to comport therewith, leaving it for you and me to grapple with the difficulties which were involved, and dispose of them as best we could.

And now, as to the question of derivation. The Lexicon of course must decide that. There can be no doubt of it in the mind of any one who is sufficieutly acquainted with the Hebrew, to enable him to "look it out," as it is said, if he will but take the trouble to do so. The mere tyro in that language, may satisfy himself of it at any time; while the riper scholar will be convinced of it by a single glance at the characters which are to compose the word. The appeal, therefore, is to the Lexicon; which, in the estimation of many, is the last appeal.

There may be instances in the Hebrew, as there are in all other languages, in which words occur, composed of the same elementary characters, yet derived from different roots, implying, of course, a difference in the meaning. As is the case in our own lauguage undoubtedly, with the words, Board, Bear, Bile, and many others, whether used as nouns or verbs. (But of this more hereafter.) Their import, however, is fixed and permanent; and no effort of those who speak or write the language to banish them from it can succeed. Their true import, in such cases, is always determined by circumstances connected with their use,—or more correctly, *by the relations they sustain to other words in the sentence.*

Nevertheless, it is not to be denied, that an appeal to the Lexicon is not only one of the first among the steps that are taken, with a view to ascertain the import of a term, but it is one of the most important. And it is thus, simply on the ground that it is an inquiry into *the derivation* of the word. When we go to the Lexicon for the meaning of a term, we do it, or hope to, by seeking out its parentage. This is the declared object of the lexicographer, or the student in searching for the root of a word; or in endeavoring to trace it, as it is said, to its root. With a view to ascertain its true meaning, we go to its root, with the expectation that we shall find something there which will at least furnish us with a clue to the meaning of the word under consideration. For it is a well-known law of language, *all* language, whether living or dead, that an element in the meaning of a derivative word will infallibly be found in the root from whence that word is derived. It cannot be for the purpose, therefore, solely or principally, of determining where such word is made, (in the language of a grammarian,) whether in this or that declension, mode, or tense; but to settle its import by that law to which I have referred. Its true meaning is believed to be shadowed forth in its root; just as certain lineaments or features in the countenance of the child are seen in the countenance of the parent.

With a view to illustrate this point and give its full weight to the argument, we will suppose that a teacher of the English language is listening to his pupil, who is endeavoring to explain, (or translate, if you choose,) the following declaration: "The Judge held the accused to bail in five hundred dollars bonds." The pupil complains that he cannot understand the term "*bonds.*" His teacher, with a view to instruct him in the safest, most direct and practicable way, inquires of him if he knows from whence the word comes; and is answered, that it evidently comes from the verb "*to bind.*" "But," he adds, "I find the word, '*bond,*' defined to mean, 'anything that binds; a chain, a rope, a cord;' *in the plural*, 'chains, imprisonment, captivity, fetters.' But," he continues, "I can see no reason, in saying the Judge placed the prisoner under five hundred dollars—chains; five hundred—imprisonment or fetters." "That is very probable," replies the instructor; " but you *can* see the reason or propriety of saying that the Judge bound the prisoner to appear before him, at a specific time and place, by compelling him to give security to that amount. In other words, the Judge so arranges his affairs, that in case the accused does not appear, he forfeits the sum of five hundred dollars: this is *binding* him to appear, at the specified time and place. Hence, the word '*bond*,' as coming from the verb '*to bind*.' And hence, we add, the plainly perceptible element of *the act*, expressed by that word, in the condition of the accused."

By the same rule, precisely, the word "*bundle*" is traced to the word bind, as its root; belongs to it because derived from it—and in its import distinctly implies that which may be found in its root, or primitive form. And by the same law we are to be helped not a little on our way towards determining the meaning of the word, שׁוּעָל Shoo-âl, tracing it as we do to the verb שָׁעַל Shaw-al, as its root.

With a view to sustain this position, we shall proceed to show that the word, which is properly a derivative, retains at least a shade of thought in its import or meaning, which may be certainly found in its primitive, or root. We introduce a few examples taken at random, as it were, from the Lexicon: שְׂעוֹרָה Se-o-rah; barley, grain—from שָׁעַר Shaw-ar, "he weighed, balanced, estimated;" because of the ancient as well as modern custom of determining the amount of grain by weighing it. Also—צֹדְנִית Tzai-de-ne-oth, "hunters," from צָדָה Tzah-dah, "he thought, purposed to kill, lay in wait for blood—hunted, sought to slay." *This is the term*, as we

have already remarked, which should have been used to
express the act of Samson in procuring his *foxes;* that is,
on the supposition they *were* foxes, or any other kind
of animals. La-chad, signifies " to take, to seize, as in
haste." The element of hunting, or procuring by the
chase, is found only in the former word. So also—
עֲנָוּה A-na-wah, " mildness, meekness, humility, is from
עָנָה A-nah, " he listened, attended to, obeyed. Again,
יַצִּיב Yatz-tze-va, " truth, confirmation;" from יָצַב Ya-
tzav, " he constituted, made sure, established." In all
of which may be seen an element of *the import*, or
meaning found in the root. מַעֲמָסָה Ma - a - ma - sah, " a
burden—a load;" from עָמַס A-mas, its root; the import
of which is, " he loaded, heaped up, burdened, over-
loaded, placed or laid upon." Our English, amass, " to
heap up, to gather together," is from the same.

There can be no manner of necessity, however, of
multiplying examples: the bare suggestion of the position will be sufficient, we think, for any reasonable man.
It is so with every language, whether a living or a dead
one. Even *wash*, when used to signify the debris, roots,
decayed leaves, and loose substances which the showers
or torrents have washed from the hills, retains an element of its primitive: *set*, when used to imply a class or
a rank, shows its derivative from the term which signifies the placing of things in ranks, or setting them in
specific places. The derivative in *all* cases must contain
an element in its meaning which may be certainly
found in its primitive, or root, just as the branches of a
tree, even to the smallest twig, and every leaf must contain a portion of the sap or nourishment derived from
the root. Hence the foundation of the metaphor, *root*.

This point fairly established, and we proceed to inquire what there is in either the qualities, character, nature, or in fact anything else, belonging to a fox or a jackal, corresponding to the idea of "binding, squeezing together, compressing;" all of which are found in the root from which the word in debate is derived? Herein is our surprise, and we cannot but repeat it—that the translators of the "textus receptus" should have rendered the term שׁוּעָל Shoo-âl as they have. They must certainly have known its parentage: they could not have been ignorant that it was derived from שָׁעַל Shaw-al, its legitimate root. And this word was defined, as we have seen, "He compressed, squeezed together, bound," *every part of which, in a most emphatic sense, the husbandman performs when he binds up his grain into a sheaf or bundle.* Any man who has a lingering doubt may go into the harvest field, station himself by the harvester, as he takes up a gavel, as it is called, (a pile of unbound grain as it is laid from the hand of the reaper) with a view to bind it into a bundle. He will see him throw his arms around it, "compress it, squeeze it, *bind*" it, into what? *a fox? a jackal?* Not by any means; *into a sheaf—a bundle.* So obviously is this its meaning, as it is used here, that even if the word had not been derived from its well-known root, we should have supposed that it would have been thus rendered. For, it is well known, there are many words in the Hebrew, whose root, like the true pronunciation of several of the letters of its alphabet, is irrecoverably lost. When this is the case, there is in fact no way by which to ascertain the true meaning of a word but by a regard to its position, or, in other words, *to the relation it sustains to the rest of the sentence.* This law, as it seems to us, would have led a translator to almost any conclusion, rather than that to which it seems he arrived who professed to have translated the passage before us.

But it may be said, as it probably will be by some, "this is not entirely satisfactory. The case is *too* plain, the absurdity is too glaring. No one whose knowledge of the language which he professed to be translating, was such as to justify any degree of confidence in him, would have so rendered it, if it had been possible to have made out any other meaning." It would seem so we confess; but here it is, and we have to meet the difficulty some way or other. We frankly confess, that this consideration itself is the most formidable objection to our theory which we have felt, or which we expect will be felt by others. The case is so plainly and palpably absurd, and it is so difficult for us to see how they who translated it, could have supposed or even *thought* they were correct, we almost involuntarily fall back upon the belief, that there is somewhere a reason that we have not seen. We are compelled to admit, that our translators, in full view of all the difficulties in the case, put it down just as we find it in our Bibles; and in addition, we know the word on which the whole hinges, is so rendered in several other passages of scripture, in some of them, confessedly right. Besides, as it seems to us, these translators must have seen and felt the absurdities involved in their translation, as keenly as we feel them at the present day. They must have known too, as well as we, the meaning of the word and its derivation. How, then, could they have thus rendered it?

But some will say, as we in fact have heard them

already, " we feel no special difficulty in regard to this passage, not any more than in respect to many other events we read of and which we most cordially believe; such as the " ten plagues," the feeding of Israel with manna; the destruction of Pharaoh and his hosts; in fact, any of those miracles which are so oft referred to. Why, then, should we be required to give this up, and not the others?"

Our main and final answer to this remark is reserved to a subsequent page; for the present, we are satisfied with simply appealing to the reader, if there is not something exceedingly suspicious in the fact, that seldom or never does he hear this event quoted, or see it referred to by those who evidently believe the Bible; and more especially, (which is the grand argument against it,) never is it referred to by the subsequent writers of the Bible. This is a fact, that cannot be accounted for, but by supposing, that the Hebrew scriptures, when read by those who perfectly understood that language, and just as they are with us to-day, contained no such story. There was Samson setting fire to the standing grain of the Philistines; but it was, as we have showed, by taking bundles of grain and placing them so they would burn, then setting them on fire and suffering *the fire* to run off into the standing corn, to " burn up their vineyards and olives."

While, therefore, we cheerfully make the above admission, we do as cheerfully subjoin, that it has not the slightest tendency to impair our confidence in our own theory, or the arguments by which our position is sustained. The book of Judges, that which contains the passage under examination, is, as all know, one of the earliest books of the Bible. The events it records were among the earliest in the history of the nation. After this period, and subsequent to the time when the Judges ruled over Israel, there was a period of some 10 or 12 centuries, during which men of God lived and wrote as they were moved by the Holy Spirit; and they were in the habit, as their writings now show, of referring back to great exploits and marvellous works, as well as unquestionable miracles, which were wrought by those who had lived before them; yet, not *once* is the reader reminded of Samson's measures for destroying his enemies' grain, either through the miraculous agency of three hundred foxes, or anything else. His name occurs occasionally; he is referred to several times, as one of those who had done great things " by faith," or through the potent agency of " confidence in God," and the *works* which he performed are many of them named; but his exploit of burning up the hopes of his enemies by sending among them a hundred and fifty spans of foxes, is not once referred to. This fact, we say, we can not account for, but by supposing that such an event never occurred.

Besides, we do most firmly believe, that were there no translation of this passage extant, either English, Greek, or any other, and were the Hebrew as well understood as it is at the present day, no living man, we firmly believe, would ever think of rendering it as we have it in our Bibles. Of this we are as sure as of anything, outside of consciousness or intuition. We should not be one whit more surprised to see a translation sent forth, affirming that " Samson went forth and caught three hundred *eagles*, and turned *them*, " tail to tail," as he is said to have placed his three hundred foxes, putting a lighted torch between each two, and sending them forth on an errand of mischief, than to find it as we do now.

However, it may be some relief to the reader, for us to say what we are sorry to be compelled to, inasmuch as it may shake his confidence in the trust-worthiness of the common translation as a whole, that there are several other passages, at which we are not less surprised than at the one we are at present considering. Were we to undertake to account for the introduction of Joshua x. 12, 15, into the sacred Record, or how it could have been regarded, at any age, as the record of an event that ever transpired, in any sense whatsoever, we should find it as difficult as we do in the case before us. The passage itself, assures the reader, that it is no part of the Bible : and if it did not, the last sentence, "And Joshua returned and all Israel with him unto the camp at Gilgal," (v.15) shows that it is not; for as the very next verse affirms, Joshua and all Israel with him, "are still at Makkedah to dispose of the five Kings, who are there found hid in a cave." And we cannot but feel, that it is a most unaccountable oversight in any one who reads this passage, that he fails to notice the care, the special *pains*, as I may say, which was evidently taken by him who had the temerity at first to introduce it,—to inform the reader where it came from and where it might thence be found, viz: in the "Book of Jasher;" not the Bible. How, then, came it there? And what the object of introducing it, are questions which they must answer who can. For ourselves we are compelled to say, *that faith*, which, after knowing all the circumstances and considerations involved, can receive either of these passages as the word of God, can evidently believe too much. We prefer to believe less, and have the comfortable feeling that our faith is that which we can defend.

The case, however, which we regard as more nearly allied to the one under review, is found in the 22d Psalm, 16th verse. (Hebrew, 22d, 17,) which we read as fol·lows: "They pierced my hands and my feet." A fair and accurate translation of the whole passage would read thus: "For dogs have compassed me about; the assembly of seducers, (or those that cause to work wickedness) have surrounded, '*as a lion*,' my hands and my feet." A slight change in the vowel-points, makes a very important change in the sense. We have no knowledge, however, of the grounds upon which our authorized version, in respect to the above translation, is based.

The whole difficulty, however, we think is fully met by the hypothesis, that in the Hebrew, as in other languages, there are words which are spelled alike, accented alike, and of course pronounced alike; which, after all, have very different meanings. The case under examination, we believe to be an example of this kind. Then, again, there are instances in which the same word, in different relations with respect to the rest of the sentence, will have a very different import. As for example, the word, *fare*, in our language. When used to express the price paid for being conveyed in a coach, or in the cars, it means a very different thing from what it does, when we use it in reference to food in general, or even any kind of food in particular. And in either of these cases it means a very different thing from what it implies, when we use it as descriptive of that particular *treatment* which we receive from others, whether it be good or evil. So, as we have seen elsewhere, the word, *board*, when used in its first and most common acceptation, means something very different from its import, when we say, " we have to pay so and so for our board." The noun bear, when the word is applied to a well-known beast, is spelled precisely, (though not pronounced,) as when it is used to designate a particular kind of barley or grain; as in the north of England, and in Scotland. This *last* case is so markedly like that in Judges xv. 4, 5—that we cannot refrain from noticing it with the utmost particularity.

Let us now suppose, that at the distance of a sufficient number of years, when the English language, like the Hebrew of the time of our common translation, is no longer spoken or has become a dead language, an individual translates a passage in which the word, *bear*, occurs used in the sense of barley, into another and a living one where it is made to represent that well known beast; his simplicity would make even a statue smile.

Apply these considerations, now, to the case before us. Say, with the authors of our present version, that שׁוּעָל Shoo-âl means fox, or with Mr. Calmet, that it means jackal, and you must render all the remaining terms of the passage so as to conform most strictly to that meaning. Then, you must contrive some means for Samson to get his " three hundred foxes," for שָׁלשׁ Shee-lish cannot well be defined by any other term than our numeral " *three*," and שְׁלשׁ מֵאוֹת She lish me-oth must be put down as in our authorized version, " three hundred." This difficulty surmounted and we come at once upon another. Whatever were these "three hundred" agencies of destruction, whether foxes or bundles of grain, the text, both Hebrew and English, requires them to be placed in a specific and very peculiar position, in order that they may either be made to burn themselves, or to convey fire to something that will burn. But animals, thus placed, can neither run nor burn, for they must be tied; but if tied, only in their caudal extremities, they can no more run than if their feet were all made fast in fetters.. The Hebrew and the English are both of them silent as the grave, in respect to Mr. Calmet's *cord*, or any other means for fastening them together in that position. And when these embarrassments are all fairly met and removed, you come directly upon others, if possible more formidable still. These fire-brands, or "*lamps*" as they are said to be, must be fastened one between each two. The scriptures provide no means for this, whatsoever. Again, Samson is represented as taking "fire-brands," לפדים La-pe-Dim. But he is said to have applied only one to each two of his agencies, or between them. Next, you are met by the troublesome consideration, that if you must regard these agencies, as foxes, and must employ them to scatter fire among standing grain, *one* of them, in a team, is better than two; and three teams, or couples, are better than "three hundred."

The very measures, then to which you are driven by this Πρῶτον Ψεῦδος, this rendering the word foxes, compel you to adopt others which involve you still more and more. And for all these, neither the Hebrew text, nor any translation with which we are acquainted affords relief. The original as well as the translation, represents Samson as setting something on fire; and then as letting something go into the unreaped grain of the Philistines:. If now you understand the שֻׁעָלִים Shoo-a-lim to be foxes, you must understand the whole as the translators have done; that it was "the foxes" that were set on fire; and the same that ran off into the grain. Mr. Calmet saw no other way to understand the passage. But the Hebrew, as we have shown, requires no such construction. It says only, "he let go;" *Samson* let *something* go into the standing corn; it does not say what: undoubtedly the sacred penman did not think it possible that he should be misunderstood: and having affirmed that Samson went and took so many bundles of grain, and turning the butt ends of each two together set them on fire, he presumed as you and I would, had we been in his place, that every reader would understand him as saying or implying, that it was the fire that ran off to do the mischief. And this is the construction that the original demands.

But, suffer it to stand as in our translation, i. e., regard those agencies as so many animals, and you must, as the translators have done, supply the word, "them," with the implied belief that it referred to those animals. And what is more, *if the Hebrew historian* had understood it as our translators did, he would have introduced the word אוֹתָם O-thâm, the acc. plural of שֻׁעָל, for this is the only form in which that language could say as our translators have said, "these foxes ran off into the standing grain;" or Samson let them go, etc. At the bottom of all is the painful feeling, underlying every other, that all this machinery, so to speak, is called into existence by the miraculous power of God: or more correctly, this miraculous power of God is made necessary, yea, indispensible to *the creation* of this machinery; then equally indispensible to the working of it; and for what purpose? to burn up the standing grain of his enemies! Absolutely incredible!

We now would inquire with unaffected seriousness, if the Bible must be regarded as a bound volume of inconsistencies? if not then, of course, this "confusion worse confounded" is no part of it. There is not one grain of deduction to be made from the assertion, that if the object of Samson was, as is plainly implied, if not said, to set fire to the unreaped forests of his enemies, he could not have devised a more awkward, inappropriate, impracticable measure than that which he is here represented to have done. We cannot trust ourselves to speak of it as we feel, lest our *feelings*, instead of our arguments, should be imparted to the reader, and we be found guilty of endeavoring to carry our point by other means than those which are required for the defence of truth. We prefer, therefore, to leave the whole subject to its own intrinsic ugliness and absurdity.

But we hope and expect to be inquired of, or asked if the word which has caused so much difficulty does not mean "fox"? We hope the inquiry will be confined to the single point whether there is another word in the Hebrew which is properly translated by that term? We shall frankly answer, we do not know of any; still further, we presume there is no other; yet we cannot perceive that this will militate against the view that we have taken of the subject; any more than the facts to which we have already referred, should prove that the word "fare," "board," or "bee" could never be misunderstood, or mistranslated. Any one may see, that if the word *bear*, be used in a connection that would require it to mean a kind of grain, and yet in being translated into another language it should be regarded a beast, there would be some confusion in the statements that would be made. And this is all that is required in the case before us : The use of it as in the text may have been purely accidental, or it may not ; we cannot say. Our difficulty is not with the original, as the reader very well knows. but with the translation. Were any man at the present day to undertake the rendering of this passage from the Hebrew into the English, and were he to come out with the translation we have in our common Bibles, his services as " Professor of Hebrew and sacred Philology" would not be very zealously sought in any of our schools or theological seminaries. However, this may be set down as nothing more than our opinion.

For the purpose of setting forth the embarrassments which are at once introduced into a passage, when one of its principal terms is misunderstood or misconstrued, we will give one instance more, of the various and opposite uses of the same word. A law of Edward III. forbade all ecclesiastical persons from purchasing provisions at Rome. The word " provisions," as will be seen is a most important word in this law : In fact the statute would scarcely have any meaning without it. Its import now is the common one, that of victuals ; *all* kinds that are used in the ordinary walks of life. But suppose a translator, in construing the law, should put down a term that signified just about that ; that is, the various kinds of food, he would make Edward " an hard man," indeed ; and his law one of the most cruel, despotic, inhuman, that could be found in any language or among any people. It would certainly be regarded as an attempt on the part of the king to *starve* every ecclesiastic that should see fit to visit Rome. But when it is known that the import of that term, *at that age*, was "ecclesiastical livings," the law is rational enough and its meaning clear.

The fact is, the words of our language, and we believe of every other, acquire their true import, in many cases very much as men do their character ; from the company they keep ; or more correctly, from the connection in which they are found. Relation originates law in the department of letters as well as in the affairs of men : the word, *baptize*, in 1 Cor. x. 2, is evidently used in a sense, not only peculiar, but in one which is calculated to throw much light on the vexed question of the mode and perhaps the subject of baptism.

Nothing is more common than for a word to have a specific and I may say peculiar meaning in one age of the language to which it belongs, and wholly to ignore that meaning in an age that follows. In our own language, for example, let, in the present age, conveys the the idea of *permit ;* but at a period no longer ago than the translation of our present version, it meant directly the opposite. "Thou shalt work, and who shall let it ?" who shall hinder, or prevent it ? see also *prevent*, which formerly implied the direct opposite of what it now does. *Help at this very day*, and according to the best usage, is *putting off* its former meaning, and assuming one which is wholly subversive of it. So of the term shoo-âl, it may have thrown off its original meaning and put on another; or it may have taken that meaning *on*, at a subsequent age. There are many ways to account for its present import, without adopting the violent alternative of the common version, or supposing that it has lost its true and original root.

We shall now cite the various passages in which the word שׁוּעָל shoo-âl is found, every one of them, with a view to ascertain whether it must always and invariably be translated *fox;* or whether the very nature of the case does not sometimes *demand* a different rendering.

It is found in the scriptures, in all six times: all of them with which we are at present concerned in the Old Testament of course. Nehemiah, chap. iv. 3, Judges xv. 4, 5, (the passage under review,) Psalm lxiii. 10, Cant. ii. 15, Lam. v. 18, and Ezekiel xiii. 4. It will be found we think, upon careful investigation, that in several of these passages it *should* have been translated by another word With the first example, Nehemiah iv. 3, we are fully satisfied; as the fox is proverbially light of foot, and as it is evidently the object of the speaker in the case to set forth the unsubstantial character of the wall which the Jews had been building, the figure is not only expressive, but most appropriate. In fact it is difficult to see how a more expressive figure could have been used. The second example, as we have said, is the one under ivestigation. The third, which is found in Psalm lxiii. 10, should evidently have been translated in some other way, as it is not known that foxes, under any circum· stances, prey upon human flesh, or even attack man; and the Psalmist is evidently imprecating evil upon his enemy, calling for destruction upon him through the agency of wild beasts. Cant. ii. 14—most certainly by some other term. It is not known that the fox, especially *"the little fox,"* is in the habit of making depredations upon the vines at the time specified; i. e. when the "vines have tender grapes." But it *is* known to every vine-dresser in the land, that certain portions of the vine itself have to be carefully removed *at precisely the period specified;* that is, when the vines are loaded with young grapes, and that these portions are sometimes called *"bindings,"* or "little *young vines*;" they are sprouts which not only spoil the vines, but prevent their bearing fruit. In this passage, therefore, the word we are examining would seem to require the same or a very similar rendering with that which we claim for it in the passage under debate. The original is somewhat peculiar and marked שֻׁעָלִים שֻׁעָלִים shŭ-â-lim shŭ-â-lim, "foxes of foxes," or, as we are disposed to think, *"vines of vines;"* the young sprouts of the vines at the time of the springing of grapes. In respect to the last example, Ezekiel, xiii. 4—we are unable to decide. It is not known that the fox has any habit peculiar to the desert; but, should we regard the word as properly rendered *vines*, as in the former case, then the meaning would be clear; as vines in the desert are either barren, or they bear only "the clusters of Sodom and the grapes of Gomorrah;" so those prophets of which Ezekiel complains were either barren of instruction, or they bore false and polluting testimony. Perhaps Lam. v. 18, should be noticed. But it will throw no additional light upon us.

Let us next consult those passages in which the word *bundle* is used, to see if we can gather any light there. It may be thought that these, in some way or other, will enable us to determine whether the word which is thus

rendered is either that which is under consideration, or
whether that which is used in these passages could have
been consistently employed to designate bundles of grain.
I Sam. xxv. 29. The soul of my Lord shall be bound in
the bundle of life. צְרוֹר Tze-dod, "*bundle*," is from
צָרַר tza-dad; which is defined, "he restrained, shut
up, bound up, as the waters of the deep." In no part of
which is the idea of gathering together grain, with a
view to bind it into bundles. Cant. i. 13. צְרוֹר Tze-
dod, "a bundle of myrrh is my well beloved to me."
That is, "a handfull;" or what one would naturally carry
in the hand, as a nosegay. Isaiah lviii. 6, and Amos
ix. 6, are from another word; one which signifies a bundle, or quantity of herbs, or straw, (not bound) "a band
of men;" (not bound in bundles of course.) These are
the only terms in the Hebrew language, as it is used in
the Old Testament, which would have been employed to
designate a bundle; but in none of them is the idea of a
bundle of grain, a sheaf of wheat, or the act of binding
grain. Nothing of that "compressing, squeezing, binding," into a bundle, which are seen in every instance of
the binding of a sheaf, and which are most favorably
expressed by the root שָׁעַל Shâ-āl, from which our word
is derived. אֲלֻמִּים El-um-mim, "sheaves," is from אָלַם
A-lam, the import of which is "to tie up, bind as a sheaf,
to be silent, dumb, quiet, calm, resigned." A word
which would have been as proper as that which was
used; but not more so. The husbandman of that age,
undoubtedly as of this, was in the habit of using these
words, either of them, indifferently. As often sheaf as
bundle, and bundle as sheaf; both meaning the same
thing.

We are now prepared to close this argument by apply-
ing these considerations to the passage under review :—
Admit that the term שׁעל shoo-âl means what we have
so many times affirmed, "a bundle, a sheaf," just as the
exigencies of the case require, and every difficulty vanishes in a moment. The whole is then easy, natural, unen-
cumbered,—and free from even the shadow of absurdity.
But place the word *fox* there, as our translators have
done ; or jackal, as Mr. Calmet proposes,—and there is
not another passage, I will not say *in the Bible*, but in
any book with which we are acquainted, which, for
unbounded absurdity, or unutterable inconsistency will
compare with it.

The common acceptation of this passage, as we have
already remarked, cannot be maintained, except on the
ground of a miraculous display of divine power,—commencing with the first and ending with the last step. So
far is this in accordance with the truth, that we have yet
to see the effort of one to defend it, as it is in our Bibles—
without falling back on God's miraculous power; unless
we consider Mr. Calmet's an exception. Cruden, who
is but an echo of Calmet, after administering a tremend-
ous rebuke in advance, against all infidels in general,
and those who doubt this passage in particular, proceeds
to remove all the objections that he can conceive possible,
by supposing that Samson was assisted in his enterprise
by both God and man. So far is this the obvious implication, that no one reads what is thus written, without
getting the impression that it is a clear case of miracle ;
and that it was the intention of these men thus to represent it. Yet, not the slightest proof can be found, that
anything of the kind was either claimed or desired. It

is as we have seen, an example of one who overcame "by might and by power," and "not by my spirit, saith the Lord."

Had this literally taken place, or as it appears in the transaction, it would have been confessedly a great miracle: and, like *all* of that class of works, it would have been referred to again and again by the subsequent writers of the Bible. There can be no doubt, that it is Samson to whom reference is made in Hebrews xi. 34; who, as it is there said, "turned to flight the armies of the aliens." But nothing is said of his setting fire to their fields of grain by the agency of an army of foxes. No other passage can be found in the Bible, where it is evident that his exploits are expressly referred to: it would seem incredible, therefore, that his name should stand with that of Jeptha, Gideon, David and Barak, as affording, by their works, the most eminent examples of the power of faith, "waxing valiant in fight; out of weakness, being made strong;" and not one word be said of this—the greatest of all his works.

The reader, we think, can scarcely fail to see the force of this argument. Let us remind him of the fact, that *not a single well authenticated miracle*, recorded in the Old Testament Scriptures, particularly those which were wrought at or near the beginning of its history, that is not made the subject of *repeated reference*, in the subsequent portions of the Bible, by "those who spake as they were moved by the Holy Ghost;" whose words are left on record for our instruction. Even those miracles which initiated the emancipation of the Jews from Egyptian bondage are so frequently referred to, that the reader cannot doubt as to the belief of those men who have referred to them; these men were *inspired:* And the faith, or argument, or even *reference* of an inspired man, cannot well be an error.

Suppose, for example, that the miracle of the passage of the Red Sea, had not once been referred to by any of the subsequent writers of the Bible, either patriarch or prophet: that single consideration would have stood forth, a silent, yet unanswerable evidence against it, however well authenticated in other respects. The same is true of the miraculous supply of quails in the wilderness; the furnishing of water from the rock; the overthrow of Amelek at Rephidim; the supply of Israel with manna; the giving of the law; or in fact, any other of the well-authenticated miracles recorded in the scriptures. It was evidently the intention of the Holy Spirit thus to designate the genuine and incorruptible evidences of inspiration, and effectually distinguish them from those that are both spurious and false. In this way we are furnished with reliable testimony, on that important subject, to the end of time. Some portions of the Bible, such as the cvi. and cvii. Psalm, are almost wholly made up of these references. In none of them, however, do we find anything of the matter in hand—no reference, not even the slightest, to the arrangements of Samson for scattering fire over the unharvested fields of his enemies, through the potent agency and miraculous co-operation of his "three hundred foxes." Hence, and for various other reasons, as we have already said, we conclude that it was never done.

For these reasons, all of which seem satisfactory and quite conclusive, we have been constrained to believe, that the שֻׁעָלִים Shŭ-a-lim of the text should have been translated *bundles*, or sheaves; instead of foxes: and this is what we had proposed to do.

With the reader's permission now, we will say a word in explanation or defence of "that inordinate *length*," to which this chapter has been extended. And first, the object which it aims to accomplish is one which from its nature cannot be reached in a few words. The reader himself, whose mind has been employed in endeavoring to follow the argument, has undoubtedly thought of a great many things, which, as it seems to him, might be advanced in support of an opposite theory; and unless he be in this respect forestalled, the argument, however conclusive, will not be followed by conviction. In order to be conclusive, in the estimation of some, an article of this nature must anticipate every consideration that would be likely to come into the mind of any man that should attempt to peruse it. So long as a single suggestion, reply or rejoinder can be made, the argument is not thought to be complete.

Then again, it is no very easy task to overthrow the faith of one in a passage like this. If upon first looking at it, at least, with some degree of seriousness, his conscience does not accuse him of having been led to believe what seems likely to prove an absurdity, he will be likely to cling to it with a tenacity, which is generally in proportion to the weakness of his cause. He will, perhaps, insensibly aim to make up all deficiency of evidence or argument, by a kind of extra effort to explain away what seems to militate against his long and fondly cherished theory. Besides, when an argument is offered which seriously embarrasses his theory, if he can recollect at any time, to have had that consideration under examination, whether he succeeded in answering it or not, the fact of his having even looked at it, is abundantly sufficient to leave the impression upon his mind, that it is not of any great weight. A consciousness of having seen it, and of having made up his mind to believe as he does, notwithstanding it now answers all the purposes of a most satisfactory solution of this apparent difficulty.

Then the bare presentation of the argument on a subject like this, would be about as satisfactory, and about as much to the purpose, as the naked frame of a house to dwell in in a cold winter. The writer himself must be permitted to put on a covering. His argument is a thing in which his reader is quite as much interested as he is. It is a cause which consults the reader's comfort and happiness, quite as much as it does his own. And it is surely a less task to read than to write; especially if the writer is attacking, as in the present case, the long and fondly cherished views of many who have sincerely received the scriptures as the word of God. Still more, if the writer's object be, as it certainly is in the present case, to confirm and establish the reader's faith by removing from its foundation whatsoever is inapposite or unworthy of his confidence, he has undertaken a very difficult task. He has first to show, that it is not as the reader has long regarded it; next, he of course, undertakes to show how it is. No man likes to be convicted of either sin or folly, but more especially of *credulity*. Of the first, we have not sought to convict the reader; of the second we may have said that which implies the bare possibility. But he may set up in defence, that this is a kind of common calamity. Of the third, which is *credulity*, he is undoubtedly guilty, for if at any time he has regarded the translation which we have endeavored to overthrow, as worthy of his confidence in the least, he certainly can find a verdict against himself, for having believed what is evidently absurd, simply because others have believed it.

Of one thing, however, we are abundantly certain; he who has followed us to the end, will never more have confidence in the passage we have examined as it stands. At any rate, not in the present translation. So sure am I of this, that I would be willing to risk that upon the question, "has he read the article? has he duly weighed the arguments that have been offered in support of the amended translations?"

And, should this be the extent of all we have accomplished; should our labors go no further than to undermine the confidence of the reader in the passage as it stands, failing utterly of convincing him of the correctness of our own views, we shall regard ourselves as not having labored in vain. No man was ever yet benefitted by believing error. But we hope for things in advance of this.

Finally, we are satisfied of at least one thing more. The reader, whatever be his views on the question of a new *translation* of the Bible, will have been convinced, that at least a new *version* is imperiously demanded. For if any translator can be convicted of having (what shall I call it?) made such a mistake? adopted such an an absurdity? as is here involved, he certainly has proved himself unworthy of that confidence which we ought to feel in one who is attempting to translate the word of life. However, this is a question which I propose to consider in another place and at another time.

CHAPTER II.

THE DIAL OF AHAZ.

II. KINGS XX. 9, 10, 11; AND ISAIAH XXXVIII. 8.

" The word of the Lord is right." Ps. xxxiii. 4.

" And Isaiah said, This sign shalt thou have of the
Lord, that the Lord will do the thing that he hath spoken : Shall the shadow go forward ten degrees; or go
back ten degrees ? And Hezekiah answered, It is a
light thing for the shadow to go down ten degrees : Nay,
but let the shadow return backward ten degrees. And
Isaiah, the prophet, cried unto the Lord; and he brought
the shadow ten degrees backward, by which it had gone
down in the dial of Ahaz."

" Behold, I will bring again the shadow of the degrees, which is gone down in the sun-dial of Ahaz, ten
degrees backward. So the sun returned ten degrees, by
which degrees it was gone down."

FEW, we believe, have read the Bible with becoming
seriousness, that have not found difficulty with these
passages. Perhaps I should speak of them as one; they
are, in fact, but one. There is an odor about them, that
will scarcely fail to attract attention; even though they

be passed over, as they often are, with but slight notice. Those who cheerfully subscribe to the doctrine of miracles; who believe, that the inspiration of the scriptures has been sustained "by many infallible proofs"—who regard this kind of evidence among the best, are as often troubled with this passage as any are. Not that they deny that there was a miracle wrought here—but they are in difficulty as to what that miracle consisted in. There is evidence enough of the miraculous power of God; but the question, as to what was done to furnish the trembling Hezekiah with "a sign" that he should live and not die, is attended with rather serious difficulties.

It cannot be denied, there are those, who, when passing over this portion of the sacred record, step lightly and with caution, lest their tread should awaken that which they cannot readily account for, or dispose of. They find it far easier to say, they believe it all just as it stands, than to stop and clear up the difficulties which evidently confront them. They have that which passes for faith in the word of God, and have it in great abundance; which, after all, is not one whit better in its influence, either upon our mind or heart, than the blindest credulity, if not unbelief itself: for, if the mind of one is conscious of a lack of confidence in a passage, or of a desire to know its true import, or perhaps whether it be at all understood, it will not, *can* not rest till it has employed all the means at its command to satisfy itself of its truthfulness or falsity.

Many considerations can be easily imagined, that would persuade almost any one to pass on and not stop to inquire into a matter like that before us. It has been so long received as truth by the wisest and best of men, so many commentaries have been written upon it, not one of them pretending to find any difficulty with it, that the common reader chides himself for stopping to notice anything in the way of objection. Those whose knowledge of the original languages was evidently such as to enable them to decide in respect to it, if any could, have all, or nearly all, passed it by as if there were nothing to distinguish it from the known and accredited testimonies of God. Then, again, there is the "odium theologicum," which justly attaches to unbelief; and last, though not least, *the hard study* it will cost to investigate the question and clear up the difficulty.

Many, therefore, prefer to cast in their lot with the multitude, believing it entirely safe to receive it as the word of truth, even though there may be something which to them is not quite intelligible. They seem to be satisfied with the assurance, that it will not injure them, more than it has others, even should it be proved erroneous. They very much prefer not to expose themselves to the censure of good men, or to the charge of having called in question the correctness of our authorized translation. A principle of interpretation has been employed, as it seems to them, which would invite disaster into other passages; but then, they may be mistaken. Not many are willing to meet the eye of well-educated and intelligent men, after it is known that they have doubted what these men have believed.

One thing, however, should be carefully borne in mind : No man, whose aim it was to comment upon the whole Bible, has ever yet lived long enough, or had time, to devote to the investigation of *all* those passages which are known to be so very difficult of interpretation. In fact, some portions of the Bible, small portions too, have employed the pen of those who may be safely classed among the most learned and wise, no inconsiderable portion of their professional life. Where is the biblical student, that has not read essay after essay on Romans viii. 18—23, or theories for explaining it, till it would seem no new thing could be advanced? The same is true in respect to the 7th of the same Epistle: what care-worn, hardy soldier of the paper war, that has not tried the temper of his steel (pen) on this passage? Each one thinking he could certainly settle the question as to whether a Christian, or only a legalist is here described? That part of the chapter, which is included between the 13th and 25th verses, has caused an immeasurable amount of bitterness; arising from the fact, that it has come to be regarded a kind of test, in the question of orthodoxy: And yet, it is well-known, that the number of those who construe it as Augustine did the latter part of his life, is not much superior, if any, either in piety or learning, to those who accord with Arminius. Many are so strenuous in respect to this matter, as to regard him an heretic and no Christian, who refuses to adopt it as explained by the most rigid Calvinists.

From the very nature of the case, therefore, those passages of scripture which are difficult of interpretation—are likely to remain unintelligible and obscure; and in respect to that portion of the Bible, which is easy of comprehension, we *need* no comment upon it. The plain and intelligent reader can be far more profitably employed than in reading long-drawn and fine-spun theories, or expositions of passages that are perfectly plain at first.

This, upon which we are about to remark, is one which has given employment to not a few. And those who have paused long enough to look at it carefully, will find no difficulty in assigning the appropriate cause.

That the reader may see the result to which a most laborious and learned commentator has come, after a long and careful investigation of it, we shall give at considerable length, his views on the subject: particularly, those which are embraced in his concluding remarks. The following is his translation of the passage.

"Behold, I will cause the shadow of the degrees, which has gone down on the degrees (the Dial) of Ahaz by the sun, to go back ten degrees. And the sun returned ten degrees, on the degrees on which it had gone down." (Isaiah xxxviii. 8.)

After giving at some length the views of Mr. Calmet and others, he, thus, in summing up, gives us his own.

" In regard to this miracle, it seems only necessary to observe, all that is indispensible to be believed, is, that the shadow on the dial was made to recede—from any cause. It is evident that that may have been accomplished in several ways:—it may have been by arresting the motion of the earth in its diurnal revolutions; and by causing it to retrograde on its axis—to the extent indicated by the return of the shadow: or it may have been by a miraculous *bending*, or inclining of the rays of the sun out of their natural course. As there is no evidence that the event was observed elsewhere,—and as it is not *necessary* to suppose that the earth was arrested in its motion, and that the whole frame-work of

the Universe was adjusted to this change in the movement of the earth, it is most probable that it was an inclination of the rays of the sun, or a miraculous causing of *the shadow* itself to recede. This is the whole
statement of the sacred writer; and this all that is necessary to be supposed. What Hezekiah desired was a
miracle; a sign that he should recover. The retroces-
sion of the shadow in this sudden manner, was not a natural event. It could be caused only by God; and this
was all that was needed. A simple exertion of divine
power, on the rays of the sun, as they rested on the dial,
deflecting those rays, would accomplish the whole result. It may be added that it is not recorded, nor is it
necessary to an understanding of the subject, to suppose
that the bending of the rays was permanent, or that so
much time was actually lost. The miracle was instantane-
ous, and was evidently satisfactory to Hezekiah, though
the rays of the sun, casting the shadow, may have again
been soon returned to their regular position, and the
shadow restored to the place in which it would have
been, had it not been interrupted. No infidel, therefore, can object to this statement, unless he can prove
that this *could* not be done, even by Him who made the
sun, and who is himself the fountain of power.

"*By which degrees it was gone down.*" That is, by
the same steps or degrees on which the shadow had
descended. So far the LXX express it. "So the sun
reascended the ten steps by which the shadow had gone
down." It was the shadow on the dial which had gone
down: the *sun* was *ascending;* and the consequence
was, of course, that the shadow on a vertical dial would
descend. The *sun*, here, means evidently, the sun as it

appeared; the rays, or the shining of the sun. A return of the shadow was an effect, such as would be produced by the recession of the sun itself." (Barns on Isaiah, chap. xxxviîi : 8.)

The reader will not have failed to observe that this extract proceeds upon the ground that *there was a dial*, or something by which time was measured; and that too, by the sun's shadow, as at the present day upon our common dials. But this same reader must be made to understand that there is no such word as dial in the passage, of which our extract professes to be a correct translation. Nor is there any word there which signifies a dial. There is, in the Hebrew, the word מַעֲלָה mâ-â-lâh, from עָלָה â-lâh, "to ascend, to go up." As a noun it means "*ascent, a step*;" and in the plural, "steps, *a flight of stairs*;" which is unquestionably its import in the passage under examination, though translated, "degrees." In I. Kings x. 19, and Ezekiel xl. 26, 31, 34, its import is undeniably "steps;" as when we speak of these in a flight of stairs. The same word is used in 2d. Kings xx. 9, 10, 11, where it must be translated steps, or stairs, whatever becomes of our translator's dial.

There is but one defense which can be set up for "the King's translators;" and that happens to be one which no sane man would offer. It may be said, "there is no word in the Hebrew which means *dial*, if this does not." Equally true would it be to say, "there is no word which means 'the mariners' compass,' if this does not." And had they translated it by the term clock, or watch, or any other, which is used to designate an instrument for measuring time, the absurdity would have been no less than now.

What could have suggested to the translators of our common version, the idea of *a sun dial*, we leave for the reader to conjecture, if he can. For ourselves we are obliged to confess we see nothing, except that it was evidently a device of some kind or another for measuring time, or dividing the day, by means of the shadow of the sun ; a chronometer, as uncouth as every thing of the kind must have been at that age of the world ; and used by Ahaz, the father of Hezekiah. Josephus understands the word which is here used just as we have rendered it, " a flight of stairs," in the palace of Ahaz. He supposes " Hezekiah desired the Prophet Isaiah, that he would cause the shadow of the sun, which had already gone down 'ten steps,' on the stairs of his palace," (for as the sun should *ascend*, the shadow must of course *descend*,) " to return again to the same place ; thus making it as it was before." The LXX find themselves obliged to translate the word just as Josephus has done, " a flight of steps, or stairs ; " thus proving, incontestibly, that at *that* age of the world and of the Jewish nation, there was no knowledge of any sun dial, nor even anything of the kind for measuring time. Had the language of the Jews contained any term for the designation of a device for the above purpose, it is undeniable that it would have been used on this occasion, instead of the one which was employed. They, (the translators of the Alexandrine version,) understood the whole statement as Josephus did, as referring to a miracle which the Prophet Isaiah wrought, by causing the shadow of the sun to return ten degrees upon the stairs of Ahaz's palace. The marginal reading of the passage will show some of the difficulties which both they and we have to encounter ; for example,

4*

"degrees by, or with the sun." Hebrew, literally, "which has descended on the steps, or degrees, or stairs of Ahaz, by or with the sun. בַּשֶּׁמֶשׁ Bash-she-mesh; that is, by means of the sun; or caused by the sun."

Mr. Calmet says, "the dial is not mentioned in the scriptures before the time of Ahaz, who lived 726 years before Christ. Nor is it certainly known, that even *after* his time the Jews generally divided their days into hours. The word hour, ($\chi\alpha\iota\rho\iota\chi o\varsigma$) occurs first in Tobit; and it has been supposed, that the invention of dials came from beyond the Euphrates. About 300 years after the age of Homer, or before Christ, about 500, Pherecydes set up a sun dial in the Island of Syria, to distinguish the hours. But this was at least 200 or 230 years *after* the days of Ahaz. The Greeks affirm that it was Anaximander who first divided time by hours. He lived about 550 B. C.; or about 200 years after the reign of Ahaz. Mr. Calmet further observes; "the Chaldeans were early distinguished for their attention to astronomy. And it is probable that it was in Babylon that the sundial, and the division of the day into hours, was first used: and that the knowledge of these was conveyed in some way or other to Ahaz.

Yet it will strike the reader, we think, as a somewhat difficult undertaking, to get a sun-dial for Ahaz or anybody else, from Chaldea, some 200 years before *he lived*, who is said to have been the inventor of it. Besides, we are sure to find terms for the designation of such things, quite as soon as they are invented. Wherever fire-arms have been found, whether among the people that devised them, or among those that have adopted them, the language of that people has soon been found to possess a word by which those arms were known. So in respect to every thing else; but especially, we think, in respect to chronometers—of any and of every description: astronomical instruments; the mariner's compass; surveying utensils, etc. etc.; *the names by which they are known*, and even many other terms connected in one way or another with their use, *would find their way into a language* about as soon as the things which they designate are known among that people.   And when once there, we believe that neither history nor tradition would drop them, whether the language were a living or a dead one.

Moreover, the fact that the Septuagint, or Alexandrine version, (a work which was undoubtedly made somewhere between 280 and 290 years before Christ,) contains not the slightest knowledge of the dial; but, on the contrary, translates the passage before us by a term which fully corresponds to the Hebrew original, is proof that no such instrument was then known.   Why did the authors of that version, when translating the passage under review, consent to use a term whose import is, as we have said, only that of "a flight of stairs," if there was in the language they were translating, a term, or even the elements of one, to express the idea of a chronometer known by that name?   Would God, *our* translators, or those of the king, had felt themselves bound to do in like manner.

But as this is a consideration to which we purpose to attend still further on, we dismiss it for the present, only premising that if the language be a *living* one, spoken by a people as intelligent as were the Jews, "in the days of Uzziah. Ahaz and Hezekiah," and as firmly bent on improvement as they evidently were, we have little room to doubt, that the introduction of such an important thing as *a sun dial*, an hour-glass, the compass, or any the like device for measuring time, or navigating the sea, or measuring the land, would soon procure for itself a word by which it might be known, and that term would become a part of the language. Ahaz, it seems, was so much in favor of improvement, that when he found an altar at Damascus which highly pleased him, he sent the fashion of it to Jerusalem, (2d Kings, xvi. 10,) that one might be constructed after the fashion of it. Is it credible, that he who should have procured *a sun dial* from Babylon, or anywhere else, *would have left its name behind?*

Perhaps we shall be excused for introducing an incident at this place, which, though not of the utmost importance in itself, is nevertheless, not without its use or application. The writer was once, in company with some 8 or 10 others, traveling in a stage-coach. Among the number was a learned Mormon, if the expression be not too great a paradox. He, the said learned Mormon, was soon put upon his defense and upon that of his religion, (if we must thus name it,) and was most diligently kept there. During the discussion which followed thereupon, one of the party, who, it seemed, was quite familiar with "the Book of Mormon," or in other words, the Mormon's Bible, put the following question to the said Mormon. "When was gunpowder invented?" He was answered, though not by the Mormon, for it was evident *he* did not know, "about five hundred years ago. The Moors used it first about that time." "Very well," replied the enquirer, turning to the Mormon, "your bible, as you call your book of Mormon, contains an account of a voyage or expedition, said to have been undertaken by one Nephi, about the reign of Cyrus, the Persian, which was some seven hundred years B. C. And, in that account, your book represents them as having been furnished with *guns and bayonets*, pistols, compasses and charts." The poor Mormon's eyes were very attentively fixed on something or nothing, as the case may be, in the bottom of the coach, where they remained till he was relieved by the device of a fellow-passenger, who suddenly introduced another topic, evidently to the great relief of the Mormon. The simple mention of gunpowder, in a work which purported to have been written full two thousand years before that article was known to the world, was of course, sufficient proof that the whole story connected with it was a falsehood.

To return to our argument. So utterly silent is the Hebrew language, in respect to the *instrument* we are considering, that the sacred historian, in giving an account of this important matter, *is obliged to use a term whose plain import, as we have many times said, is only that of a flight of stairs!* And he is compelled to use this word because there is no other to apply to that which was then before him, which was a contrivance of of some kind or other, by which Ahaz was in the habit of measuring time, or judging of its flight. Cyril of Alexandria, and Jerome, both suppose that this arrangement for measuring time, was in fact, only *a stair case*, so disposed as to enable one, while the sun shined, to form something like an estimate of the flight of time by the shadow's descent from one stair to another.

Why did those most ancient commentators regard it

thus ? Why were they compelled to call this device, as they did, *a flight of stairs*, if there was in fact another and a proper word for naming it ? The answer is, they evidently knew of no other term to be applied to that which was then before them, a means, or contrivance, employed by Ahaz, for measuring his days. Being perfectly familiar with the language of the Jews, they knew of no term to be employed here, but the only theory used : And certainly, our translators, or more correctly " the kings "—could know of none, if Cyril, Jerome and Josephus did not. How then, come these same men, (the translators) in possession of an idea that the conversation which passed between Isaiah and Hezekiah, concerning the speedy end of the king's days—was where they could both of them look down upon a common sun-dial, and talk of the shadow's going up or down, forward or backward ?

"But," says the reader, " if we understand the writer, he admits that there was something before Hezekiah, by which the king, as well as his father Ahaz—was accustomed to divide his day : What matters it whether it be an hour-glass, a dial, or " a flight of stairs," provided this latter device may be made to subserve the purposes of a dial, or any other instrument for measuring time ? " What matters it !"   " Much, every way." For, as the passage now stands, the impression is made upon the mind of the reader, that a common sun-dial, with its regular characters and figures, its lines and circles, degrees, etc. etc., in a word—every thing that goes to make up one of those faithful monitors of the flight of time, was there before the Prophet, and that in answer to his prayer, a mysterious and unseen hand had been put forth

to move the shadow back the number of degrees which
had been specified ; whereas, it is evident that nothing
of the kind was there : that in no part of the world, not
even in Chaldea till hundreds of years afterwards, was
there any device for the measuring of time, that bore
any very marked resemblance to that instrument so well
known among us.   To meet the conditions of the statement in our authorized version, we must have the literal
sun-dial, stationary and placed where the king Hezekiah and the Prophet Isaiah can look down upon it, as
it would seem, while the former is reclining upon his
sick bed,—and can see with his own eyes the shadow
return the specified number of degrees.   I cannot resist
the impression that this was the view which the translators took of it, and that it is their intention to communicate that idea to all who shall read what they have
written.

But it is proper for us to inquire as to the miracle itself,
viz : the lengthening of the days of Hezekiah, or the sign
which was given him as an assurance that his life would
be prolonged.   It was evidently some change in the
shadow of the sun, as that shadow rested upon a flight
of stairs, in, or on the outside of the palace of Ahaz.
This shadow, according to the statement before us, is
made " to return," or to retrograde ten steps, or degrees,
down which it had descended.   If we continue to understand this as taking place upon a flight of stairs, the return of the shadow or the coming back of it, the specified distance, is as expressed in the Bible ;—its coming
back, or *up* ten degrees down which it had gone.   The
question which now concerns us, is *as to what must take
place in nature in order to produce such a result as this.*

We can conceive of but two causes that could produce this result : the earth, by the omnipotent power of its Creator, must have been made to pause in its diurnal revolution, and *roll back* a sufficient distance to produce the desired change ; or—as suggested by Mr. Barns and many others, the shadow of the sun, made to return by the bending of the rays of light out of their natural course. It cannot be denied that He who made all things, can do either of these : he can stop the earth, and cause it to roll back, so as to produce that effect or any other in that direction ; or he can cause the rays of the sun to bend from their natural course sufficiently to produce it. Either of these is possible with God. And he could keep everything in its natural place, while the earth was being moved so as to accomplish this : no one can deny it.

But the inevitable result of at least one of these would be the lengthening of the day : it might not be to quite the extent indicated by the writer of the book of Jasher, when, as he tells us, Joshua commanded the sun and moon to stand still : but, if the steps upon the flight of stairs were such as to divide the day into hours, it cannot be denied that a considerable fraction of a day would have to be added, as the result of the shadow's return.

Now there is not the faintest intimation, either in the original Hebrew, or in any translation with which we are acquainted, *that the day was lengthened a single minute.* This could not have been the case if the earth had been stopped in her diurnal revolutions, as we have seen. Nearly one-half of a day must have been added. Besides, if anything like this had taken place, it was an event which would have been noticed on every sun-dial in existence; and Mr. Calmet seems to think that in Chaldea there were instruments of this description at that age. And as to the lengthening out of the day, *that* is a phenomenon or result which must have been witnessed over the whole earth; at least on that side of it which was at that time turned towards the sun. In respect to the other hemisphere, its inhabitants, (if there were any,) must have thought they had a very long night; and that the sun. had forgotten to rise. Those who occupied a position on the surface of the globe, which• enabled them to see the sun, must have stood aghast, on witnessing the bright luminary of the heavens suddenly pause and turn back; with others, there must have been equal dismay at the fearful prolongation of the night. These are facts which every reflecting mind will at once perceive are results that must have been caused by the stopping of the earth and its movement backward.

Accordingly, many have supposed, that 2d Chron. xxxii. 31, is, in fact, an allusion or reference to such an event. They think that the king of Babylon, with all Chaldea, witnessed this remarkable appearance; saw the lengthening of the day, and all the other results of this "wonder in the land;" and having heard of Hezekiah's sickness, as well as his recovery therefrom, and that it was through a miracle wrought by the prophet, that he was restored, "the king of Babylon sent unto him to inquire of the wonder that was in the land."

Nothing, surely, is more natural than this, or more reasonable for us to expect. We are not surprised that the so-called "father of history," (Herodotus) should be summoned forward to testify of the wonders which, "tradition says," the Egyptians saw concerning the sun and moon. That famous *tradition* is sufficient, it seems, to account for every thing of the kind. The standing still of the sun and moon, as recorded in Joshua x. 12, 15, is actually proved by it! Loose, jointed and sleezy as it is, it is abundantly sufficient to account for any number of such phenomena.

One word further "en passant," in respect to this tradition of Herodotus. He states, that "the priests of Egypt had a tradition, that in very remote ages, the sun had four times departed from his regular course; having twice risen where he ought to set; and twice set where he should invariable rise." This sad and melancholy departure of the sun from its orderly course, could not have been very remote, so far as respects *one* of the cases referred to, if the miracle in the case of Hezekiah be considered as intended. Herodotus himself lived very near that period, (490 years B. C. !) within two hundred and twenty years of it at the farthest!

But the most formidable consideration about this tradition is this: It is the testimony of certain travelers, who in the earliest ages of Egyptian history, wandered so far south as to cross the equinoctial line; and having supposed with all the rest of the world, that *the earth was a great plain*, and that on every part of its surface, *the sun would be* BEFORE *the beholder at noon*, these travelers having found themselves where, in an unaccountable manner, the sun had contrived to get round behind them at that hour, so as to shine upon their backs, they were unable to account for what they witnessed, except by the supposition above referred to: "The sun had

risen where he ought to set; and set where he ought to
rise !"

It seems to us not a little strange, that men who have
taken upon themselves to explain so difficult a passage
as this, should allow themselves to quote a tradition of
this nature, without even stopping to show its proper application or relevancy to the event which they wish to
account for. Suppose we admit, "for the sake of the
argument," the tradition referred to : it states that " the
sun has twice so far departed from its natural course, as
to rise where it ought to set, and set where it ought to
rise." What is there here, even if that were so, that is
applicable to the stopping of the earth, and the rolling
of it back in the case of Hezekiah, or the stopping of the
sun and moon, in the days of Joshua? How does it
apply to either of these cases, any more than it does to
the destruction of Jerusalem, or the conquest of Britain
by the Romans?

It is a maxim in logic, sound and good, that " an argument which proves too much, proves nothing." That
axiom seems to have a most direct bearing upon the present case ; for, if there was anything, at any time, any
event, any catastrophe, which could have laid the foundation for this tradition among the Egyptians, *other than
that which we have supposed*, and ours, it must be
remembered, *is an historical fact*, it was an event which
undeniably disqualifies it for an application to the case
before us. The record we are considering does not represent the sun as rising or setting where, or when it ought
not to. No mention is made of disorder, or wonder in
this direction. It is not said, that in order to bring the
shadow back ten degrees, upon the device of Ahaz, the

sun went down in the east: it is not even intimated that his position there is altered in the least; but only, that his shadow is made to return ten degrees, by which degrees it had gone down. All we have to do, therefore, is to say, in plain English, what this means; and our guide to this is, as it should be, *the original Hebrew*. There is no intimation that the arrangements of nature were subverted; the earth convulsed; the heavens thrown into a confused mass, in order to furnish Hezekiah with the satisfactory sign that he should recover. On the contrary, "order reigns," above and below; while in answer to the prophet's prayer, "the sun returned ten degrees, on the degrees which it had gone down;" and Hezekiah regards it as a satisfactory proof that he shall be permitted to recover from a sickness which was at first thought and declared to be unto death.

The reader must not understand us as feeling uneasy at the evidences of a desire on the part of learned commentators and others to find something, *some tradition*, some scrap of history, in respect to the ages that are past, of a catastrophe or event, that can be made to answer the exigencies of this case. On the contrary, we think such a desire altogether reasonable. We are fully persuaded, that if *we* had come to the conclusion, that "the sun once stood still in the midst of heaven and hasted not to go down for the space of a whole day," (understood, of course, as it was intended to be, that he paused there and became stationary, or at least appeared to,) or that it had been arrested in its flight through the heavens and made to move backwards, so that its shadow should retrace its steps "*ten degrees*," we should certainly employ no little time, if our life were given us, in searching among the traditions and records of the past for something to confirm and establish our faith. These are events, that in respect to their effects *must have reached every part of the globe ;* just as did those of the deluge.   Why, then, should we not look for some knowledge of them every where, wherever man is found ! The waters of Noah have written their own history upon the mind of the world.   No nation or people, no considerable portion of the human family any where upon the face of the earth, that cannot tell you something of the flood. But in respect to a certain day, which was as long again as any other day, and still another, one in which the sun paused in mid-heaven, as if he had forgotten something and left it behind him in his bed-chamber, and was about to return in search of it, both tradtion and history, (that which is called profane,) are as silent as the grave.   We do sincerely appeal to every intelligent reasonable man ; *ought* we not to expect to find some knowledge of such an event, if such had ever occurred ?

Instead of saying anything, therefore, in the way of *discouraging* these investigations, we would most heartily approve of them.   We believe that those who differ from us, in regard to the nature of that " sign," of Hezekiah's recovery, so far as to believe that the sun was arrested in his course through the heavens, and made to return, (we are obliged to use language here as it was used in the days of Isaiah,) we think they cannot be better employed, than in looking up something, either among the traditions of men, or in the history of the past, to meet their particular case.

The tradition referred to by Herodotus, however, will

not answer the purposes or object for which it is cited. The supposition to which we have already referred, to wit, that the tradition was to be traced to the account given by those early travelers, is the only one, as it seems to us, which can be assigned as its cause. Had those same men gone far enough in *the opposite* direction, they might have reported, on their return, that the sun, for the space of several days had refused to set at all, either in the east or west; that he persisted in showing himself for several months directly in the north, at midnight, bright as at noonday, and that in the course of a few weeks afterwards he had wholly refused to rise at all. This would have been a far greater wonder at that age, and one that would have been regarded as altogether more incredible than to see the sun turn about and sink back to his chamber in the east.

Another consideration, and one which is of some weight in determining this point, is, that if there were literally and truly a sun-dial used on this occasion, it must have been constructed very much as they are at the present day, with their circles and lines dividing the day into portions, if not hours, yet periods which very nearly answered to them. But it is evident that the Hebrews, neither at the time referred to, nor for hundreds of years after, knew anything of such a division of the day, as that which is now known by the term hour. Their language, however, is not as in the former case, wholly without a word to express a very short, and probably indefinite period, and one which is called an hour. שָׁעָה shâ-âh, (the import of which we have just suggested,) means a very short period. See Daniel iii. 15, and iv. 33. In the books of Moses, and in other Hebrew writings the term "hour," is used to signify *the season*, a specific time, whether more or less, its length depending on, or determined by the circumstances under con sideration.   For example, in the place just referred to, Daniel iii. 15, " but if ye worship not, ye shall be cast *the same hour* into a burning fiery furnace," that is *at once*, or as soon as it can be done.   Another example we have in Daniel iv. 19, which must be understood in the same way, since the term שעה shâ-â, when used as a verb signifies to see, as at a glance or in a moment.   The noun, therefore, which is derived from it must express the same idea ; a sight, or at a glance.   Daniel, Tobit and Judith are our earliest authorities for using the word to signify a division of the day, or a part of the night.   In every case, however, the import is not only indefinite, but it is indefinitely short.   The Greeks appear to have been quite ignorant of this division of time, at the period referred to, and can trace it no higher among themselves than to Anaximenes, or Anaximander, in the reign of Cyrus, or towards the close of the Babylonish exile. " The result," says Mr. Calmet, " to which we must come on this subject, is, that the use of time-measures, or sun-dials, and the distribution of the day into hours, is more ancient in the east," (meaning Chaldea or Persia,) " than among the Greeks ; that the author of the invention is not known, and that *we cannot tell in what manner the ancient Babylonians and Chaldeans divided their hours of day and night.*"

All this, in the form of a very hearty concession, as we perceive, from the very man who stands high with the world as a Biblical critic and oriental scholar, and who, some time ago, as the reader will undoubtedly remem·

ber, informed us that "the dial of Ahaz" was undoubtedly brought from Babylon!

But we will not pause here. The night was divided into four quarters, or greater hours, termed *watches;* each watch containing three lesser hours. These watches were also called by other names, according to that part of the night which closed each one. The first was called "*the even,*" the second, "*midnight;*" the third, "cock-crowing;" the fourth, "the dawn." See Mark xiii. 35, "Watch, therefore, for ye know not *when* the master of the house cometh; whether at even, or at midnight, or at the cock-crowing, or in the morning."

The word hour, therefore, is evidently used with great latitude in the scriptures. When *first* introduced, and for a long time, it was altogether indefinite, in respect to its length, being used very nearly in the sense of the Greek, "ἐν ταχύ," or the English "*at once,*" or as soon as possible. Towards the age of the Apostles it became more fixed and definite. Yet there are passages in the New Testament where the term hour would seem to embrace *a whole watch.* Matthew xxvi. 40, "What! could ye not watch with me one hour?" one space of time allotted to that duty? See also, Revelations iii. 3, Matthew xxiv. 43, 44, and xxv. 13.

"The word hour, in the scriptures," says Mr. Robinson, "signifies one of twelve equal parts into which the day was divided, which, of course, were of different lengths at different seasons of the year. This mode of dividing the day, prevailed among the Jews, at least, after the exile, and perhaps earlier. Anciently, however, the usual division of the day was into four parts; morning, heat of the day, midday and evening. But when the Jews became subject to the Romans, they adopted the manner of dividing the night into four watches, as above described.

The reader will be careful to remark, that for all these various divisions of time, the Hebrew has a specific term; one by which a particular portion is meant. But when we come to the age of Daniel, we find a term in the Chaldee character, which is properly translated *hour*, though evidently used, as we have seen, to designate one of the shortest divisions of time; one which scarcely admits of the idea of duration or continuance.

What now, are we to do with the passage under consideration? In the translation which is given us in reference to this whole matter, a language is used which sounds very much as if it were a record of a much later age, and of far more recent events. Nay, it seems as if we were using the language of to-day. After introducing the dial, the term *degrees* strikes us very much as if we were standing by an instrument of that kind, which we knew had been in use at the longest but a few years. And what is said of " the shadow," is very intelligible, so long as it is represented as passing backward or forward; but when we find the representation that of *as*cending and *de*scending, (unless we understand the former as approaching xii o'clock, and the latter as that of sundown,) it becomes rather difficult for us to ascertain what is meant.

Many have felt this difficulty, and in order to obviate it, some have supposed the dial, as it is called, was a kind of pillar, standing in the court of the palace. But whatever it was, or stand where it might, it must have been constructed on essentially the same principles upon which instruments are constructed at the present day for measuring time by the sun, in order to justify the language used in the translation before us. And if thus, the day must have been divided virtually as now: all which we conceive to be incredible if not impossible.

Whenever we sit down to the perusal of a history which proposes to inform us of that which has taken place in any part of the world at an age this side of the period at which *printing* was invented, if we know that art was in use in the country of which we are reading, we are not surprised at witnessing references, in one way and another, to something connected with that art. But when we peruse a work like that of Homer's Illiad, or his Qdyssy, and find in neither of them the slightest re-ference to anything connected with the art of writing, we are constrained to admit the probability that *that* poem, however perfect, was evidently composed, either as a whole, or which is far *more* probable, in short, fugi-tive pieces, and gathered into its present form at a period when the art of writing was but little if at all known. So in respect to fire-arms, (if I may be excused for returning to this illustration, once more,) any of the terms which are used at the present day, in connection with their use, or as descriptive of their effects, are en-tirely out of time and without meaning, when employed in a writing which purports to have been in existence at a time and place where fire-arms were unknown. Among civilized nations, at the present time, a shield is scarcely known as an instrument of warfare, any more than was a gun and bayonet in the days of Abraham: while the sword is common to almost all countries, if not all ages.

The reader will permit us to say, by way of explanation, we are endeavoring to set before him, in as clear a light as possible, *the law*, though unwritten, which pervades the world in reference to this matter. They who are attempting the history of any people, or a description of any event, whose object it is to portray an evil or describe a practice among men, are shut up by this law to the use of terms which would be altogether inapposite, when employed in any other age, or applied to any other subject. The painter who attempts to delineate with his art, a scene or an event, historically belonging to another age, must carefully study the history of that age, lest he introduce upon the canvas characters or circumstances which were unknown to that age, and which, of course, will convince an intelligent, well-educated man who looks upon his work, that the author was himself unacquainted with that which he attempted to impart to others. For example: a painting representing the fall of Jerusalem, when taken by Titus Vespacian, that should clothe the beleaguered walls of the city in the smoke and thunder of modern warfare, would only provoke the pity of every intelligent man that had occasion to look at it. So, he that should attempt a description of the Crusades, and in any way, whether by mistake or design, should say what implied the use of those "carnal weapons" which are peculiar to a later age, would stand before an intelligent age convicted of an unpardonable blunder. The writer himself once had the pain and mortification of witnessing the so-called assassination of either Cæsar or Belshazzar, he cannot now tell which : but the terrible deed was done by a man on horse-back with a common horse-pistol !   Nor are his feelings very dissimilar, when, as he reads the history of David and Jonathan, he sees it stated, that " Jonathan gave his *artillery* into the hands of the lad, sending him away to the city." 1st Saml. xx. 40.

We have often asked ourselves, whether, at the period or age of our present translation, *the simple bow and arrows of an ancient warrior* were designated by that formidable word, " *artillery?*"   If so, it is evident, that word has undergone a change in its import, that would render it fatal to the reputation of a translator, or even a writer, who should use it to express that idea.   Artillery, great guns, in the days of Saul and Jonathan !

We are obliged, however, to confess, that our feelings are not wholly unlike these, when we read the passage under examination, as it stands in our authorized version.   We are pained to find such sad and melancholy proofs, if not of carelessness, of a lack of something which ought ever to be unheard of with a translator— *a sound judgment ;* or, as John Milton would say, " a good, sound—round about sense."   We cannot fully protect ourselves against fears, that he who has been guilty of such an oversight as this, in circumstances as important as the translation of God's message to man, cannot be trusted, as a translator, anywhere.   Were there not a kind of sacredness associated with the names, and attached to the very characters of those who took part in this venerable translation, such examples of disloyalty to the Great Author of the original would destroy our confidence in their ability to perform what they had undertaken.   We never sit down to the investigation of this great subject, (the question of a new, or corrected version of the scriptures,) without perceiving our mind slowly but most firmly being made up in favor of it. Hitherto we have been among the most confident that the time had not come by a full century or more, for moving in that direction; but our confidence has forsaken us in this matter: Our reasons for suffering the old version to remain intact, have sunk down, one after another, until all, or nearly all, have disappeared.

Still we cherish for the present version, notwithstanding its undeniable imperfections, the most profound respect. We love beyond all else, in the department of letters, the sound and substantial tone of almost all its declarations. The ease and man-like skill, with which the translator comes to the selection of the very best terms for the expression of a truth, or the enunciation of a precept, we regard as worthy of all acceptation. This, however, only leads us the more deeply to deplore those instances in which we see, or think we see, the indisputable evidences of error, or want of judgment. That power and precision, with which they have expressed those nice shades of thought and feeling, especially in the Psalms, cannot but command the respect and approbation of all who have been the subjects of those deep, religious emotions which are there described. How oft, when engaged in religious exercises or devotions, our thoughts confined to what was then passing in the council-chamber of our own mind, have we turned from every form of expression, from every mere human or uninspired effort at description, to those which we found only in the word of God! Look, for example, at the 139th Psalm: "O Lord, thou hast searched me and known me: thou knowest my down-sitting and my up rising ; thou understandest my thoughts afar off." That is, "Distance doth not dim thy sight." "Thou compassest my path and my lying down, and art acquainted with all my ways." "Thou compassest my path:" Marginal—"thou winnowest my way;" just as the husbandman winnows his grain to separate the chaff from the wheat! And in the 51st Psalm—"Create in me a clean heart, O, God; and renew a right spirit within me. Cast me not away from thy presence, and take not thy Holy Spirit from me. Restore unto me the joy of thy salvation; and uphold me *spirit free.*" Sadly marred is the sense of this important passage ; besides being made to convey a wrong idea. It is the prayer of David, that *his* spirit may be made *free ;* free from the bondage of the flesh, no longer in subjection to sense. No traces of that singular prayer which is found in our common English Bibles can be found in the original Hebrew. The word which is rendered, "*free,*" and which our translation represents as expressing a quality of the Spirit of God, means—*princely, liberal, free*—as opposed to the idea of narrow, selfish, slavish.

The reader will perhaps smile at the idea of praising a book, which in the estimation of every intelligent man on earth, is *above* all praise : but—our object in what we have said, has been, not only to give our voice in favor of every true excellence, in the present version ; but also to set forth the reasons or considerations which have led us to decide in favor of a new, or corrected version. There can be no manner of difficulty in sending forth an edition of the sacred volume, which shall retain all the desirable qualities that are possessed by the translation before us; and with these, a correct and most perfect version; one that shall be free from all the errors, whether of translation or anything else, which are undeniably found in that which is now in general use. We want to see a version in which you shall search in vain for the foolish and mischievous story of "Samson and his Foxes;" or that of the Dial of Ahaz; or the profane and false declaration that "Joshua commanded the sun and moon to stand still, and they obeyed him." We wish to see an edition of the Word of God by men that will permit it to speak for itself, whether its testimony shall harmonize with the developments of modern science or not. We are waiting to see the first passage, which when properly understood, shall conflict with the plain and obvious deductions of either science or philosophy.

But it was not our object, in this essay, to set forth the reasons, which we are confident may be advanced in favor of the enterprise we have just named: Still, we see no impropriety in expressing our convictions of the necessity of such an undertaking; adding as we may, the assurance, that our present investigations have had for their ultimate object the *proof* of such a necessity. We do not wish, as ministers of the gospel, to spend our time in meeting and removing objections to the sacred record, which belong only to the translation. Too many, at the present day, are virtually in the position in which Voltaire found himself; filled with all malice against the whole Bible, on account of an absurdity here and there found, which belonged exclusively to the translation. After having vented his spleen at the whole book, pronouncing it a bundle of absurdities, he was coolly informed by the Jews of Amsterdam, that his quarrel was with an incorrect translation and not with the Bible, properly speaking. We have no doubt that thousands of amiable and sincere persons, in their patient endeavors after truth, have had their whole mind and soul hopelessly soured against that truth, which otherwise would have made them wise unto salvation, from having found in the word of God, bound up with the story of the Cross, and apparently a part of the divine message, the silly, absurd and utterly incredible stories to which we have already referred. Our life is too short, our time too precious, to be wasted in the most patient and humble endeavors to remove absurdities which belong only to the errors of uninspired men.

And since we are fairly engaged on a theme that we have already repudiated, we will only add, what would seem to be too obvious to need proof, that no man is ever benefited by believing an error: Evil, unmixed and infallible, must come to any man, who regards that as truth which is only its opposite. It would almost seem that some have a kind of idea, that if they believe *every* thing, they will of course believe all the truth there is in the world. But every man that compels himself to say or even *think* that he believes what his conscience assures him he does not, and what his reason tells him he cannot believe, very soon, and very easily brings himself to think as lightly of that which he knows to be true, as he does of that which he knows to be false.

But to the work before us : Instead of being opposed to new versions or new translations, criticisms, strictures, essays, any thing in the way of candid and serious investigations of the word or truth, we greatly desire them.

We believe that truth, just as Christ its author, in the presence of doubting Thomas, *challenges* investigation. We believe also, that the present is an age, peculiarly fitted for such an undertaking as that which we have indicated; and that the sacred record has nothing to fear from even the most thorough and searching investigations.

It surely is a source of no little satisfaction to us, and we think it is to many others, that the God of truth has so arranged the affairs of his providence as to make it more and more difficult to propagate error, and increasingly easy to defend the truth. It has evidently been his aim from the first, in some way or other, to multiply witnesses for the truth; to station them along the pathway of righteousness; that they may cheer and encourage the heavenward traveler, and rebuke, with terrible effect, the man that will allow himself to trifle with the ways of God.

This " cloud of witnesses" is composed sometimes of such things as the world calls *circumstances :* sometimes of events which are of a most serious and interesting character. But whatever their form or name, they ever point as with the finger of God, to those truths which their testimony is intended to sustain. If, for example, in Geology, there is *a particular dispensation*, there are a multitude of facts which belong to that particular period: they must all of them be classed with a specific series of events; for they can be explained with reference to these events and no other. In the department of Comparative Anatomy there are certain characteristics, or features, which belong to the bones of an animal; no man errs, or is *exposed* to err, who makes these characteristics the basis of his description of that animal,

5*

in regard to his habits, modes of life, etc. etc. Those
that live on land will carry certain characteristics or features in their bones, to distinguish them for ever from
the remains of those animals that were created to in-
habit the waters: and these will be furnished with those
which will sufficiently distinguish them from the am-
phibious tribes.

Precisely so in respect to religious considerations;
there is a language adapted to the Mosaic economy: its
terms, modes of expression, order of exercises, forms of
worship, etc. etc., look only in the direction of Moses;
so much so, that the reader of the Epistle to the Hebrews, at the present day, will not fail to see one mode
of expression there, which will assure him, that, at the
time when this epistle was being written, the temple in
Jerusalem was still standing, and those sacrifices which
were accustomed to be offered there had not ceased.
The simple announcement in the gospels, that the shep-
herds in Jewry were keeping sheep, on the night in
which Christ was born, that they were out with their
flocks in the open fields, keeping watch, "when suddenly there was with the angel a multitude of the
heavenly hosts praising God," etc., cannot be reconciled
with the idea that Christ was born on the twenty-fifth
of December, for at that season of the year, it is cold in
Judea as in any other country occupying the same latitude.

There is a costume for every thought; a specific vest-
ment for every historic age, and for every fact. No
statement can possibly be made by an uninspired man,
in respect to anything that *now is*, that shall foretell as
God in Prophecy, the events of the future. Man has

power in this matter only to misrepresent; he can make statements in regard to *the present*, that are obviously untrue; and that every man of his generation can affirm to be so; he can also declare in respect to *the past*, what can be demonstrated as false; but in this demonstration we must use those things which are *facts;* things known and read of all men; *arguments*, employed to disprove a proposition which is untrue, like those which are brought forward in support of the true, must be such as to commend themselves at once to our notice as so many *facts*, things or results which cannot be accounted for but by the supposition that it is, or is *not*, as affirmed.

Accordingly, the term *sun-dial*, or "*dial*," as it is used in the passage under review, is a term evidently born out of due time. It is not old enough for the idea that it is made to represent in that passage, by many hundreds of years! In looking for it among the records of antiquity, we find ourselves placed in circumstances not unlike those in which we should be placed, were we to go in search of the Electro Magnetic Telegraph in the days of Columbus, or one of Colt's Revolvers in the days of the Crusaders.

Whatever, then, be the age, the state, the institution; whatever be the law, the ceremony or the rite, there will inevitably be certain peculiarities in the terms which are used, which cannot be explained without a direct reference to the subject to which they belong. And they will be of a nature too, that will render it impossible for them to be used, except where they are evidently in place, as applicable to that economy which they were appointed to explain and perhaps support.

Let these considerations be applied to the case in

hand. The conversation which passes between the Prophet and his King, is all very natural and in keeping with the age. But when the translators refer to an instrument for measuring time, which, as is well known, belonged to a much later age, and which, perhaps, was never employed by the Jews at any period, if indeed ever known to them till after the Christian era, we are conscious that something more than curiosity directs our attention to that matter at once. A language is employed in reference both to the sun's ascension and declension, a statement made concerning the distance which his shadow has passed over, and which it is said to have re-traced, that strikes us very forcibly as belonging to a much later period of the world. Instead of being engaged in listening to the conversation between a Prophet of the Lord and his king, at a period some seven hundred or eight hundred years anterior to the days of Jesus Christ, we find ourselves standing by an instrument of modern date, listening to the free and familiar use of terms that belong to modern improvements in arts and science.

We have said above that the " dial " was probably *never* in use among the Jews. Our reasons for this belief, as we have many times said, are the utter silence of the language, in respect to a term which should express or represent such an instrument. Whenever the Mariner's Compass has been known; or wherever it has been introduced, it has at once *compelled* the people that have received it to furnish a name by which it should be known. When the steam engine was first introduced, there was no word by which it could be designated. Its inventors, or those who first used it were obliged to contrive for it a name, as best they could, and on the shortest notice. So with respect to everything connected with its use, or the use of steam, whether in navigation or in propelling machinery. What success should we meet with, should we attempt to find among the works of antiquity, even no further back than the history of the English nation, the terms we have just named? And thus in respect to the Telegraph, it has an existence both here and elsewhere over most of Europe; and it has a name, such as it is. But should we be likely to find it among the records of our nation, or the reports of our literary societies, previous to the year, or thereabouts, of its construction?

Endeavoring to get around this difficulty, many have advanced the hypothesis to which we have already adverted, viz: that the dial was probably brought, as they express it, "from the east." By which is meant, as we suppose, from Chaldea or from Persia. Let it be admitted that it was brought from the east; was it known in the country from which it came without a name? And how long did it remain in that to which it was brought, without that very important appendage? The Magnetic Telegraph is a native, so to speak, of this country. It has already been introduced into almost all the countries of the civilized world; but it has carried its name with it. It matters not whether it be that by which it has been known here, or whether it is by some other. Undoubtedly there is a term by which it is readily known, wherever it is found; so that in describing it, or its magic power of conveying intelligence from one place to another, or in speaking of it any way, a writer of the age in which we live would not have to use a term which meant only "a flight of stairs;" unless, in fact, a flight of stairs, *was the Telegraph.*

This point settled, and we may apply the reasoning to the case in hand. Our argument is this; the utter silence of the Jews, in their language, the undeniable absence of a term for naming, or designating such an instrument, amounts to little short of demonstration that no such instrument was known there, at the period referred to. A child is no sooner born, whether of Christian or pagan parentage, rich or poor, bond or free, than it has a name bestowed upon it. But here is a plan, a device for measuring time; an instrument for informing man of the rapid flight of his days; but, unhappily there is no term for distinguishing it from a pruning hook, a battle ax, or " a flight of stairs"! Impossible.

We feel compelled for a moment to notice the language which is used by the translators in another respect. Like that which is employed in " the Book of Jasher," where Joshua is represented as commanding the sun and moon to stand still, and they obey him, *it is evidently founded on erroneous views of natural science :* Nothing is plainer than that they who translated this passage (Joshua x. 12, 15) and left it as we have it in our Bibles, believed, in accordance with the old and exploded notion, that the earth was stationary; and that the sun, moon and heavenly bodies revolved around it. This was the almost universal belief, as late as to the middle of the sixteenth century. Even Luther, when arguing in support of this theory, refers to the passage in Joshua, saying "sun, stand thou still on Gibeon, and thou moon in the valley of Ajalon." "This," says Luther, " could not have been, had the earth revolved upon its axis : No ! the earth must therefore be *stationary ;* and the sun, moon and stars revolve around it."

Now, it cannot be denied, as we have already remarked, that to produce that effect, the apparent stopping of the sun and moon, *the earth* must be stopped : some tall arch-angel must be commissioned, or commanded to apply the brakes ; or roll a great globe into its path ; or what is more consonant with our subject, *God must stop it.* There is no other way for bringing about even an *apparent* pausing of the sun ; unless we adopt the hypothesis of Mr. Barns, to wit, that " the sun's rays, by a miraculous display of Divine power, were bent out of their natural course, so that the shadow should seem to be turned back, the requisite number of steps."

Mr. B. takes precisely the ground, in respect to the case we are considering, which the late Professor Stuart took in regard to the standing still of the sun and moon. When the writer of this article was engaged in preparing his *first*, on that subject, he wrote to Mr. Stuart for his opinion on the general subject : The Professor replied by saying, he had long regarded it as taking place *only in appearance* ; κατ οψιν, as he expressed it. He supposed the rays of light were so bent from their natural course as to make an additional day ! How the professor managed to get the earth and *time back* into their former relations, or movements, neither he nor Mr. Barns informs us.

That would do but little, however, towards helping us out of the difficulty. It is evident enough, that the Jewish historian, when recording the miracle which Isaiah performed, neither saw nor felt any necessity for providing for an increased length of the day. It is fair, therefore, for us to conclude, that in the narrative, as it came from his hand, *there was no stopping of the sun;* for this would of necessity have increased the length of the day. *Jasher*, when he had represented Joshua as stopping the sun, immediately provided for the natural effects by adding, " so the sun stood still about the space of a whole day." This was not only natural; it was, so to speak, unavoidable; for, as the journey of the sun through the heavens, (I speak of it as it appears) is that which produces the day, so the stopping of it any where above the horizon must prolong that day the full length of time that it has been stopped.

The reader must not accuse us of spending unecessary time on this part of our subject : we are too well aware of the strength of this, our present position. If it be proved that the day was not prolonged, it will follow, as we have just seen, that the sun was not arrested in his journey through the heavens : and another result will be, the miracle which was wrought will be found to be some thing essentially different from what it has been supposed to be.

Now, that the day was in no sense increased, is evident, in the first place from the total silence of the Jewish historian on that subject. It does not seem to have entered his mind, that what the prophet had done to satisfy the anxious Hezekiah of his recovery from sickness, had produced even the slightest effect on the length of the day. We therefore feel justified in adopting the opinion which we have just expressed; that the earth was neither stopped in its diurnal motion, nor was the day in any measure increased as to its length.

And further; if that had been the case, as we have already intimated, it would have been noticed, by man all over the world ; and though he might not be able to fur

nish those who lived at a later period with any assurances of it, except in the way of his traditions, yet in
these, he certainly would have preserved a most faithful
remembrance of it.

This consideration is duly noticed by Mr. Barns,
in his comments on this passage : he admits, as of course
he must, that if the day had been prolonged, (as it certainly must have been, if the sun had been made to
either stop or retrograde,) *it would have been noticed by
every nation and by every people upon the earth :* and
he correctly construes the universal silence of the world
on that subject ; regarding it a most sound and irrefragable proof that there was no such event.   Still ; Clark,
Scott, Henry and some others, think, as we have already
said, that 2 Chron. xxxii. 31 is a reference to a recognition of it in Babylon at least.

However ; a single reference to the record will satisfy
any one, that quite another subject is referred to ; "*The
wonder* that was in the land," and that " the princes of
Babylon were sent to inquire about," was " the splendor
and wealth of the house of his precious hings; the silver
and the gold, the spice and the precious ointment ; and
all that was found in his treasures : there was nothing in
his house nor in all his dominion, that Hezekiah showed
them not." See 2 Kings xx. 13.   The reader will observe
that no mention is here made of the miracle which had
been wrought, as there certainly would have been, had
there been one of the nature supposed, the stopping of
the sun, or the lengthening of the day, and had it been
the object of these princes in coming to Jerusalem to
inquire into it.   And when the Prophet called on Hezekiah, to remind him of his folly and to assure him that
this freak of his pride and vanity would cost him all his
treasures ; and that his sons should be made to serve in

the palace of the King of Babylon, as a punishment of his folly, there is not the attempt at a defense on the part of Hezekiah, as there certainly would have been, had his folly consisted only in showing them what God had done for him in restoring to him his health : nothing can be more certain than this.

Then again; where this subject is noticed once more, in the passage above referred to, (2 Chron. xxxii. 31,) the record is even more explicit : it is there evident enough that it was in respect to the king's *wealth*, that it is said " the Lord left him to try him, that he might know all that was in his heart." If this " wonder," which they had been sent to inquire about, had been the miracle that had been wrought, there would of course have been no mention of his indiscretion as consisting in showing them his riches. We cheerfully admit the probability that the translators thought otherwise : they undoubtedly supposed, that it was the miracle which Isaiah had wrought, as is evident from their inserting the word " *done*," as they have. A small matter this, to be sure ; but small as it is, it makes a great difference in the import of the passage ; even all there is between what *is* and what is done. We may also admit, that their opinion is of great weight, without regarding it infallible : they were not inspired ; nor were they furnished with the advantages or helps for giving to the world a correct translation, which are enjoyed at the present day. Besides ; they had no means for knowing what was *the errand* of those ambassadors, that we do not possess, they come to a conclusion, in respect to this matter, from premises or circumstances that are lying here before us now : what hinders *our* knowing as much about it as they ? still further, in 2 Chron. xxxii. 27–30 a more particular account is given us of the immense riches which belonged to Hezekiah ; as if to convince all who should read that they *were* " a great wonder in the land," From the manner in which they are mentioned, and from the frequency with which they are spoken of, we should judge, that the king of Babylon was not alone in thus regarding them : they are here enumerated with great particularity, *after* due notice had been taken of the miracle ; as if, in the estimation of every one, they were far *more* wonderful than the sign which had been given of Hezekiah's recovery.

We regard ourselves as admonished in the twenty-fourth verse of the chapter last mentioned, not to be hasty in our decisions as to what was actually *done*, which constituted that sign. The passage reads as follows : "In those days was Hezekiah sick unto death, and he prayed unto the Lord; and he spake unto him, and he gave him a sign." Marginal, " wrought a miracle for him." There can be no doubt what the sacred historian refers to here ; but, if this sign that was given, or miracle that was wrought for the benefit of the king, consisted in causing the wheels of time to roll back, or the shadow to return ten degrees on a literal dial, why is there not an allusion to it in some way or other ? The historian whose words we have here, regarded himself as being sufficiently definite. There was a miracle wrought, and that miracle, whatever it was, was a sign to Hezekiah that he should recover from his sickness. Why is not this on the whole rather a plain intimation, that *that* is all we are to know about it ? It certainly could not have been, that he who wrote the second Book of Chronicles did not *know* in what that miracle, consisted as well, at least, as the translators of the present version did. Hence we have been led to think the more of *the manner* in which that historian has thought fit to leave the subject.

But I must neither close the discussion nor leave this part of it without a reference, (a single one further) to the fact, that if such an event ever happened as is stated in the translation before us, there must have been found, in some parts of the earth, a scrap or fragment of it in the shape of a tradition. Among the nations of the earth, if not now, yet at some former period, there must have been some knowledge of a day unlike any other "in all the hoary registers of time." Especially must this have been the case with those nations that *then* lived, and perhaps now do in and about Palestine. And I wish it to be distinctly understood, that tradition most certainly would have been of a very peculiar character ; it must and would have been such as to have *suggested* something more than the mere fact which had originated it ; just as in the case of the flood. In every nation which was then upon the earth, you not only find a tradition of that catastrophe ; but that tradition always approaches, with more or less particularity, to the main circumstances in the case. Among the aborigines of our own country, the tradition is, that once there was a mighty chief, who, seeing the increasing waters, gathered his family into a great canoe, and set forth in search of dry land ; that after floating about upon the waters for a long time, they landed upon a high mountain, etc.

We cannot of course go further in describing this tradition, nor need we ; the same particularity in detail of circumstances is found in the traditions of every nation ; so much so, that nothing but obstinate blindness will fail to see in these that which corroborates the great truth, that in the days of Noah the old world was destroyed by a flood.

To apply this reasoning, then; had there been in existence a tradition of that event which is said to have been the prolonging of the day, by the retrograde moving of the sun,) that tradition would have been something like the following; especially among the nations around Palestine: "In the times past, the sun, on a certain occasion, suddenly *stopped ;* and without pausing, hurried back to the chambers of the east ; from whence he set out again on his journey for the day," etc. Among the barbarous tribes still west of that country, to whom the sun was of course just rising, the tradition would have been varied so as to accord with an earlier hour of the day. The half-clad savages of Europe, especially of its western borders, would have gazed in utter dismay, to have seen their fiery god turn suddenly back, as if to seek something which in his haste he had left behind him in the morning; and, to the latest generation, the chief or head of each family would have entertained his posterity with a full length history of the strange event in all its particulars.

Another consideration, bearing upon the main question, should be presented ere this discussion is brought to a close. Whenever anything is found in the volume of Inspiration, which, in fact evidently conflicts with the facts of science, it amounts to a certainty, that it is either not understood, or it is no part of the word of God. Not that Revelation " borrows leave to be," from science, or science from Revelation ; for what God has said in vol. I., of his works, or, in other words, in the works of Nature, is, and must of necessity be in harmony with what he has said in vol. II., which is the word of Inspiration.   The testimony of either, on any point which comes within its appropriate jurisdiction, is abundantly sufficient, and if properly understood, is the end of debate.   Man may misunderstand the works of Nature, may misinterpret them, just as he may misunderstand, or mistranslate the word of God.   Yet that is no fault of the Word, nor any infraction of the Rule.   For example, the Mosaic account of the creation, found in the first chapter of Genesis, without controversy, and beyond all dispute has been so misunderstood.   Many were the hours of deep anxiety which were passed by us in the examination of that passage, with a view to ascertain whether it could be so construed as to harmonize fairly and honorably with the undeniable developments of science.   And many were the reproaches from men of high standing, both in the literary and religious world, which were cast upon us and all like us. who were unwilling to *cut*, instead of untie the knot, who preferred patiently to investigate the subject, with the conviction that when correctly interpreted, both records would be found to agree.   We were sometimes denominated *semi-materialists*, said to be altogether inclined to the rationalistic philosophy, and regarded as unworthy to be trusted with expounding either the word of God or the lessons of science.   Yet, there stood the Mosaic cosmogony, (or account of the creation,) with the evident consciousness of its own rectitude, and the weight of six thousand years resting upon it.   There too, lay the geological record, cold and hard, though evidently written with the finger of God in the solid rock ; and many were they who were afraid to stoop down and read it, lest they should find that it contradicted his word.   Well do we remember the relief that it gave us to find that the two records were not only written by the same hand, but, that when correctly understood, they actually sustained each other. In point of fact, with men of thought, those whose lives are devoted to the study of the word of God, there has as great a revolution taken place within the last half century, (an exegesis of Genesis, chap. i,) as was witnessed during the sixteenth century, among the most learned of earth's population, on the general subject of Astronomy. It would be as difficult now to find an intelligent man advocating the theory of literal days in the history of the creation, as it would to find one of the same class endeavoring to support the position that the earth was stationary, and that the sun, moon, and stars revolved around it.

And how has this change been brought about? We answer for all. It has been by subscribing to the sentiment, or principle, that what God has said *in science*, is just as true, and just as worthy of all acceptation, as that which he has said in the volume of Inspiration.

Now we neither affirm nor deny, that God, who made the world, *might* arrest it in its revolutions, and *hold* it there, or compel it to turn back, so that the sun should actually set in the east. We think that fact, however, should go but a little way towards persuading us that such an event has ever taken place, or ever will. We are in the habit of placing just as much confidence in the uniformity and immutability of nature's laws, as we do in the promises or assurances of God's word; both are alike sure. And what is more, we regard all these views in perfect harmony with an intelligent belief of the word of Inspiration; our mind is fully made up, in respect to the passage upon which we have so long dwelt, it is unquestionably another, and a most melancholy case of *mistranslation*. We believe that since there is no word in the Hebrew language that signifies *dial*, the translators assumed a fearful responsibilty in thus translating the passage. We think with one whose words we have many times quoted, that we receive as revelation, all that God desires us to, when we suppose that the Prophet Isaiah was assisted of God to work a miracle, for the purpose of assuring Hezekiah that he should certainly recover from that sickness, which had it not been thus arrested, would have proved his last. We believe that the miracle consisted in causing the shadow of the sun, *in some way or other*, to move in a miraculous, or supernatural way upon some contrivance of his father Ahaz, something employed by him to measure time by; it may have been the shadow of a tree, or that of a tower, either of which describes a part of a circle, and by careful observation may be so divided as to be employed in dividing the day into very nearly equal portions. If this device was in fact " *a flight of stairs*," as would seem probable, if not entirely certain, from the word in the original Hebrew, then, *it should have been thus translated*, whether our translators could have understood it or not. Their efforts to help us understand the passage, we are constrained to believe, have led us for a long time to misunderstand it, which is all the verdict that we find against them.

There is, however, another view which may be taken of it, which differs materially from the one we have already given, and which—after all—may be the correct one. The whole transaction may be only an example of God's forgiving love towards Hezekiah, whom he had determined to cut off on account of his sins, but who, by repentance and submission had placed himself within

reach of the mercy of God, just as Ninevah had succeeded in averting that doom which overhung that city,
by timely repentance and faith.   In this case the whole
event, from first to last, would require to be placed on
record just as it occurred,—for the purpose of setting
forth God's willingness to forgive sins upon repentance
and faith : in other words, it was a gospel sermon,
preached by Him who devised the gospel.   Then, the
various expressions upon which we have dwelt, may be
considered only as examples of highly wrought poetry.
It is no uncommon thing for men at the present day,
when speaking of one who was evidently drawing near
to death, to say—" his sands are almost run :" meaning,
of course, that life was near its close.   And it was undoubtedly as common to use that expression, *or one
which is equivalent*, in the days of Hezekiah as it is now.
There is, in fact, a peculiar force—or expressiveness in
such a declaration.   Let the sands in the hour-glass be
regarded as the representatives of our moments here on
earth, and the figure is exceedingly expressive and beau-
tiful.   But the hour-glass was then unknown ; hence the
expressions of the passage before us.

Let it now be supposed, as it certainly must be, that
Ahaz had something, we cannot tell what, nor is it necessary that we should, by which he had been accustomed to mark the lapse of time.   The passage, as we
have often said, requires us to suppose that it was " a
flight of stairs," by which, in all probability, he was
accustomed to ascend to the top of his palace, at the
close of the day to enjoy the cool of the evening.   The
shadow, as it passed along down, step by step, is strikingly emblematic of his declining years.   The declaration, then, that the Lord caused the shadow to return

ten steps or "*degrees*," (if you will be careful not to associate here with the idea of a dial,) is simply that he caused the life of Hezekiah to be prolonged "fifteen years." God had so far restored the king's health as to permit him to go up unto the house of the Lord; and this partial recovery, or return to life, is both the symbol and earnest of his entire recovery. Let it still be borne in mind, that this recovery, partial though it was, was in answer to the prayers of the Prophet, accompanied as they were by those of the royal penitent. It thus became "a sign " given of God, and as truly a miraculous display of divine power as the restoration of the widow's son to life. The shadow is the emblem of life; its decline represents the king's waning years; its "return on the steps by which it had gone down," would of course represent his returning health, and the consequent prolonging of his years. In their prayer they both ask this, and it is granted. The pen of inspiration, in making a record of the event, puts the thing signified for the sign; which is, in fact, the cause of the misconception of the passage before us.

Should any one object, that neither of the views which we have taken appears to take any notice of the conversation which passed between the prophet and his king, in regard to the nature of the sign which should be given; we have only to reply that the idea of causing the shadow to pass on in advance of its natural speed, as Hezekiah suggested, would certainly be attended with no less difficulty than the causing of it to return; so that we cannot see that this consideration in any measure affects the supposition : it is as applicable to one as to the other. Besides; it seems to have been his opinion, that to hasten the shadow *forward* would

be an easy matter—even for any one to accomplish.
How,—easier? we ask.   Can there be any other meaning to this, than that which we have just given; the
king calls his *life* a shadow, and then affirms that it
would be an easy matter for Isaiah, or anybody else to
do that which would *hasten* its decline?   If we may
suppose that the Prophet acted in the two-fold capacity
of prophet and *physician*, (and the whole record justifies
this conclusion,) we can easily conceive that the declaration of the king had a fearful meaning to Isaiah.

A single consideration further, we think should be
noticed; the two records which we have of this event
differ very materially, on one or two points.   That
which we have in the Book of Kings contains no reference whatever to a certain "writing," us it is called,
which Hezekiah is said to have written on the occasion
of his recovery from his sickness.   This "writing"—
extending, as any one may see, from verse 9, chapter
xxxviii., in the record made by the prophet, to the end
of verse 20 of the same chapter—is poetry; while that
which precedes, and that which follows it, is the gravest
prose.   Professor Hengstenburg of Berlin, (for reasons
unknown to the writer,) rejects this "writing," altogether, as spurious and unworthy of our confidence: an
opinion in which we feel very much disposed to concur,
when we compare its style with that of the rest of the
record; in connection with the fact, that no mention is
made of it in the previous copy; or that which is found
in Kings.   What, the bearing of this upon the main
question—or whether any at all, we pretend not to say.
It would seem, however, to be sufficiently obvious, that
if the two records are both true, they should harmonize

on a point of as much importance as that under consideration.

It would seem, too, that we have something to learn from the consideration so carefully noticed in both records; to wit—that Isaiah prescribes an application of figs, in the form of a plaster, laid on to the boil. And this would appear to be thus noticed as an intimation that it was the means, under God, of Hezekiah's recovery. If so, why is it not proper to regard this fact as the miracle which Isaiah performed? Hezekiah's sickness was so severe, as that his life was despaired of, even by the prophet; yet an application of a very simple nature is blest to his recovery. Is there any thing extravagant or absurd in the supposition, that this was the wonder, or marvellous event at which we are to look in this transaction? And why not regard the fact of Hezekiah's recovery, so far as to " enable him to go up to the house of the Lord, on the third day," (the third from that on which he had been assured by the prophet of his recovery, instead of his death;) why not regard *this* event, as *the earnest*, the sign of the king's recovery? The return of the shadow, upon the steps, or degrees, upon which it had gone down, in highly figurative or poetic phrase, would be simply the revocation of the divine edict, and the consequent prolonging of his life. All this would be expressed most forcibly, though poetically, by representing the current of life as being turned back " ten degrees;" (ten, in Bible language, signifying a sufficient, or requisite number.)

There is then, in our humble opinion, nothing further to be said in regard to this passage: what we have affirmed in various ways is, that nothing *certain* can now be determined as to the nature, or character of that device, which Hezekiah, and his father Ahaz before him. had used for measuring time; but that certainly it was not, it could not have been *a sun-dial*; since nothing of the kind was known on earth till centuries after. We think it far better, and more in accordance with our duty as expositors of the word, to say, frankly, we do not know what this contrivance was, than to affirm, with our translators, that it was an instrument which probably was never known among the Jews of any period. Far better not to decide a point like this, than to decide it erroneously: for the tendency of this latter course is to ignorance, skepticism and infidelity; while the former is evidently in perfect harmony with an humble faith in the word of the living God: And this we hope ever to cherish.

CHAPTER III.

THE RESURRECTION OF THE BODY.

In the present paper we propose to meet two very plausible objections against the resurrection of the body; as, I. Death destroys the identity of the human body: II. There is not room for the dead when raised to stand upon the earth.

In other and more explicit terms, it is asserted, that if the dead should be raised, and in the resurrection, should occupy as much space as when alive and upon the earth, they would cover every foot of its surface, (the land) to the depth of *ten feet*, or more.

The doctrine of the resurrection, as taught in the Bible, is peculiar to the religion of Christ. It is evidently found in the Old Testament; but only shadowed forth there, in its relations to the great and sublime doctrines of the incarnation of the Son of God, his crucifixion and death.

No reason can be assigned, however, why we should make any distinction between the religion of the Old Testament and that of the New: It obviously is but one great system of truth, differing only in respect to the methods employed by Infinite Wisdom to impart that truth to man. For, if Christ sought to be explicit

on *any* subject, it was, that he meditated no change in
the system of doctrines in which the Jews had been educated; except, perhaps, in respect to an increasing degree of light; or, as some may express it, a change from
shadow to substance.   In some form or other the idea of
improvement, or more correctly, *progress*, is kept before
the mind of the reader in every part of the Bible.   Advance is inscribed on every page; just as in respect to
those who have embraced its doctrines: They are represented as daily making progress.   To stand still, is impossible to the believer; he is either advancing in the
divine life, or he is not of God.   There may be seasons
of sad and melancholy declension, such as would make
angels shudder; yet the true child of God will survive
them, as did Peter his denial of Christ, and David, his
fearful sin in the case of Uriah.   Spiritual life, at such
times, is like those cases of suspended animation, in
natural life; or, to use another and perhaps a more correct comparison, the heavenly traveler, in ascending the
hights of Zion, at such times, crosses a deep and perilous
ravine.   Therefore, they who claim for the system of
doctrines taught in the scriptures, that it is a perfect system—a claim which all prefer who regard them as given
by inspiration of God—must of necessity subscribe to the
idea of progress in those who have embraced that system.

In affirming, as we have, then, that the doctrine of the
resurrection of the body is peculiar to the Christian system, we have intended to say, only, that nowhere but in
the religion of Christ, do we find this idea entertained—
or this doctrine advanced.   No other form of religion,
however near it may approximate to the true, in other
respects, knows anything of that which Christ advanced

in the declaration, "I am the resurrection and the life: he that believeth in me, though he were dead, yet shall he live."

Many of those systems to which I have referred, embraced the idea of the immortality of the soul; *some*, of a future state of retribution: yea, most of them do; but in what way or by what means is evidently unknown to them. Obscurity, on these important points, is evidently a prevailing element in every form of religion but that which is the true.

Here we have the cause, undoubtedly, of that obstinate skepticism which exists on the general subject of the resurrection. Men are born sadducees: they witness the event of death; whether it be the death of a fellow-creature, or that of a beast; they see, that decay immediately commences; and, that in the course of a few hours, "Dust returns to dust again." Every intelligent man knows, that the same material laws obtain in regard to the dust of all mankind, which he sees employed in respect to the remains of an animal; or, in fact, a plant: that these laws, continually in operation, pick up each separate particle of matter and hasten to combine it with others, those which are employed to form another organization: that while not one atom has been lost or annihilated, every element of which the former body was composed, is scattered abroad as if never to be gathered again; or it is wrought into new forms and "brought out in a new edition, beautified and improved by its Author."

The exclamation of the Poet, "where is the dust that hath not been alive?" is not only a very important one, it is most natural, and worthy of our attention. There would *seem* at first sight, a plausible ground for the belief, that already "there *has* been upon the earth a sufficient number of the human race to cover its surface several feet in depth." This *seeming*, or theory, in the form of an objection to the doctrine of the resurrection of the body, it is the object of this paper to refute.

The author of the first Epistle to the Corinthians, (chap. xv.) judged correctly in supposing that the two great objections to the doctrine under consideration, were, as he there expressed them, "*how* the dead are raised; and with what body they come forth." He met these objections everywhere, in the course of his labors, as a minister of Christ. At Athens, they formed the butt of ridicule to "those who mocked;" and of a most painful solicitude to those who feared.

PART I.

The question with which we are at first concerned, regards *the identity of the bodies when raised from the dead, with those which were buried.* Are they the same with those which, as the Apostle says, "were sown?" What grounds or reasons have we for saying, 'the same bodies are raised from the dead, which we saw buried?' There is, indisputably, not a particle of matter in "the new edition," according to the expressed declarations of the word of God, which was there before; not *one* which was employed to form that body, during the day of probation, that can be found in it after it has been raised from the dead. Where, then, the propriety of affirming that it is the same body? Possibly the question of identity *may* turn on that of *atoms*, or elements of which the body, during its mission in the present world, was composed. If so, we are certainly without hope in respect to the resurrection of the dead.

This was the form of the objection which Paul first endeavored to meet. Accordingly, he referred his reader, (or anyone else, who should be troubled with this objection) to the well known fact, that grain, any and every kind, "was not quickened," that is, did not spring to life, "except it first died." In other words, there was, at the very out-set, in every instance where grain, such as wheat or corn, or any of the cereals were sown, the utter and complete dissolution of the particles of matter, composing the seed that was sown, before it could grow up. Its elements, so far as human observation could determine, were as widely scattered as those of the human body, which had been left to decay on the parched sands of the desert. And yet, no man, either in his conversation or thoughts, was ever understood to doubt the identity of the grain raised with that which had been sown. His language ever was, like that of revelation, "God giveth it a body as it has pleased him ; *and to every seed his own body.*"

But some may be inclined to examine this article, who do not cherish any very marked respect for the declarations of the Bible, either on this, or on any subject. They may be ready to admit, that Paul believed undoubtedly and most firmly, in the resurrection of the dead ; and yet, they may affirm in accordance with their *unbelief*, that no such event can possibly take place. They may, therefore, *object* to our method of expressing the sentiment, or argument in the language which, as we believe, "the Holy Ghost teacheth." But they certainly can find no fault with us for using the expressions as we do, when we affirm, that it is only out of respect to the Bible that we employ them. We do not by any means deny, that we regard our position as *doubly proved*, when we can find, as in the case before us, a declaration as in the word of God, covering precisely the ground of our argument. But we do maintain, that when this *first* objection, to wit: that death destroys our personal identity, is removed by every instance in which the husbandman succeeds in growing grain from seed, and that no man in his senses supposes either that the seed which is sown is annihilated, or that that which comes up and bears grain, is identically the same with that which was sown, if the question of identity, must turn on that of atoms or elements; the objector, whoever he may be, as it seems to us, should not only be silenced but satisfied forever. Because, if the question here were worth arguing, we might ask, on the supposition that it required the identical particles of matter to form the seed, where is there room for increase ? The cultivator of the soil, if he is so foolish as to employ himself in this way, might sow his bushel, take good care of it, and when every kernel came it would have just one kernel, and he would reap just his bushel.

The man, therefore, that objects to the doctrine of the resurrection, that it cannot be true, because the identity of the body sown is destroyed, must, in order to be consistent with himself, affirm that the whole business of raising grain is altogether absurd and incredible ; because there is no such thing as identity in respect to any body, or corporation, unless the identical particles or elements are employed in both cases. In fact, a denial of our position will place one in a very difficult situation: he would be obliged to deny the identity of every tree in the forest ; every leaf that grows ; every spire of grass ; every plant that springs from the sward : every animal that lives; every *man* that draws the breath of life : for no one of these, or of ten thousand other things that might be named, is the same thing for the space of two consecutive minutes, in the course of its existence as to the sameness, or identity of the elements, or parti- cles of matter—of which it is composed. No river, or lake, or even pool, is the same *now*, that it was one minute ago : every stone, or mountain ; every thing with which we are acquainted, here on earth,—or with which we expect to be acquainted in the world to come,—all are subject to one and the same law in respect to their identity ; that must be maintained without supposing an identity of materials in its composition, or it cannot be at all. He, therefore, who affirms—that a thing cannot be the same to-day, that it was yesterday, unless the identical atoms or particles of matter be found in it at both periods, makes a clean sweep in respect to the ques- tion of identity or even individuality. Under his law nothing can grow, any more than be diminished,—with- out annihilating itself. The child when he comes to be a man, must not be held responsible for what he did in childhood, for he is not the same being. The Psalmist had no occasion to pray—that God would not remember against him the sins of his youth. And the evil doer, whatever his crime, must be suffered to "go unwhip- ped of justice," unless he can be taken and punished in the very act; because a retribution which does not reach him instantly, reaches not *him*, the man that did the evil deed, but another and a very different being. The sick, when he recovers, may be prosecuted for the payment of his attendant physician and nurse, yet he can always enter an *alibi*, in his defense : he was not there · *he* is not the man that was sick; on the ground of the objection which we are examining, he to whom these services were rendered is nowhere. It will not be denied, by any intelligent man, that matter in any, and all its various forms, is constantly changing its position, passing from one organization into another; that there is no place, where, for any considerable time, it may be regarded as stationary. Experiments have many times demonstrated, that in the course of a very short period, every man, so far as he may be said to be composed of matter, undergoes a complete and thorough change. His very "*bones*," in the language of Job, may "be full of the sins of his youth;" but his sins are not matter: were they, in this respect, like either bones, or flesh, or blood; in other words, composed of matter, they would of themselves pass away, without waiting to be purged by "the blood of the everlasting covenant."

Identity, therefore, in respect to man, as well as in respect to almost every thing else, must be allowed to rest on something besides an identity of elements combined in its organization; or the thing must be given up as the wildest chimera: those nations that have been upon the earth, three, five, or fifteen hundred years—are the same *nations* they were a thousand years ago, though there is not among them a single individual that was found there a hundred years since. Take any of the rivers on the earth; there is not in any of them a gallon of water, perhaps not a drop that was there a century ago. We talk of the Mississippi, the Ohio, the Amazon, as if we felt that every body would understand us, and know for a certainty the identical river to which we referred, yet if this must depend on an abiding and unchangeable sameness of the waters which go to make up those rivers, we have only to station ourselves upon the bank of any one of them, and look upon its passing current to see our river pass away. Old ocean, itself —is subject to the same mutations: and earth, with all its continents and islands—to hold it in an unchanging position, is by no means stationary: every moment a change is taking place in the elements of which it is composed; so that to-day it is any thing rather than what it was when God created man and placed him upon it, to go no further back: yet a man could not make himself more ridiculous than to assert that it was not the same. Its waters are being solidified, and thus passing into forms somewhat more substantial; while at the same time, its rocks and mountains, by no very slow process, are being broken down, and becoming dust. That day which was seen in prophetic vision, when "*there was no more sea*," is evidently not far distant. Nor will this changeless mutation (forgive the paradox) cease, even here. "It doth not yet appear what we shall be." We have *no* idea, nor can we have, of the appearance or true state of things in heaven or earth, or in respect to the human race, when things have reached that result for which they are and were created.

If now, the question of identity, either as regards a person or thing, must be conditioned upon its *immutability*, not only in respect to its elementary principles, but any thing else, there is evidently no such thing, *never* was, and never will be. Whatsoever may be predicted as resultant of this, must also be given up; identity, on such grounds as this, is impossible. The reader is not the same individual he was when he commenced this chapter.

But it is not; there are considerations which have

no reference whatever to the nature or number of elements combined in the formation of man, which fix in him an identity that is just as immutable as the throne of God.   Every man that exists, every child that is born, *sustains specific relations*, not only to every other creature, but to God the Creator.   These relations, in respect to moral beings, are not only at the foundation of moral obligation, they are the basis, the true, unchanging basis of that which we are in search of, *man's individual or personal identity*.   No two beings that ever existed may be supposed to have sustained precisely the same relations, one towards the other, or towards all others.   Nor can any two be found among the myriads that have been upon the earth, or that may yet *be* upon it, that shall sustain precisely the same relation to their Creator.   No two that have existed or that ever will exist, have had identically the same thoughts, the same moral feelings, one with the other.   No two that have performed precisely the same acts, or, that in all respects have occupied the same ground in regard to human responsibility.   A fixed and unalterable diversity obtains through all the universe, which no being can ever modify, much less change; and on this unchanging structure depends that identity we are in search of, and which is itself unchangeable.   Sir Isaac Newton, when busied in those investigations which, in their results, drew a sponge over the philosophy of the world, was the same individual, identically the same, with that small boy who bore that name a few years before, who had like all his schoolmates, to learn his A. B. C.   And had he lived a thousand years, and been permitted to prosecute his studies as successfully to the end, as during the days of his mightiest achievements, he would have been only Sir

Isaac Newton. The position which God had assigned him from eternity, was a position for which no other being in the universe was made, and one to which no other was or could be adapted.

The same is true of the poorest, or most obscure, or most neglected of the sons of men. There is a position in the great family of men, which belongs exclusively to him; a place for which he was created, and for which no other being was; a station, with all its dependences, whether they be few or many, which no other being in the universe could occupy, and for which he alone was created. This fixedness of being, this immutability of character, is a resultant of *the law of existing relations.* Everything in morals turns on this law, man is not a man without it; an animal is not an animal, except through this all pervading and omnipotent Rule. The whole is not greater than a part, except as the result of that law on which we predicate human, as well as universal identity.

In regard to moral or responsible beings, the law is more stringent, if possible, than in respect to anything else: the reason therefor, is evidently this, there is more involved here than in any other part of the creation of God. Lazarus, lying at the gate of opulence and *starving* there, covered with the evidences of human infirmity and sorrow, abandoned of all his race, and cared for only by his canine physicians, is yet a being that has a fixed and changeless mission, a responsibility which none but Lazarus can meet.

In this alone is personal identity; man, so far as *matter* is concerned, is not the same, any two periods of his existence. At the moment of his creation, he sets forward on a journey, which is never to terminate. He commences to follow a line which to some may seem a literal circle, ending in itself; yet, he never returns to precisely that point which he occupied at a previous stage of his existence. That unchangeable Ego, which came into being at his birth, whether he sleep or wake, be well or ill; abide at home, or be a lone wanderer without name or nation, moves on to that eternity for which he was created, and from which there is no return. Consciousness accompanies him all the days of his existence, to assure him of his identity with that being who has endeavored from the heart to obey his Creator God, and who has never knowingly departed from that obedience; or, to annoy him with the sad and melancholy assurance, that he is the same, identically the same intelligent being, that often and long had known his Maker's will, but had done it not. This it is, which shall lie down with his body in the grave; and it is this, which at the sound of the arch-angel's trump, shall come forth either to the resurrection of the just, *which is unto eternal life ;* or, to that of shame and everlasting contempt.

To return, then, for a moment, to the objection against the doctrine of the resurrection, as it was urged in the days of the Apostle Paul; and to its answer by the same apostle, we say of identity, it is that principle of life in the grain which passes over from one stage of its existence to another *unchanged.* It may lie perfectly dormant, thousands of years, and then be made to germinate; as has been recently demonstrated in the case of grain which was taken from the wrappings of an Egyptian Mummy, and caused to spring up and bring forth its appropriate kind. So long as the attendant circumstances were such as were required by the nature of the case, no change could reach that principle of life. When passing from one stage to another it must necessarily *put off*, so to speak, lay aside, never to be resumed that body with which, from the first it had been invested. Those particles of matter with which this mysterious principle had been incorporated, by which it had been preserved, had, to the very last one, like those which compose the human body, been dropped in the grave. Yet, through the arrangements of an everwise Providence, others stood ready to become the covering and defense of the new corn in that new life into which it had risen.

Here all the essential principles involved in the resurrection of the human body, are not only seen but acknowledged, in respect to a fact, or event of a wordly nature, as we say, why should they not be admitted in respect to that which is of vastly more importance, an event which differs from that other only in respect to its containing the principle of an immortal soul which is to rise to immortal life? The consideration suggested by the Apostle, viz: "that which is sown a natural body, is raised a spiritual body," does not in the least affect the main question; for the objection looks only at the circumstance or consideration, that in the death of man, the body which he occupied on the earth is left in the grave, and it takes the liberty to infer from this the extinction of his being; but if such a result as this is to follow, then surely there is no grain to be expected from ever so liberal sowing, for every kernel thus deposited leaves *its* body in the ground. Like that which once invested the undying spark of human existence the kernel of wheat, the body which enwraps the principle of life in the seed, is left in the earth, while "God giveth it one, as it hath pleased him ; and to every seed, his own body."

"But," says the objector, " this is all very well as far as it goes ; we remember, however, that *illustrations* are not necessarily arguments; a thing may be very much like another, which is true, and yet not be like it in this respect; the kingdom of heaven 'may be' like unto a house-holder, who called unto him his servants and delivered unto them his goods," etc. etc. while it may be true, that no such event as that ever existed, except in the imagination of him who spake the parable. So in the case before us, there may be many things in the philosophy of sowing and reaping taking in the whole history of the thing, which are strikingly analogous to something else, which something else is only an imaginary thing. It is obvious enough to any one, that this objection would have some weight, were it not, that the thing which it regards as imaginary, or hypothetical, is that part which is inspired, or more correctly, the comparison is one which Divine inspiration has brought forward, adopted, and sanctioned, and therefore, is not only just but evidently reliable. Nothing indeed, can be clearer, than that the writer of the Epistles to the Corinthians, most firmly believed in the resurrection of *the body :* a body, which, though not composed of the same materials that were once employed to form it, yet sustains precisely that relation to the undying spirit which once inhabited it, which was sustained by that in which the spirit dwelt before its decease. And this same writer, while under the guidance of Divine inspiration, is endeavoring to convince his readers of the truth of that doctrine which he so firmly believes and which he regards as a most important doctrine. In doing this he uses the comparison, or illustration of which we have spoken. It would seem therefore to be clear enough, that this illustration is in fact a most reliable argument.

Look, for a moment, at the objection; death destroys the identity of the human body; we who survive our dead, have the testimony of our corporeal senses, that the body of our friend who has been called away before us is scattered to the four corners of the world; that not one particle of matter can be identified as that which belonged to his body while here in the flesh: how then can we believe? This is the question; and the Apostle proceeds to answer it, by showing, that the husbandman on the ground of the doubter, cannot believe in the growing of grain: because, from the period in which it was sown, (or soon after) to that of the harvest, (or very nearly,) no man can find one particle of that which was sown. He may go at any time, after the lapse of a few days, and dig about the plant, he can find nothing of the grain that he sowed there; any more than an Oriental traveler as he examines the tombs of Petra, can find the dust that once belonged to the bodies that have been carried and laid there.

We are willing the reader should understand, that we regard this illustration so important, so appropriate and satisfactory, as to need scarcely anything in addition, for the support of the doctrine under discussion: especially, since it is one with which everybody is more or less acquainted. No man needs to think but a moment, if his mind is troubled about the resurrection of his body, on the ground that the particles of matter which once composed it are evidently and widely scattered abroad—he must in like manner be troubled about the rearing of his corn ; a matter that his corporeal senses, (the self-same witnesses that assure him of the dispersion of the dead body) have assured him of: in this case, therefore, he must not believe what he sees, and what he has seen thousands of times. If he would be just to himself, just to his principles, and just to his senses, he must stoutly deny the whole. His *friends* may come forward and unite their testimony to his to any number that can be desired; yet he must not believe: he saw the grain put into the ground; he saw a green blade spring up where that grain was buried, he went to inquire what had become of it, and lo ! he could find nothing of it : now, let him believe, that " he shall find it after many days"— *if he can.* Those witnesses, (his senses,) whose testimony so much troubled him in respect to the dissolution and dispersion of the body of his friend, are equally confident and positive, that " the full corn in the ear" is identically the same with that which was sown; but these same witnesses have assured him, over and again, that every part and particle of the grain that was planted is gone !

In fact, the author of this argument on the resurrection—I speak of the Apostle Paul—seems desirous to put it out of the power of his reader to disbelieve, or even doubt: he selects a well-known fact—a fact with which every one is conversant—a fact in respect to which no man who ever knew anything, ever had a doubt—and writes upon its very front this undeniable assurance; "you must disbelieve *this*, before you can feel at liberty to call in question the resurrection of the dead."

A word further in respect to the character, or nature of the comparison: We have already said, that it was drawn from the common and ordinary events of life. Every one may be supposed to know all about it. Hence the utter impossibility of any one's being deceived by it. Herein is its great strength. Paul has carefully followed the Great Teacher. Instead of doing as many religious teachers, at the present day, cite a passage from fabulous and shameful heathenism, with a view to illustrate, as it is said, (that is, throw light on his subject,) he copies the example of his Lord and Master; takes his reader, his disciple, to a subject with which he is not only familiar, but which he knows to be true, however mysterious.

Permit me to draw a little further upon the patience of the reader. I wish to speak a word of the Saviour, as a Teacher: especially, since, as I have already said, the Apostle has so faithfully adopted his method of instruction.

No doubt, one of the powers to which they referred, who returned from a vain attempt to apprehend Christ, and affirmed that "*never* man spake as this man," was—that his instructions were made plain; that while other men, in endeavoring to give instruction, used comparisons, figures of speech, metaphors, and illustrations, drawn from unheard of and unknown subjects, the Lord Jesus Christ made use of those, with which, they to whom he was speaking, must of necessity be familiar.

We may regard him, in accordance with the custom of the age, as walking forth with his disciples, that he might converse with them upon the momentous subject of his mission, and the various relations he sustained to them: before him, and probably at no great distance, a shepherd appears leading forth his flock in search of pasture. Then comes the declaration, which John has so faithfully recorded: "I am the shepherd; ye are the sheep." A stranger instantly appears and calls to the sheep as if to persuade them to abandon their rightful shepherd and protector and follow *him :* " but the sheep hear not his voice; they refuse to follow a stranger." Then, in the distance, "a sower is seen going forth to sow." Now follows " the parable of the sower and his seed." On another occasion, they witness a vine, clinging to whatsoever it can reach, and endeavoring to raise itself up so as to bear fruit. Then follows the declaration: "I am the vine; ye are the branches: ye do abide in me, and I in you. The branch that abideth not in me, is cast forth, and men gather them in bundles, and they are burned."

Now, we cannot too much admire this trait of character in our Lord and Redeemer, considered only as Teacher. As we have already said, it puts it out of the power of the teacher to mislead or deceive: he is enabled to give light on subjects that otherwise are inscrutably dark and unintelligible. If it be possible to impart a clear and satisfactory knowledge of that which before was utterly unknown, it is to be done in the way adopted by our Lord Jesus Christ; compare it with things that *are* understood; illustrate it, by saying it is like this, or like that, taking special care to have *a this* or *a that* which is well understood. Much may be learned in this way, that can be in no other; much which is of the greatest importance.

We are by no means sure, that the course we are endeavoring to discountenance, or perhaps censure, is as objectionable to others as to ourselves. For as we have cast our eye about upon an audience, when a speaker was endeavoring to illuminate his pathway by frequent references to heathen deities, or by the most free and liberal use of pagan agencies ; by declaring for instance that the point he would explain was " like the effect of Circe's cup upon Eurylocus and his companions ;" or that something was " dark as Erebus," " faithful as Patrochus," " affectionate as Minerva, by the side of Jupiter"—we have thought, most, if not all, could affirm with Ahimaz, " I heard a great tumult, but knew not what was there." Under pretence of making himself understood, but in fact to display his so-called learning, he has referred them for illustration to that which they knew nothing about, and of course has only increased their darkness.

But, suppose there *was* an age, in time past, so familiar with these things as actually not to be embarrassed by a reference to them; their knowledge could in no sense benefit them; it was at best but a belief of the fabulous: consequently, the time would most surely come, when the generations upon the earth would know nothing of it at all : an attempt to illuminate a subject, or illustrate a difficult point by a reference to these things, would most certainly increase the darkness in which it was already involved, add to the embarrassment of the hearer, while it pointedly displayed the want of good sense in the speaker. Long before the dawn of the millennium, we believe all knowledge of pagan mythology, but especially of this *use* of it, will have vanished away.

Not so with respect to those subjects to which the Lord Jesus Christ refers, or from which he draws his illustrations. The time will never come when the human race can do without the sheep, or the sheep without a shepherd. While man shall dwell upon the earth, there must be sowing and reaping, gathering into barns and preparing the grain for food.   So long as the world shall endure, he that readeth the parable of the sower and his seed will understand it; as an illustration, it can never pass into disuse.

Now, the beauty or excellence of the means which the apostle employed, for answering the objection to the resurrection of the body, which we have been considering, consists in the fact or consideration, that the time will never come when men can live without bread; or have bread without growing wheat.   But, if they must grow wheat, they must sow it; if it must be sown, it will have to sprout and grow up, in order to give bread: but every kernel that sprouts and grows up, demonstrates that the objection we are considering has no foundation whatever.   The husbandman may examine his wheat any time, after it has germinated and grown up—he will find *nothing*, not even a particle of matter that belonged to the grain he sowed; yet, when the harvest is come, he shall assuredly gather in the identical grain he sowed: no change has reached a solitary grain, which has in the least disturbed its identity; there lies before him, in every kernel, a practical illustration of the absurdity of his position, if he has so much as thought in his heart, that the doctrine of the resurrection cannot be true, because death destroys the identity of the body.

Possibly, while we have been insisting, with such earnestness on the relevancy or appositeness of the illustration which we have used, and for which we have claimed special attention, on the ground that it is selected from what can never be unknown, or pass into desuetude, it has occurred to the reader, that this same apostle from whom we have received it, has seemed to sanction the practice which we have so much condemned—an attempt to illustrate important truths by a reference to what must soon be unknown, and which cannot be too soon forgotten. There are, as we are well aware, frequent refeiences, in the writings of Paul, to certain games among the ancients, those of Olympia in Greece, for example. These seemed to have been a favorite source of illustration to him: he scarcely attempts to urge us forward in our way to heaven, without some reference to the race : whenever he would persuade us so to live that our influence in all its weight shall be felt in favor of the religion of Jesus Christ, he refers us to himself as our example, declaring that he "so fights as not to be found beating the air :" *he* does not allow himself to be employed in hurling his blows at nothing : that is, he is careful to make every blow *tell :* he does not lose a moment or an effort.

To reply, so far as necessary, we have only to say, that the apostle's reference is to something which did at least *exist,* or was not wholly fabulous ; and which, though a practice of no very exalted character, in respect to its moral influence, was, nevertheless, far less injurious than that which we have endeavored to discourage. It cannot be denied, that in order to be understood, we must often refer to that which is outside of our subject and will soon pass away. The Spirit of inspiration, in his attempts to communicate knowledge to man, must needs use the language of man ; must refer to things with which man is *acquainted :* and it is on this principle, or in obedience to this law, that Paul introduced into his argument for the resurrection of the dead, the fact, or consideration, that every kernel of grain, which germinates and grows up, loses its identity just as truly and in the same sense as the human body which is raised from the dead. His object is, as we have many times said, to set forth this great and important truth, that if we refuse to believe that the dead shall be raised, on the ground or because it has seemed to us that the identity of the body has been destroyed by death, we must, in order to be consistent, refuse to believe that the grain which the husbandman has reaped is that which he sowed : the identity consisting in that mysterious individuality, that something which is itself and not another ; that which, in man, is the *egomet*, the myself, in distinction from every body and every thing else.

PART II.

·But it is time we considered the *second* objection which is our purpose to notice in the present paper, against the resurrection of the dead. The reader may complain, that his patience has long since been exhausted ; that a question that evidently rests on revelation should not be exposed to the assaults of those who have no respect for anything but that which is reached by unaided reason.

We are by no means sure that all, or even a majority of those who shall read this discussion, will admit the propriety of calling this second objection anything more than a freak of infidelity ; a kind of side-issue, or something of that nature. What if there be not room on all the surface of the solid earth for the family of man to stand and be judged ? Will it follow, that there will be no judgment ? Are we to be told, that He who created all worlds, cannot arrange for so great a matter as the trial of mankind, unless he can find room upon this foot-stool? Suppose it should be *proved*, that if all the bodies of the human race, which have already been upon the earth, when raised from the dead, shall occupy the same space, each for itself, as when alive and inhabited by the spirit, that part of the earth which is land will be covered to the depth of ten feet or more—what would follow? that we must give up the doctrine of a general resurrection and of a judgment? or may we be permitted to believe, that God will *make* room for that fearful day and its vast assembly, when and where he shall need it?

It is evidently unnecessary, that we should answer this question, or any other of a like character: the objection we propose to consider, however absurd in the estimation of some, is, nevertheless, a very serious one in the view of others; and one that must be fairly and satisfactorily removed, or in their estimation the doctrine of a resurrection must be given up. All this is clear to any one who has watched the developments of a few years past, or made himself familiar with the teaching of several "*isms*," which are beginning to work themselves into notice, in the different parts of our country. A thing may be abundantly satisfactory to the reader, and to the great *majority* of readers, while it would be quite *un*satisfactory to others: and that which is an objection—a most *serious* objection to some cardinal doctrine, in the opinion of one, may be unworthy of notice in that of another. Nevertheless, whether it be so or not, in truth or justice, *the effect* upon his mind may be the same as if it were what it seemed to be: and consequently should be thus treated.

Some twenty or twenty-five years ago, the writer was

providentially seated in a church, listening to *a funeral discourse* from a minister of another denomination; in the course of which the speaker made the assertion we have just made, and which forms the objection we are now considering. He seemed to be aiming at the doctrine of "original sin," as it is called; or that view of it which supposes that all sinned in Adam and fell with him, and that the guilt of this first sin was so imputed to his posterity that it became truly and properly theirs. What was his object in directing the hearer to that doctrine *then* we could not see: neither could we clearly perceive whether it was, that he wished to express his *dissent* from that dogma, or not. Sometimes it was with an air of doubting, as to its validity; and sometimes there was an apparent unwillingness to be regarded as an unbeliever of the doctrine we have just named.

In the course of his remarks, he stated, "that if all that had been on the earth, were to be raised from the dead, and each body was to occupy the same space that it did, while in the present world—the *whole* surface of the ground—or all the face of the earth—would be covered to the depth of at least *ten feet!*" He did not seem to notice the bearing of his remark upon the doctrine of the resurrection, or to know that it would have any at all. The thought, that he was contributing to the aid of skepticism, did not appear to cross his mind: but he passed on without attempting either to prove, or modify his assertion, with a view to prevent its unhappy bearing in favor of infidelity, and of course, against the whole system of religion as revealed in the scriptures.

The circumstance that many of my own congregation were present, led me to feel more anxiety as to the impression which was made on the mind of the hearer, than

I otherwise should have felt, perhaps, though I know not that I could have been placed in *any*, where I should not have felt. The idea was so startling, so out of the way, so shockingly absurd, and yet there was a something about it, which served very deeply to impress it upon the mind of the hearer. Without pausing to look at the consequences, or rather, its *bearing* upon the Christian doctrine and hope, many, I was persuaded, would greedily embrace it, and an idea once honored with a cordial reception, will linger long after its unutterable absurdity has been exposed, as if determined to be finally and permanently established in the mind, solely on the ground that it has been once favorably regarded.

I returned to my study, and taking up my pen, demonstrated by the aid of common Arithmetic, in less than fifteen minutes, that every soul that had been on the earth since the creation, with the body it had inhabited, whether that body were one of a giant or an infant, might have been interred as we now bury our dead *on less than one-third of the territory of the State of New York!* It may well be supposed I did not fail to correct the impression that had been made upon the minds of the people as soon as I had an opportunity; and it may be well enough for me to add, that I had the pleasure of receiving assurance from several of my most intelligent hearers, that their own minds had been greatly relieved by the timely refutation of the error.

Some few years afterwards, in a different section of the country, and on a similar occasion, I heard the same sentiment advanced again. Just as in the former case, without seeming to know he was strengthening the feeble knees of infidelity, and loading with fetters of grievous dimensions, the mind of every thinking person in his audience on the subject of the resurrection, the speaker made the astounding declaration, that "if all that have lived since the creation, (when they shall be raised from the dead,) shall occupy the same space on the surface of the earth, as when here during their probation, they will cover every foot of dry land to the depth of fifteen, (some say *forty*) feet !"

While from my inmost soul I pitied the man, that he should have been so unwise as to receive such an assertion without stopping to inquire into its nature or tendency, or whether it was true, or what he wanted of it, even if it *was*, on that occasion, I felt to pity his hearers still more; if on the former occasion I was astonished and grieved, on this, I was even more; for his discourse was occasioned by a most melancholy providence, (a lady of high standing and intelligence, with her two lovely children, burned in their own dwelling); what *could* such a statement as that do towards comforting the afflicted, surviving husband ? What could have been the motive of the speaker, unless to startle and overwhelm with unutterable extravagance? But the evil was done, and it must of course be met.

The day following, as the writer was conversing with a brother in the ministry who had heard the discourse with himself, several persons coming up, paused to hear what was said of that singular declaration. One of them remarked in the way of inquiry, I suppose you are aware, gentlemen, of the place, or the work where that sentiment was found? and of course where he obtained it? It is in the last number of the Democratic Review! I then proceeded to give them, in as few words as possible, an account of what I knew of the matter just as I have given it in the foregoing pages; assuring them that any man whose knowledge of common Arithmetic was sufficient to make plain calculations in simple multiplication, could demonstrate the unutterable absurdity of the whole statement. One of the by-standers, an officer in one of the churches of the place, remarked, " the man that could do that, (that is demonstrate the absurdity of the statement,) *ought* to do it, for it was evidently of most mischievous tendency and import. Besides," added he, "the writer in the review fortifies his position with quotations from Professor B. of New York; so that you perceive the gentleman from whom we heard it yesterday would seem not to lack authority for his views."

We parted, and in the course of a few weeks there appeared in one of the religious periodicals of the day, the following refutation of that shameless sentiment. I propose to give it somewhat expanded or enlarged, without any other apology for its length, or for the length of the foregoing introduction to it, than its obvious importance. I know not, kind reader, that you and I can be better employed than in hanging the " Plumb-line " of a just and accurate investigation by the side of that wall which has been daubed with such untempered mortar as this. We have too much interest in the question, or doctrine here involved, to make it wise in us to complain of weariness in our endeavors to know and hold fast the truth, and in addition, to free that truth from every form and element of error.

We commence, therefore, the demolition of this strong hold of unbelief, by saying that the number of inhabitants now on earth, according to the most accurate estimates that can be made, is 1,200,000,000. These.

having sprung from Noah and his three sons, must of course, be the joint production of three families : consequently, 400,000,000, is the number that one pair, in the course of 4,200 years, the time that hath elapsed since the Flood, would bring into existence.   This calculation is made with a view to ascertain the number of Adam's posterity, down to the period of the Flood.   I have set down the number of years, from the creation to that period, as being 1660 : the common estimate being 1656.   According to this estimate, or in other words, allowing 400,000,000 to be the number which would spring from one of the sons of Noah, in the course of 4,200 years, (the time from the Flood to the present,) 15,000,000 or thereabouts, would be the number that would spring from Adam, as his posterity, during the time which would elapse between the creation and the Flood ; (1660 years.)   But, as man lived much longer then than now, and as it is written of them " begat sons and daughters," it is probable we ought to *increase* that number by at least its full amount, so that, in round numbers we should put down 30,000,000, as the sum total of earth's population, " when the Flood came and took them all away."   This number, as every one may see, must now be diminished by arithmetical *diminution* if the reader can conceive of such a process, till we find the *mean* number, that which would be found on the earth, not only during a particular year, between the creation and the Flood, but *any* year, and consequently *every* year.   Instead of being as *after* the Flood, and at the present day, three generations in a century, we must give to every generation of Adam's posterity, *before* that event, the age of at least three centuries.   Men lived on an average then about 500 years, as they do

7*

now, or are said to live 70. If, under the present state of things, we must call the years of one generation ⅓ of a century, we must say there were only some *five* generations of men on the earth, before the Flood. Taking the mean number 20,000,000 and multiplying it by five we have in round numbers, 100,000,000 as the sum total of those who were on the earth, previous to the deluge. Since that period we have had 140 generations: now 500,000,000, the mean number of inhabitants, each year, since the days of Noah, multiplied by 140, the number of generations, we have 70,000,000,000 as the number of inhabitants which has been upon the earth since the days of Noah. To these add the 100,000,000 of antedeluvians, or, with a view to make that number as large as some would think it ought to be, we will call it double that, 200,000,000. These added to the number of post deluvians, (70,000,000,000,) multiplied by 3, we have a grand total of 210,200,000,000 ; as the sum total of those that have been upon the face of the earth, and for which we seek a cemetery, " where we may bury our dead from our sight."

Our next measure is to ascertain the number of human beings which may be buried on a single square rod. In doing this, as is evident, we must take the human race as death takes them, that is, of every age, from the infant of a span long to the giant " whose spear's handle is like a weaver's beam." For the purpose of making all plain and intelligible we will draw a diagram, or square, which we will call a square rod ; and on which we will place the different ranks of human beings, as they are cut down by death.

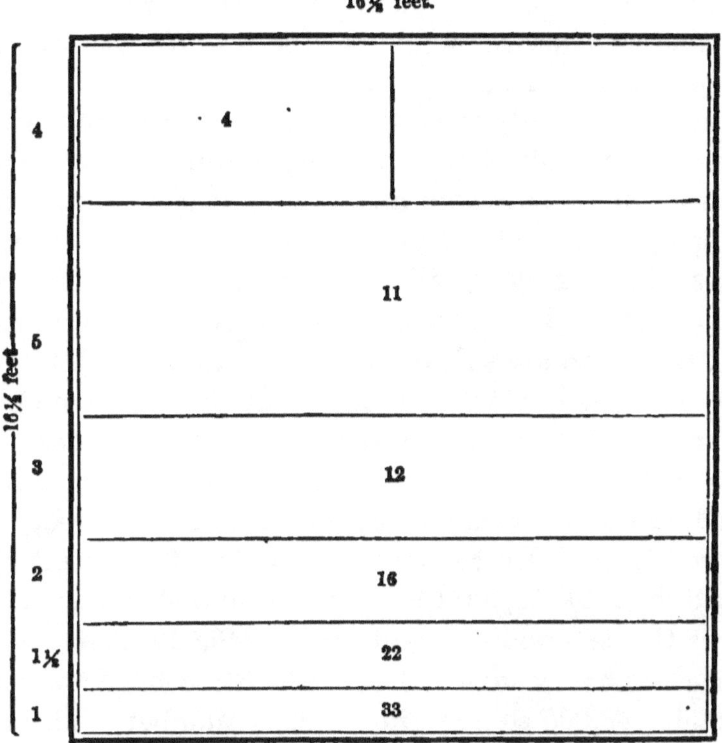

A large proportion of the human race (a full third or more) are cut down by death by the time they reach the length of one foot; we will therefore lay off their portion of the burying ground, first by drawing a line supposed to be one foot from the lower side of the diagram. An infant of that length will not occupy a space more than six inches in width: consequently as many as 33 can be laid in this row, without one overlaying another. We next mark off a strip one foot and a half wide: on this we propose to lay 22, as an infant of that length cannot need more than nine inches in width. We next take two feet; on this we lay as many as sixteen. Next one of three feet in width; on this we place easily as many as twelve. Again, we measure off a strip five feet wide, on this we place as many as eleven. We have now a strip 16½ feet long by four feet wide. We propose to cut this directly in two, or in other words, divide it in the middle, making it a territory for the tallest of the sons of men : those who measure eight feet three inches in length; of this class we bury four, two in each division; making in all ninety-eight on a square rod. And since we have set down the number twelve in rank No. three, we are safe in saying that at least two more may be added, which will bring out the round number of one hundred on every square rod. Now there are 160 square rods to the acre; these multiplied by a hundred, the number contained on each square rod, will make 16,000. Every square mile has 640 acres: 640 multiplied by 16,000 (the number buried on an acre,) gives the astounding result of 10,240,000 that can be buried on every square mile. The State of New York contains 46,000 square miles. This number multiplied by 10,240,000, the number that can be buried on every square mile, gives 471,040,000,000 of the human race, that might be buried on the territory of this state alone. But we have been able to find only about one half or one third of that number since the creation ! In other words, *the state of New York alone would furnish grounds to bury three times the number that have ever been upon the earth !* So much, (or shall we say so *little?*) can infidelity say of its famous objection against the doctrine of the resurrection of the body.

I recollect, distinctly, that in the calculation *first made*, the result was somewhat different. In that the territory of New York was found sufficient for something over two burying grounds; the state of Virginia something more. But the explanation is, in *that*, I allowed *too many*, for the number of inhabitants since the Flood. In this I think it not unlikely, that I have not allowed quite enough. But place that matter anywhere within the bounds of reason, and the territory of the state of New York will furnish as many as four cemeteries for the burial of the human race; taking every one in whom the breath of human life has been, without placing them where one will overlay another; and the state of New York, as all must know, is but a small portion of the whole earth.

But we have room for a larger and more favorable result than this. The objection we are considering contemplates a different position to the human race; one which will make a still wider difference in the result. Our answer is based upon the idea, that we are to find room to *bury* the human races; the objection asks only that they may have room to *stand*. We shall see a very wide difference here. And we will endeavor to reach it in a few words.

Taking the square rod, as before, we place *in a standing position*, 33 on the *first four inches* of the diagram; as many as 30 in *the next six;* as many as 25 on *the next eight;* which makes only one and a half foot of the square occupied in placing 88. Now, in order to place them in as compact a position as possible, we turn round the next course, making them all face the right or left of the position before taken, and allowing one foot of the diagram. A child, large enough to be twelve inches across the shoulders, would be about six inches through the breast upon an average; this position would give thirty-three more upon the square; and only two and a half feet are occupied. Next we take a strip one foot wide, having the position of the child the other way again, and his age that of ten years or more. In this row we place twenty-two more. Again, we take one of a foot and a half in width; here we place, (facing the other way,) as many as twenty-seven. We take another piece of one and a half foot; facing the occupants to the front; in this we place twenty We have now occupied six and a half feet of the diagram, and on it are placed as many as one hundred and ninety. Now, as these are hypothetically the smallest specimens of the human race, and as we have occupied only a little over one-third of our diagram, we will set down the entire number that might be placed upon it, in a standing position, at three hundred; and on this, as a basis of our last calculation, we proceed to ascertain how many square miles it would require.

The acre, as we all know, consists of one hundred and sixty square rods. These multiplied by three hundred, the number that can stand on one square rod, will give 48,000. But as we have been somewhat moderate in our calculations of our numbers on our diagram, we give 50,000 as the amount that may stand easily on a square acre; taking the human family as death finds them. Now, there are 640 acres in the square mile; these multiplied by 50,000, the number standing against the acre, give 32,000,000, as the number which may be placed on every square mile of earth's surface. The state of New York, as we before said, contains 46,000 square miles. This number multiplied by 32,000,000, the number standing against the square mile, gives the astonishing result of 1,472,000,000,000, as the number. One billion, four hundred and seventy two thousand million, that might be placed upon the soil of the state of New York.

This result is reached by a calculation which is based

on the following number, (210,200,000,000) as the
amount, in round numbers, that have been upon the
earth, of all ages and all sizes, including the 5,000,000,000,
which is believed by some, may have been found of
ante-deluvians.   These numbers, we admit, are only an
approximation, yet were we required to vary them, with
a view to find a *nearer* position to the true one, we
should feel constrained to *diminish*, instead of increase
them; especially, must we say this of the number of
those who lived before the flood.   1660 years, afford but
a small period for the production of so vast a number as
that of five thousand millions from a single pair; although
it may be true, that they lived much longer at that age
than since, "and begat sons and daughters."   Quite as
reluctant are we to admit, that the number two hundred
and ten thousand millions has been upon the earth, since
the flood, as the joint posterity of four families, with the
age of man reduced to comparatively a day.   Yet, on
these numbers, as a basis, the calculation we have made,
conducts us to the astonishing result of finding *more
than ten areas* of sufficient extent within the limits of
New York, for all the purposes of marshalling the human
race, even all that have ever lived, for the august and
solemn business of the day of judgment.   We have not
the lingering shadow of a doubt, that if every being in
human form, that has been born into the world, were
now in existence here, and each occupying in every
respect, the full amount of space which he occupied at
any time of his existence, all might be comfortably
placed upon *one twentieth part* of the territory of the
state of Virginia; or *one twelfth of that of Massachu-
setts.*

But a word further in respect to this objection.   It is

evident to those who have either read the preceding, or have solved the problem themselves, (for any one can do it who is familiar with the simplest rules of common arithmetic,) that—instead of such a state of things as the objection contemplates, it would require at least four millions of years for such a result. Earth's population must first be spread over every square foot of her surface, on every continent, and every island, to the full extent of her capacity, to sustain by her yearly contributions in products and fruits; and this multitude must have come and passed away millions of times—as they are doing now, and as they have been doing since the creation, before the result will have been reached, which is affirmed by the objection to have arrived already. Arithmetical calculations make sad havoc with these wild theories; facts accessible to almost any one, scatter the mists of skepticism and infidelity, if properly applied, or rightly construed. Let that dreamy credulity, by which so many of the present generation are "spirited away" to the land of shadows and mists,—of revelations and miracles, be met with cool and serious argument; argument made up of undeniable truths; and the world will be permitted to move forward in its direct line of progress, to the consummation of all things. There are, in round numbers, about 40,000,000 of square miles of land on the earth; including all the islands, of course. This number, multiplied by 32,000,000, the number that can stand on one square mile, gives 1,280,000,000,000,000 that can *stand* on the earth, and no one lean or stand on another. The earth must stand and be covered with a population dense as at present, the appalling time of 320,000 years, before its inhabitants will at all be troubled for room, even though all should be raised from the dead, and be standing on the earth at once.

A single consideration further in respect to the doctrine of the resurrection, and the reader and the writer will part. That consideration, if viewed in the light of an argument, may have the effect to silence all doubts on the subject, answering all objections before they are even started, and prompting us all to be in readiness for that day, when—"they that sleep in the dust of the earth shall awake, some to everlasting life, and some to shame and everlasting contempt."

That consideration is *the resurrection of our Lord Jesus Christ.* It was not without cause, that the disciples and primitive Christians insisted so strenuously on this fact. It was from a clear foresight of the importance of this event in the great system of salvation, that God arranged to have the evidence of it so clear and so invulnerable. The resurrection of the man Christ Jesus sustained such an important relation to that of the human race, as to make it necessary for God to accompany it with irrefragable proofs of its reality. It was *the pledge* of the resurrection of all mankind. It was an *earnest* of that important event to all the race. It was God's method of setting forth a most important truth to man, by placing an example of it before his eye. The Apostle admits, in the very beginning of his argument, that "if the dead rise not, Christ is not raised." That is, if it be an impossibility for the dead to be raised;—if the thing be such an absurdity, or such an *any* thing, as to make it certain that it cannot and will not be,—why then it will follow that "Christ is not raised, we are yet in sin, and they are perished who have died in the belief of his resurrection, or in the hope of it." In the person of

Jesus Christ, *there must be a man to suffer, a man to die, and a man to be raised from the dead*, in order to *perfect* that great system of representation, by which God reveals himself, as well as the principles of his government to man. There must be the man in the person of Christ to suffer, in order that the whole human race may be adequately represented as a suffering, lost race. There must be that same man in the person of Jesus Christ *to die*, to assure the whole family of man, not only that we must all die, but to prepare the way for the resurrection of man to life eternal: and the man Christ Jesus must be raised from the dead, to convince the whole world that the resurrection of the body is not only not an impossibility,—but that it is the arrangement on the part of God, which is best calculated to disarm death of its terrors, and the evils of life of their power to harm us. We have no dread of falling to sleep, and reposing for the night, if assured that we shall be permitted to awake in the morning.

This principle of representation underlies the whole gospel; indeed everything that God has, at any time, sought to communicate to man, has been brought before him by law, or the device of representation. The great Teacher himself, who is the Lord from heaven, claimed for himself, that he was the only adequate representative of the unseen and Holy One; the Being on whom no eye of mortal could look. This same Teacher, in his labors to instruct his disciples, and through them to instruct us, employed the parable, the simple comparison or the Apothegm. Very few were the instances in which the direct declaration is made, which, in itself, and apart from all metaphor or figure declares the thing or idea that Christ would impart. In his endeavor to give to Nicodemus a clear and correct idea of the new birth, as it is called, or more correctly, that change in man's moral feelings, as well as in his character, which is the beginning of life in Christ, the Lord Jesus had no prospect or hope of success, except by holding up before the mind, that change so important, under the figure of the birth of man, or his first entrance into life. Accordingly when this "ruler of the Jews," expressed his inability to understand Christ, he was told, that if that end had not been reached by this process, there was no such thing as accomplishing it. "If I have told you earthly things, and ye believe not, how shall ye believe if I tell you of heavenly things?" (The little word "*of*," which is introduced by the translators, embarrasses the sense.   The import of the question is this; "if after using comparisons, drawn from the most common and ordinary things of earth, (the blowing of the wind, etc.) I have failed to give you a correct idea of that change so needful to your eternal salvation, how should I hope to succeed, what shadow of a prospect have I of success, if I must present the naked, the unexplained, literal things of the world of light? You, a teacher in Israel, and cannot understand the first lesson in the school of life! Where are they that have been taught of you? What have they learned of the way of escape from sin, or the remedy provided in the Gospel?"

This plan of representaton is evidently the great central idea of God's communications to man. To set forth to the world the fearful evil of sin, to show its widespreading influence in accordance with the laws of moral beings; to exhibit its fearful tendencies and consequences, especially when sanctioned by parental example, he suffers it to spread over the whole world. All the evils which come drifting over the family of man, originating with that in the garden, are but the developments of his plan for informing the world of the evils which in the course of time or in the ages of eternity will result from a single act of disobedience!   In what other way could God so impressively have set forth to the human race, the impotency of penal enactments, as a principle of restraint, having for its object to deter man from sin, and prepare them for heaven, as by placing Adam where he should make the experiment, so to speak, for the whole human race?   What circumstances can be supposed more favorable to a successful result, than those in which Adam was placed?   The thing prohibited was of the least possible importance; there could not have been the shadow of an excuse, on the ground of any intrinsic value in the thing which was forbidden; no considerations but of sheer disrespect, could be seen or supposed to influence our first parents in the direction in which they saw fit to go.

Men are fond of persuading themselves, that if they were free from the evils that have come upon us in consequence of Adam's sin, they would find it far easier to walk the way of life than they do now. They vainly imagine that if placed where he stood, with the fearful threatening of death in case of disobedience, they should most assuredly remain steadfast in their allegiance to God.

Now it was of the utmost importance, that we should be undeceived on this point. If to keep man holy, or in the case of his defection from God, to recover and save him, something more than the influence of law, the dread of punishment, was requisite, it was no less important to the world, that this should be known, than were the interests which had been periled by sin; for, as is well known, man is naturally ignorant of any other influence, either to save or reform, than that of penalty. This is seen in all his services to his deity, where the light of the true religion has not shone. The savage recognizes nothing of the Great Spirit, except in scenes of terror and dread. And when idolatry has prompted its victim to put forth an effort to *make a god*, its conceptions of the awful and destructive are strained to the utmost, to make a monster that can *frighten* into obedience. It knows no other law; it recognizes no other influence, by which to procure submission. The earliest forms of worship in all nations are those of suffering and pain; and the nearer a people that has *ever* enjoyed the true light, shall come in their abuse of that light to that degradation and corruption which are regarded as *the abnormal* state of man, (but more correctly his *original*, in respect to superstition and bigotry,) the more deeply stained will be the rites and ceremonies of their religion with the objects of fear, the sources of pain, or causes of trembling and dread. Romanism is indebted for its abusive penances, its painful fastings and self-tortures, its bloody inquisition, and its sooty purgatory—in short, for its *every* thing which appeals only to the fears of man—she is indebted for it to the element of sheer *heathenism*, which still remains in her heart of hearts, as the center and source, if not the sum, of her being. In fact, so just and accurate is this law, that it becomes a matter of ease to determine the measure of intelligence or refinement of a people, by looking at the degree or measure of that which appeals only to their fears, in their religious services.

The first great lesson, therefore, which God would impart to the human race, is, that motives of fear or dread can never prompt to that service which is acceptable in his sight: that which is only the service of a trembling slave, is neither praiseworthy, much less meritorious in his eyes; nor will it *lead* to that obedience which will save from sin, cleanse and prepare the soul for heaven.

To demonstrate this to the abundant satisfaction of his intelligent creatures, God ordained, that our common ancestor—Adam—should be placed where the trial should be made for the whole race. He should be free from everything that predisposes man to sin, or prompts to disobedience: there left to that which some have called, "*the freedom of his will;*" by which is meant only that he is at perfect liberty to do as he chooses; act without any, even the least compulsion; he chooses the way of disobedience. The threatened penalty—*death*, that awful word, that fearful event which seems the end, not only of happiness but existence; *death* had no power to *keep* man in the way of obedience to God, much less recover him when once he had left it.

And God invites us everywhere, both in his providence and in his word, to look at this experiment and mark well its result: his silent, yet most solemn assurance to us all, is, that if placed precisely in his circumstances, we should do just as he did: in other words, that *we need some other influence than that of dreaded punishment to save our souls from sin and lead us home to God.*

Here, the world is furnished with its first lesson in the gospel: for, surely, when fully convinced of the impotency of law, nothing is more natural, than for an intelligent creature to inquire for that which shall have power to restore man to the favor of his God. "How shall man be just with God?" is the spontaneous inquiry of the soul, when once it has ascertained, that all its previous plans have been broken up.

And here is the sum total of sense or truth in the oft-repeated dogma, that " we all sinned in Adam and fell with him:" *every intelligent creature of God can see just how it would fare with him, if left to stand where Adam stood.* Adam, therefore, *is* our " federal head and representative;" not, to transact wickedness for us, nor to furnish us with a bad character before we exist; but *by fair and adequate experiment*, to assure us, that by " deeds of law, no flesh living shall be justified;" and thus preach to us a gospel which too many despise and reject.

But it was important that this principle of representation should not stop here. It was capable of setting forth to man, not only the gloomy prospects of the human race, if left to rely upon themselves, or the impulses of nature—but the God-head himself could be represented : yea, the very love of God could thus be set forth. In the person of his Son, his life, his death, we are furnished with an experiment, (if you are pleased to call it thus) by which it is demonstrated, that all may be saved if they will. The disabilities (whatever these may be) under which the race have labored, in consequence of the first transgression, have been removed and more than removed by Jesus Christ, who has procured for us *a protracted day of trial*, as well as the gracious promptings of his Spirit ; so that " where sin abounded, grace has superabounded ;" where evil has grown out of the first transgression, fearful and great as it may have been, mercy and truth have risen from this system of representation, as it is seen in Jesus Christ.

Such is the importance of the question of the resurrection of Jesus Christ, to that of our own. As he was *man*, truly and properly man, whatever may be said of the question of his Divinity, and as "God raised him from the dead," it follows, that the resurrection from the dead, when undertaken by God, is not an impossibility. There is at least *one* case in which the dead has been raised: so that the fearful assurance with which infidelity attempts to solace itself, viz., "there is no resurrection of either body or spirit," a solace at which it trembles, is broken—wholly and effectually broken; insomuch, that if the very existence of things depended on this cardinal doctrine of the Sadducee, it must utterly perish. "The dead shall be raised, and we shall be changed; in a moment, in the twinkling of an eye, at the sound of the last trump; for the trumpet shall sound, and the dead shall be raised."

There is, therefore, no hope to unbelief; if it must exist only on condition that "the dead rise not;" this single case removes forever the prospect of the infidel's prolonging his slumbers, when the clangor of that awful trump shall be heard; he may be compelled to awake. *One, surely*, has come back from the chambers of the dead, not to inform us of anything which we may not learn from the Bible without, but to assure us, all, that "*the dead shall rise*, every man in his own order; Christ the first fruits; afterwards they that are Christ's at his appearing."

Let not the unbeliever therefore lay the flattering unction to his soul, that the resurrection of Christ cannot be proved. If it cannot, nothing can be. The evidence of his resurrection is fully equal to that which proves his existence; and of this, we have better and more satisfactory assurance than we have that Socrates or Alexander, or Pythagoras lived. I would as soon think to subvert the testimony of all history, and plant the black flag of doubt and uncertainty on the very rampart of consciousness, as overthrow that which may be gathered, in favor of the existence of Jesus Christ, from the various means that men have employed to remember what is past.

In the resurrection of Jesus Christ then, we have the assurance of heaven, that the dead shall be raised, incorruptible and immortal. His people have an earnest of a resurrection unto life eternal, distinctly remembered and impressively brought forth, in that event in which the Sadducee never believed, and at which the Athenian ever mocked. But not till history is all untrue, and the testimony of rites and ceremonies, all unreliable, will the confidence of intelligent men be shaken in the doctrine of a general resurrection. Before that period, both reader and writer will have passed beyond the confines of doubt, not only as to this, but all other subjects *which are clearly revealed in the word of God.*

8

CHAPTER IV.

THE GOD-LIKENESS IN MAN.

A CONSIDERATION OF JAMES iii. 9.

" Men, who are made in the similitude of God."

IT is, perhaps, impossible for us too highly to prize this short portion of inspired truth. The subject of which it speaks, the statement it makes, in reference to that subject, together with the air of calm and solemn confidence in its own correctness, are all of them of the utmost importance; they decide in the most effectual and satisfactory manner, a most important question.

That man is not, at the present age of the world, and *has* not been, since the days of Adam, as when at first created, is the very general if not universal opinion. Almost every creed or confession of faith, which can be found among men, or which has ever been, since creed became the popular method of expressing the doctrines of Revelation, has contained the idea, in some way or other expressed, that man is but the ruin of what he once was. A great part of "the burden of the Lord," in the estimation of the vast majority among the Evangelical teachers of religion, consists in asserting over and over, that "man has fallen from the state in which he was created," and that, instead of being the exalted and God-like creature he was in the beginning, he is marred in every material or important point.

Much has been written at different ages of the world, with a view to account for this sad transition, to explain its cause and extent; to set forth, in a most precise and particular manner, the evidences and fruits of this change; and yet this change, whatever it was, would seem to have been unnoticed in the instructions of Jesus Christ!

We regard this a most remarkable fact or consideration: that a doctrine of such fearful import as that of the fall of man, was never once alluded to by the Great Teacher, in any of his discourses. His mission to this world was evidently to declare the gospel, the *whole* gospel. If, then, a part of that gospel, and by no means a small part of it, was to describe man's degradation in sin, and to set forth that result as having been reached in some way or other, in the first transgression, is it not passing strange, that Jesus of Nazareth, whose object it was to give us all the information we needed on the subject of our salvation, never once alluded to it? He was not thus behind in regard to our depravity: he more than intimated this on several occasions. But not once does he suggest, that *this depravity is in consequence of Adam's sin;* or, that it was, in fact, in any way connected with it. In his conversation with Nicodemus, he evidently predicated the necessity of the new birth upon it; but gives us no information of its character or origin.

I shall have occasion, however, to refer to this a little further on: for the present I have only spoken of it as a circumstance—or consideration very much like that which I am about to mention, viz.: the change which it is supposed has taken place in the character of man since his creation. The Bible seems to know nothing of this in the sense in which it is represented at the present day. Man is evidently created by God *now*, just as when he formed him out of the dust of the earth, —and breathed into his nostrils the breath of life. As he made Adam, so he seems to have made us all.

This view of the subject may not only be new to many at the present day, but it may be regarded as very erroneous: there is a kind of general belief that man, as he comes into being now-a-days, is a very different creature from that *first* example of which we have spoken. And yet, the Bible, at any rate, that portion which we have made the foundation of our remarks, seems to know nothing of it. God said in the beginning, "let us make man in our own image;" and after that the work is accomplished, he declares that it is done:—" so God *created* man in his own image ; male and female, created he them." And after the lapse of thousands of years, an inspired servant of the Almighty says, as in the passage referred to, " men are *now* made in the similitude or likeness of God."

Mark, it says—in the *likeness* of God : not that they are now, or ever were, a portion of the Deity, so to speak, an *emanation* from the Creator; but simple " *in his likeness.*" A thing may be like another in some respects, or in a great many respects, and yet it may be very *unlike* in others; and these, all of them very important ones. There are some things about man that really look god-like, or divine, while there are *others* that more nearly resemble certain elements in the character of a very different being.

Another consideration of a preliminary character is—that this change in man, which is generally regarded as the result of the great apostasy, consists in the loss of what is called "original righteousness;" consequently—it is affirmed that man is now created with a propensity to that which is wrong, a kind of seminal principle, which is itself an evil, while it is at the same time the cause, source and origin of all the evil which he ever does. His state, or condition, independent of voluntary action, is said to be sinful.

As this is not the place for us to attempt either a defense or a refutation of this theory, we must be content with simply saying; if when God proposed to create man in his own image, his meaning was to make him *holy*, instead of sinful, *that likeness must have departed soon as man sinned*. Consequently—man is no longer in the image of God; and the meaning of the passage at the head of our essay—is—that man was *originally* made in the similitude of his Creator; but is *not* so now. Then—another consequence must be met; man, as he is now, and as he has been ever since the fall, has been created not by God, who was the Creator of only the first pair, but by a kind of sub-agency, so to speak,—an *arrangement*, which the Almighty only inaugurated, and then left to do the work which he had to do at first with his own hand: or, if it be maintained, that God is still the Creator, that no man is brought into existence but by the special agency of God, just as in the creation of Adam; and in addition, that the entire species is now created not only in a state of utter destitution in respect to holiness, but to active hostility to every thing good, then will it follow, undeniably, that God is the author of evil, even that great *mass* of sin, which is said to lie in back of the executive in man, as a something which is itself wrong, and the origin of all that is wrong in what man does; is antecedent to all unholiness in respect to external conduct; a primum quid, a first principle, a law, a something as we have already described it, which is antecedent to all moral action—is itself the cause of evil acts and is itself evil!

How utterly without number are the embarrassments with which the common notions on this subject are surrounded! Each effort to remove one discovers a multitude which cannot be removed. Let us pause and reflect for a moment; what a strange thing in the world would be an evil, a *moral* evil,—which God himself was the author of! The very thought shocks us!

From all which we joyfully separate ourselves to the simple contemplation of the word of God, rejoicing in the instructions of our Lord Jesus Christ, on the general subject of the introduction of Moral Evil into the world, that it was "*an enemy*," and not by "the Father of lights." We are sorry for the man, and twice sorry for his creed, who, in order to be consistent, and stand firmly by the natural and unavoidable results of his system, is obliged to adopt principles and endorse laws that undeniably involve the fearful dogma, that God is the author of sin. But among all the victims of a blind and arbitrary bewilderment, on the subject of religion, there is no one more to be pitied, than he who has at last consented to adopt the principle that God can do anything and everything, even to sin, but that let him do what he will it will be right! That he can create a being with all the endowments of responsibility upon him, place him in circumstances where he cannot but sin, then, punish him forever for sinning, and yet be just, and yet be holy! We know very well, there *is* a maxim among men, to the effect, that " the king can do no wrong ;" that the fact of his elevation to the highest position in the kingdom is a sufficient guarantee that *whatsoever* he shall do will be right. A dogma sufficiently absurd to be scarcely worth rebuking, but when applied to a just and holy God, is more than horrible.

Let us then, fall back upon a first truth in morals, as it is beyond doubt a first law with God, that in the beginning he created man in his own likeness; an intelligent, responsible being, endowed with all the powers, whether of body or mind, for doing good or evil, and until good or evil was done, without character altogether. The declarations of the Bible, to the effect, that in the beginning God had made man upright, but that afterwards man had sought out many inventions, are only another attempt on the part of the Holy One and Just, to free himself from all complicity with evil. doers, or thought of having foreordained the wickedness of man. Better not be orthodox, in the common acceptation of the word, than adopt a theory which involves the character of God so as to convict him of sin.

But we must specify particulars. It is not enough for us to say, in general terms, Man is like his Creator, in that he is a moral being, a free, moral agent, a being, as we have already said, capable of doing good or evil; having all the powers which are requisite for a most perfect and upright walk with God; or for a most bitter and unrelenting warfare with him. There are concomitant qualities which lie along the pathway of man's history, or character, which were undoubtedly taken into the account in the declaration, that man is made in the similitude of God.

(1st.) And first: Man and his Creator adopt one and the same law, for the purpose of determining the moral character of actions; the law arising from, or suggested by existing relations. He is so made, that whenever the question is before him, which involves the morality of anything that is done, his first mental act is to determine the relations which exist between the parties, and from these, with as much certainty of its correctness as if it were that instant revealed from heaven, he reads the true moral character of the deed.

There would seem to be a kind of light emanating from these relations which at once reveals the act that would be right, and of course, that which would be wrong. We cannot admit the existence of a rule engraven upon the mind, or like the rod of God, laid up in the ark of the covenant, left in the inner chamber of the soul; *a line*, to use another expression, which we involuntarily, or instantly stretch upon an action and thereby obtain a knowledge of its rectitude or obliquity. *In this case we should take no notice of existing relations*, but, as if measuring a tower, or ascertaining the superficial contents of a field, we should proceed to stretch our line and at once determine the right or the wrong of the subject before us.

Instead of this we are always conscious of glancing first at the relations which are always recognized as those that are to be consulted in determining the morality of the act. We may not, at all times, be conscious of this act; but the reason is, we have at some previous day recognized these relations, given our full and hearty assent to them, and memory has made a faithful record of their teachings, so, that results involving the most important interests, and settling the most difficult questions of casuistry are reached as by intuition.

And the knowledge we thus obtain is of the most trust-worthy and unchanging character. For example; here are three young men, who are come in to recite their lesson in geometry: their teacher directs that a diagram be drawn upon the board; call it a right-angled triangle; and it is proposed to demonstrate that the square on the longest side is equal to both those which are constructed on the other sides. The teacher inquires if they *believe* this, and is answered by all in the affirmative. He inquires further if they have demonstrated the proposition, and is told they have not. " Why, then," inquires he, " why do you believe it ?" One answers for all, " because we believe you know; and we believe you are a man of truth." But, one of the three desires to know if the diagram cannot be measured ? He then takes his scale and sectors and proceeds to measure it. Here he has the testimony of his senses, in addition to that which he had in common with the whole, at first; which was but the testimony of competent witnesses. The third inquires still further, if it cannot be measured in another and more certain way ? and is answered that it can be. He is then directed to measure it in the common way, which is soon done to the satisfaction of all, *by the relations of its various parts, one to another.* By these he is pointed to the Q. E. D. with the calmness of an oracle from heaven; and while the convictions which have been reached by either of the other processes may be shaken, and perhaps overthrown; that which has been produced by the last named, the recognized relations, can never be. Man is as sure of its correctness as he is of his existence; and will as soon doubt the one as the other.

When two parties, at variance, attempt to settle their difficulties, or, in other words, determine what is right between them, they, first of all, have regard to the relation which exists between them. The father can require that of his son that he cannot of any body else; because he sustains to that son a relation which no other man does, and one which he sustains to nobody else. If, now, the justice and equity of these requirements *depended upon a rule*, any other man might demand the same things of the boy that the father does. The servant would owe the same service to a highwayman, as to his lawful lord and master; a consideration this, as it seems to us, sufficiently clear and satisfactory to close the argument.

That God proceeds on precisely this principle, in his requirements of men, is evident to any one who is conversant with the Bible. Take, for example, the law of ten commands; after asserting in the most explicit manner his own existence; and that it was he who brought the family of Israel out of the land of Egypt, (thus announcing two of the most important relations, that of Creator and Deliverer,) he proceeds to enjoin the duties which arise from these relations. Four of the commandments or requirements grow out of these relations: the remaining six, as any one may see, are based on those relations which man sustains to his fellow-men. The first of these, as in the former case—is that which he sustains to his parent; and on it is based the command, "honor thy father and mother," etc. Thence, all the way down to the faintest traces of relationship, are the duties enjoined which grow out of each. But not a claim is advanced, not a duty enjoined, without a reference either expressed or implied to some one or more relations: of this fact we say as we have said before, had there been a rule for measuring moral conduct, independent of relations, the decalogue would have embraced no reference whatsoever to God, as Creator, Deliverer, or any thing else; no division, as now, into that common one of a first and second table: no specification of duties to parents different from those which we owe to our neighbors.

As it is, we therefore uniformly find that a denial of obligation is based on a denial of relationship. " Am I my brother's keeper?" said the first murderer. As if he felt that this relation would of itself—have settled the question of his obligation to have done very differently by him than he had. And the first transgression, with all its attendant evils, would probably never have been, had not our common ancestor for the moment refused to acknowledge his responsibility to Him from whom he had just received existence. " Thus, saith the Lord, thy God, the Creator, the Holy One of Israel :" this is a specimen of the whole Bible. " He that cometh to God must believe that he is ; and that he is the rewarder of them that diligently seek him." " Here," says Professor Stuart, " are the two pillars upon which the whole fabric of religion and morals rests." Here, the first requirement is the belief of God's existence ; all mankind are cautioned against Atheism. In the second place, we are to believe that God is the moral governor of the world ; " he is the rewarder of them that diligently seek him." By fair implication, he is the punisher of them that seek him not.

Position, therefore, which is but another name for relation, is every thing in determining the moral qualities of whatsoever is required, or whatsoever is done. This fact accounts for the unwearied pains which the writer of the Epistle to the Hebrews has taken to set forth the exalted nature, character and position of the Son of God. His peerless supremacy is the basis of the Apostle's oft repeated exhortation, "Let us diligently heed these things, lest we should let them slip; for if the word spoken by *angels* was steadfast, and every act of disobedience received a recompense of reward, how shall they escape who turn away from him that speaketh from heaven?" The whole Epistle is but an inspired argument, supporting the claims of Jesus Christ to universal homage and acceptation, on the ground of his exalted character. There is, perhaps, not another book in the Bible, in which so much is proved, as in this: the writer has gathered up all the rites and ceremonies of the ancient church,—has set forth their peculiar relation to that spiritual worship which was introduced by Jesus Christ, and closed his argument by the oft repeated appeal, "how shall we escape, if we neglect so great salvation."

But the powers of language, in setting forth the indisputable supremacy of the Lord Jesus Christ, are wholly and many times, exhausted by the writer of the Apocalypse: as if it were not enough, to exhort men from heaven, and with the broad seal of God's authority to embrace the Lord Jesus; the writer lays all the elements of grandeur and sublimity under tribute, in his endeavors to set forth the exalted personage whose claims he would enforce. If he attempts to describe him, "his eyes are as a flame of fire; out of his mouth proceeds a sharp, two edged sword, his face is as the sun, shining in his brightness." And when this mysterious being speaks, all the thunders of God utter their voices. The position which is assigned him in heaven, is " in the midst of the throne ;" in the midst of power. No being but the Lion of the tribe of Judah, the Root of David, is found worthy to open the book, and to loose the seven seals, no other being, in heaven, earth, or under the earth, is worthy to look on dark decrees and gaze on things unknown. None but the first, the last, the Almighty; the Alpha, the Omega, the beginning and the end ; none but the Lamb of God is sufficient for these things.

We cannot read this book without sympathizing in some measure, with the writer, in his endeavor to find *a name* for that mysterious being who challenges the homage of all God's rational creatures. And when we remember that all these labors are performed, with a view to set forth the claims of the Holy One and the Just, we can scarcely fail to see the grounds of that law by which the magnitude of the duty of receiving Christ is exhibited, or the guilt of him who rejects this Saviour is determined ?

And why is it that in the case of him who blasphemes against the Holy Ghost, that there is no forgiveness ? Is it not, that the *relations* of this heavenly Paraclete, or those which he sustains to man, the offices which he performs in securing our salvation, are those which no other being can perform because no other occupies precisely his position.

One uninterrupted, undeviating aim, in him who wrote the book of inspiration, is observed. It is to persuade men to do right, act wisely, in respect to their salvation. It is God's method of setting forth the process which every intelligent creature pursues when determining the rectitude or obliquity of that which God requires. Take from the scriptures of the Old and New Testament the aims and labors of the Spirit of Inspiration to persuade men to obey God on the ground of what God is to them, and what they are to God, and there is little left.

(Secondly.) But secondly : Man is like his Maker in respect to his power of exerting a moral influence over moral beings.

Few subjects are more instructive, or more replete with wisdom to those who would learn, than the arrangements of God by which one moral being exerts over another an influence that shall persuade him to do or *not* do. The destiny of the human race was in an important sense committed to Adam. Not that God had employed him to transact wickedness for the world nor that he had or dained him a general factor of huge and flagrant sins : but that he might set forth this most instructive truth, that *all moral beings, exert a most powerful influence over their posterity.*

A certain man that lived some eighteen hundred years ago by the name of Paul, as he journeyed from Jerusalem to Damascus was met by the Lord Jesus Christ and converted : the same energies, which he had before employed in *opposing* Christ, he thenceforward devotes to his service. The world has felt the influence of that man ever since. About the same time, or a little before, lived one Judas Iscariot, a very great sinner. He was regularly admitted to the church of the Lord Jesus, and was " a member in good and regular standing," for the space of three years and a half; but in the end proved himself a traitor; and in the act of procuring his Master's death— dug his own grave in hell. Pilate, in signifying, that with respect to Christ, it should be as the people desired, showed that he stood at the head of a long line of infamous beings, who, for the purpose of doing their work of mischief, are found endeavoring to decide in favor of all parties, and ready to give security to the world, that if placed in worldly power, no claims of a religious character shall be suffered to interfere with the claims of the wicked. Thousands of events are transpiring every day, in solemn confirmation of the inspired assurance, that while "the memory of the just is blessed, the very name of the wicked shall rot."

But we need not go back to the history of the past for other examples or proofs of the position just laid down. In his arrangements which embrace moral beings, God has evidently so constituted man, that his influence for good or evil is felt wherever man is found. The law of Gravitation, which has by some been thought to be the developement of the Divine volition, if not that volition itself, is remarkable for this single feature; it reaches every particle of matter in the universe. There is not a dust in the balance, or mote in the sun-beam, which is not reached by that law; and not only reached but affected by it, in every instance, in exact proportion to its intrinsic weight, or importance. And in turn, the smallest grain of sand, on the shore of the sea, exerts just its own full share of inflence upon every other grain on the earth, and of course upon every rock, and upon every mountain, and upon every plant in the system to which our earth belongs; while every dust outside of itself exerts an influence over it.

Not unlike this, is the law of moral influence to which we have referred. From the heart of every man as a moral creature, there are thousands, and *thousands* of thousands of those unseen and mysterious ties, which, for want of another and more definite term, we have called by this name,—extending in every direction, or at least, wherever there is another moral being to attract or repel. Along these ties, an influence, no less subtile or mysterious than that which traverses the telegraphic wires, passes to reach some other being, to affect, in some way or other his moral character, and of course his destiny; by this influence every one that is reached is made either better or worse, more happy, or more mis· erable, in proportion as he is drawn by it towards the source of all goodness, or driven away. And this influence in man is either powerful or weak in proportion to his intrinsic moral weight in the great system composed of moral beings on the earth. The greater the amount of moral worth, in any being, the further is its extent, and the more will it effect the destiny of others.

It is in consequence of this, that the Great Creator holds in his hands, so to speak, the destiny of all other beings. He is all moral goodness, all moral worth, and of course, all moral power: he has but to will the happiness of any beings, upon the principles of his government, whether man or angels, and they are happy: he has but to order the change of any one from sin to holiness; and that man is renewed in the image of his Son.

Here too is the ground of our encouragement to pray; or rather, "*to lift up holy hands in prayer.*" The declaration "God heareth not sinners," though spoken at first by a very unlearned man, was a most profound truth. It is not in accordance with the great law of moral beings; or perhaps I should say, it is not in accordance with the great system of laws, embraced in God's moral government, for him to be influenced by the expressed or unexpressed desires of a wicked man. The Holy Spirit cannot be drawn towards unholiness; the Lord Jesus Christ cannot do mighty works where is only unbelief. He has no sympathy for that peculiar element; it is a kind of *non-conductor*, so to speak, a *medium* through which Divine goodness cannot pass. Even faith cannot exist in the same soul with sin.

As a first law, therefore, in this arrangement, man must read the following: *Be* good, if you would *do* good; *be pure in heart*, if you would be admitted to communion with him who is all purity and love. "*Be* that quality, that kind of man, which you wish others to be, throughout the sphere of your influence." "To the merciful, God showeth himself merciful; to the upright, he showeth himself upright; while with the froward he will wrestle, as it is in the margin; that is he will contend or struggle.

Nothing can be more important, therefore, than for man to know his true position in the scale of being: he is distinguished from all others, of the creatures of God, of which we have any knowledge, in that—to him is committed, in a very important sense, the moral character of those who are reached by this influence. And since this is inevitably the basis of man's happiness or misery, he should never forget, that to a certain extent he holds in his hands his fellow creature's destiny. Angels have no such prerogative; in this respect, if in no other, they are unlike their Creator; and man is superior to them. We secure or destroy each other's happiness.

(3dly.) Man, like his Creator God, is an intelligent being; he is endowed with reason or understanding;

these, combined, are called his spiritual existence. God is pure intelligence; God is a spirit.

Man's intelligence is seen, in that he is himself the cause of his own *volitions;* these are the foundations, or more correctly, the origin of all moral acts. What he does, which he does not *freely*, is of no moral character to him; his ax may light upon the head of his neighbor and cut off his life, yet inasmuch as he willed it not, he shall not be punished; it was not the result of volition.

Some metaphysicians, in order to have a consistent theory, have assigned to *motive* a power which unmakes the man. They have given to *motive* that control over mind which not only destroys free agency but annihilates responsibility. They have elevated it to the position of *cause*, efficient cause, whereas it sustains only the relation of *occasion*. Motive may *occasion* volition, but never cause it. With every moral being there must be the power under all circumstances, under ever so great pressure of motive, to say yea or nay, or the act is not a subject of praise or blame. The power of a *contrary* choice he must have as well as of acquiescent choice, or he is not free. That is but half an Executive, and hardly that, which only *ratifies* what another power has chosen; that is not free agency, absolute and full, which says " aye," because it cannot say " nay." And he is not an intelligent being who is in bondage to motive, however strong.

It is proper for me here, therefore, to refer to a single passage in the prayer of David, on the occasion of his penitence in view of his great sin. Our translators have put a petition into his mouth which David never uttered, and which he never *would;* they have made him to say "uphold me (by thy) free spirit," while the thing he asked of God, was, that he might be upheld "*spirit-free*," his *own* spirit free, instead of the spirit of God. The sin which he had committed, and at sight of which he had been made to tremble, had been in consequence of being in subjection to the flesh. Intelligence had been in bondage to the mere animal; his spiritual nature had been under the control of his animal passions. He therefore desires, in all the earnestness of his soul, that God would set his spirit free, uphold, sustain him in a state of perfect freedom of spirit or intelligence.

A single glance at this most interesting passage in the original Hebrew, will satisfy any one of the correctness of this criticism, and will also, we think, be sufficient to lead him to make the necessary correction whenever he shall have occasion to repeat this prayer.

(4thly.) But man is in the likeness of his Creator *in* respect *to the results of his own moral acts upon himself.* He is so constituted, that a deed of benevolence and mercy returns to him that performed it, a great reward, into his own bosom. Not surer does he do that which increases the happiness of others, than he does that which increases his own. Nor does he escape when he has done anything to injure his fellow man; he may run behind the law, (law of man,) for his protection, but he will find that no protection awaits him there; his Creator has so arranged that his sins shall find him out. In fact, this fearful truth is so manifest that no intelligent man thinks to deny it. He cannot do himself a moral wrong without experiencing in his own person, that which will not fail to remind him of the wicked thing he has done. He cannot have that respect for

himself after an unworthy action which he had before.
Let him use profane language, or bear false witness
against his neighbor, or basely stoop to dishonest meas
ures with a view to accomplish his own selfish ends, and
he will despise his own heart for ever conceiving such
an idea. "*Men* will praise thee," says the Psalmist,
"when thou doest well for thyself," but thou canst not
praise thyself, if doing it, thou hast done wrong.

It was my purpose more particularly to say, man is so
constituted, that if he is benevolent, kind, merciful, com-
passionate, you cannot do him a greater favor than to
place it in his power to let these traits of character flow
forth in correspondent worthy action.   You make him
happy the moment you give him opportunity to make
others happy; or, if he is at heart malevolent, you cannot take a more direct course to increase his wretched-
ness, than to give him an opportunity of doing evil.
Let the envious man be placed where his odious trait of
character shall be called into exercise, and he will be
conscious of a greater evil within him than " the rotten-
ness of his bones;" he will die by inches, and yet live
while he dieth.

Neither have I *yet* said what I had intended; thousands, as we have reason to believe, among the Lord's
poor, are so filled with love for others, so anxious to see
them in the enjoyment of the favor of God, that had
they the riches of this world, and could see that by giving, they should be instrumental in bringing others to
life in Christ, it would be the greatest happiness they
could experience below heaven.   Let those who have
large and generous hearts have means that correspond,
and opportunity to employ these means in creating happiness among others, and you need give yourself no anx-

iety as to the result, they will be happy. That father that loves his family, and is worthy of that exalted position, if a son shall have done evil and abused him, looks with strong and intense anxiety for an opportunity to extend the hand of forgiveness, and receive him back to his bosom. And the kindest act that an erring child can do to an injured and bleeding parent, is, to come where it is consistent for that parent to meet him and let his kindness flow forth in forgiveness of all that is past. The kindest act *the prodigal* ever did, and that which caused his father more happiness than all that he had done besides, was to come *back*, come where his anxious father might consistently meet him, fall on his neck and embrace him, order the best robe for him, and command the fatted calf to be killed. And if it were possible for erring man to lay *God* under lasting obligations to him, it would be by turning to the Lord, that God might consistently have mercy upon him. Woe to that cold and frozen-hearted man, that represents the Almighty as an indifferent spectator, when the terms of life are made known to dying men, and they are entreated to turn and live!

A single declaration that fell from our Savior's lips should come in here: "Therefore doth my father love me, because I lay down my life!" What, when they that crucified the Son of God, committed the greatest sin that was ever done on earth! How can this be?

I answer: sin threw obstacles in the way of man's happiness which only the death of the Son of God could remove. It shut the door of heaven upon every human soul, and nothing but the death of Christ could unbar it. In itself, the death of Christ was viewed by the Father with infinite pain and sorrow; yet, when considered in connection with its results, the Father felt grateful to the son, so to speak; since his death made it consistent for him to bestow eternal life on all that obey him. God is infinite in mercy, and has been from eternity: he has waited only for an opportunity to let his mercy flow forth; and the death of his son has furnished that opportunity. It is now safe and consistent for him, when the sinner repents, and believes in the Lord Jesus Christ, to meet him and have mercy upon him. Before the son of his love was seen offering himself for the salvation of man, the benevolence of God was as a consuming fire, pent up in his heart of infinite compassion. He *durst* not, (I speak with reverence,) he *durst* not let it flow out in action. While as yet there was no atonement; no attempt to repair the injuries of insulted justice; no arrangements to satisfy the claims of outraged but legitimate authority; it was impossible for God to forgive. Yet he greatly desired to; it was an act which he knew from eternity would, if possible, increase his own infinite happiness: yet he could not do it; he would have been unfaithful to his law: it would have been unkind to that portion of his kingdom which had remained faithful and true.

Oh, then, what rapture filled heaven, when the tidings spread from center to circumference, that the son, he who occupied the very *citadel of Divine authority*, had consented to carry out an arrrangement which would make it consistent for God to save! What gladness must have filled the breasts of angels, when poised on equal wing, they heard from the midst of the rejoicing throng that encircled the throne, the assurance, that he who alone "was found worthy to open the book, and to loose the seven seals thereof"—had offered *himself*, as the sinner's acceptance with God.

Some have believed and taught that God could forgive his erring creature, man, upon man's repentance—or without anything further. But, a feeling which under-lies all others in the human soul, like the still, small voice of the Prophet, bringing with it the most satisfactory assurances that the Lord is in it, assures every intelligent being, that some disposal must be made of *sins that are past. Legitimate, offended authority must be satisfied, ere an intelligent being can be happy.*

There is also an analogy between man and his Creator, in respect to the influence which truth will exert upon the soul; even though it may add nothing to his happi-ness. Truth, in its widest, most important sense, is an unwritten law, which every mind can read, to which every soul bows with profoundest reverence, and homage, even when he utterly refuses to follow where it leads. That much abused, much perverted passage, the seventh of the Epistle to the Romans, we give as an inspired declaration or repetition of the old adage, " video pro-boque—meliora; sed sequor pejora." I see and approve the better, but follow the worse.

The Apostle had maintained, with all the thunder of inspired logic, that *another* influence must be furnished him, than that which was derived from law, or from penal enactments: that these, instead of making him better, making him more holy,—made him worse.—But the objector reminded him, that *the law* which he ac-cused, or charged with such effects, was undeniably holy, just and good : that it was in the beginning " or-dained unto life :" "how,—then," saith he, " is that which is thus ordained, thus appointed of God, become evil ? Is that which was ordained unto life become death unto me ? Is the *law* so evil, after all, as to produce such results as these ?" From the thirteenth to the twenty-fifth verse of that chapter, you have the recorded answer of the Apostle. In the course of which, he maintains—that the law is *so clearly right*, that man, even while in sin, in love with every thing that the law condemns, *gives his unqualified testimony in its favor.* The question, which is so much agitated at the present day, to wit, "was the Apostle speaking *as a Christian ;* was he giving a Christian's experience ; or was he describing the exercises of a mind, *any* mind, *all* mind, in view of Divine truth ? This does not seem to have been before his mind at all : the thing that *he* was asserting was true of all men, whether Christians or sinners : the law of God was so manifestly right ; man, every where, was so made by his Creator, as to give his voice in its favor. His argument was plainly this ; "if my depravity is so stubborn,—if the law of sin, which is in my members, be so inveterate as to be proof against the perfect, holy, righteous law of God, so much so, that when I would do good, when I set out to reform, when I steadfastly *aim* at a life of purity and love, evil is present with me,—who shall deliver me ? how shall I escape from that which thus causes my death? I thank God I may—through J. C., my Lord.

This power, then ; this ability to recognize the purity and uprightness of law, the law of God; to feel its high sanctions respond to its claims and bow to its behests, is an element in the character of man, that distinctly likens him to God. *All* moral beings have it; it is indispensable in the formation of a responsible creature : Satan and all his sub-demons have it : they *see,* they *be-*

lieve and tremble. No matter where written, or in what character; every one whom God has endowed with *reason* can see it, can read it, and correctly interpret it.

(Fifthly.) Man, like his Creator God, can *foretell events,*—even those which are suspended upon the freest moral agency. He can predict the end of a righteous man, with as much certainty as he can project an eclipse : nor less liable is he to mistake when he exclaims, even without the aid of inspiration; "O! wicked man ; thou shalt surely die." He, like his maker, in a most important sense, can see " the end from the beginning."

This power in man underlies all his aims at reform whether in himself or in his fellow-creature : he would never " cease to do evil, and learn to do well," could he not look forward to a period, when —as he fondly believes, he shall have fully escaped from the dominion of sin, and from its fearful consequences. He would never commence in the process of law against an evil doer, arrest and bring him to trial,—try, condemn and execute him, could he not see, as he believes, the happy results upon the world. He would never preach the gospel, could he not look forward and see, as the hopeful result, men turning to the Lord ; he would never embrace it himself, did he not hope and believe that it would cleanse and prepare him for heaven.

And yet he knows very well—these results are in an important sense, suspended upon the free agency of man : yes, upon the free and unobstructed agency of those who are at heart opposed to the desired result, and will be, till converted. He looks not for man to take a step in the way of life except as he is drawn ; and yet he knows that the man steps there voluntarily. His knowledge of the laws of mind and of the power of Divine truth is such as to enable him to see, with almost omniscient certainty, "the wilderness and the solitary place, bud and blossom as the rose."

And God the Son would never have consented to come on his mission of mercy to the world, could he not have foreseen the happy result. That gracious promise which is represented in the Scriptures as having been made to him, that he should "see of the travail of his soul and be satisfied," was but the voice of the Divinity within him. That Divine influence by which the Prophets prophesied —and in the light of which they saw the latter day glory, was the same; they all looked for better days. And the whole world is "looking with anxious expectation for the manifestation of the offspring of God."

Let the sinner know, therefore, that what God has spoken will most assuredly be verified. With him it is something more than experiment: there is a certainty gathering round his work, that sanctified intelligence is fully convinced of and always looks for with pleasure.

One fact further we mention under this head : *The holier is man, i. e. the more he is like God, the stronger is his faith in the ultimate sucess of truth :* The purer his own heart, the more incredible is it to him, that eternal life should be refused by any one. The young convert cannot see how his Savior should be rejected : he thinks every body is soon to believe. And our Divine Savior, in the plenitude of his love, has represented the God of heaven, the owner of the vineyard, as saying when last of all he sends his son ; " they *will* reverence my son." In all ages, they who have lived nearest to God, as the phrase is, whose life has been most strictly conformed to him, — have been the men who have had most confidence in the appointed means of grace; have relied most firmly upon the promises of God.

In respect to the question before us, every responsible being is born a prophet: he may know much, or little, about other matters; be conversant with man, or lead the life of a hermit; he will be continually running on in advance of the present, and reading the results of moral conduct, or of the character of man. When he fixes his eye upon a godly man, one who is not only a well-wisher, but a well-doer, he affirms of him, that he "shall come to his grave in a good old age, as a shock of corn cometh in, in its season:" but when he contemplates the opposite character, the ungodly and rebellious, he says in his very heart of hearts to him, "go up, go up; do as you see fit, but if thou *do* return at all in peace, the Lord hath not spoken by me." Every man is as sure of these things, as he is of his existence: he will as soon expect to "gather grapes from thorns or figs from thistles," as see a hardened, flagrant sinner lie peacefully down in death. He as confidently expects the different results, of different courses of conduct, as he looks for the different seasons of the year, or the different fruits which are gathered from diverse trees.

With far greater certainty, his Creator God looks forward to the results of doing, whether good or evil. His fore-knowledge of these results, arising of course from his grace bestowed, is even made the basis of the elective act: "for whom he did fore-know, he also did predestinate to be conformed to the image of his Son." Moral causes are no less certain than those which are physical: he who hurls himself from the head-long precipice is not surer to be broken, than he who drops the rein upon the neck of lust, is to be ruined.

It forms no part of the writer's business to look after the fate of any set of doctrines, any dogma, or any confession of faith; the position just taken, evidently conflicts with a long and fondly cherished principle in the Calvinistic Creed: but better so than be at variance with the word of God. Will any man deny, that it is a distinguishing feature in the character of man, that though unable to pry between the folded leaves of futurity, he is nevertheless so constituted, that he can, and does foretell the results of moral conduct, with about as much certainty, (as I have already said,) as he can tell the full and changes of the moon, or predict the hour of the setting sun? And will any man deny, that this fore-knowledge on the part of the Creator, especially since in him it is liable to no mistake, is not even limited but extends to every event, whether possible or impossible, practicable or impracticable; and shall enable him to go forward and build the whole superstructure of the elective act on this foresight of events, that after all, are suspended upon the freest moral agency?

(Sixthly.) We look in the next place at the fact, that man is made like unto his Creator, *in respect to his capacity for knowledge.* If he is sufficiently intelligent to be a responsible being, he is indisputably so made, as to bear, in this respect, the most plain and marked resemblance to the omniscient One. It can be said of him, in a sense altogether praise-worthy, instead of being charged upon him as a crime, that he can be " ever learning and never able to come to the knowledge of the truth;" if by " *the truth,*" you mean every thing that is possible for an intelligent being to know. Is it not a fact, undeniable as man's existence, that in respect to his capacity for knowledge, his power of treasuring up and retaining, the more he has, the larger his capacity seems to be? the *more* he learns, the more easily he treasures up knowledge, and the surer it seems to him, as well as to all who know him, that his capacity, small as it seemed, at first, can never be filled?

Herein, if we mistake not, is a sound and most irrefragable proof of the immortality of the soul; independent of Revelation, in the common acceptation of that term: for though we regard *every* thing, which man learns of himself—or concerning his moral constitution, as being in a most important sense revealed to him; yet we do not speak of it as resulting from a special communication from heaven.

But we return: The seemingly unlimited capacity of the soul for knowledge: is this *only* in appearance? Is it a fact, that the *more* we learn, the more easily we acquire knowledge, the larger becomes the inner chamber of the soul, where that knowledge is treasured up? Does increasing knowledge make it increasingly easy to know?

If we pause here to inquire into the nature of this treasure; or more correctly, as to *how* this knowledge, be it more or less, is treasured up and made to remain in the mind, we know of no theory that at all meets the exigencies of the case: That of Des-Cartes, which supposes that every new idea, received into the mind, is a new impression made in, or upon the material of the brain; a kind of incision made in that delicate organ; and consequently, knowledge, which is the clear and distinct perception of fact, or recognition of that which is; the perception of the agreement and harmony of our ideas, or the disagreement or repugnance of the same, *is made to depend on these impressions.* The result, therefore, of increasing knowledge must be the exact opposite of what we all of us now know it to be. In proportion as we increase the number of these impressions, in that proportion, as it seems to us, shall we approach a period when it must be said, "man cannot know any more than he *now* knows, because there is no longer any room for this knowledge in the mind. The material of the brain is wholly occupied with impressions."

Our experience, on this subject, is, that every day of man's life, if not every hour, he is learning something that he never knew before; he does not make room for this increasing knowledge in the mind, by *forgetting* something already there; nor by expunging an idea or two, that he may occupy their place with others, those with which he thinks he shall be more in favor. We have said, he does not make room for these new elements of knowledge by *forgetting* something already known; for, we regard it susceptible of almost demonstration, that we never forget anything. A fact, once received into the mind, and made a part of its furniture, so to speak, can never be annihilated, or become as if it never was. Any man who has been careful to observe the operations of his own mind, has been furnished with every desirable amount of evidence, that he never forgets anything he has once known. He may have lost sight of it for many years, just as he has of a nail, or a gimlet which he had used when *building* his house, but which he dropped and left under the floor, and which had been brought to light by the removal or the demolition of the edifice. In like manner, we think, when our *earthly* house of this tabernacle shall be dissolved, and we are clothed upon by that which is from heaven, we shall find everything in a state of most perfect preservation, just as it was in the beginning, and where we left it when we were there before. And here we have *another* proof of the immortality of the soul.

In respect to the consideration last noticed, of this we are most sure; no man can by any means forget his sins: if he never remembers anything else, or which amounts to about the same thing, if he shall forget everything else, he cannot forget his own evil deeds. His sin will not only find him out, but he will find his sin out. He may forget, as the phrase is, his own name, and for the time being seem to be unconscious of his existence, yet—if at any time, in the course of his life—he has committed any flagrant offence, he will find a record of it some way or other made where the eye of the soul, in spite of all he can do, will rest upon it; and he will exclaim to himself, "I am fearfully and wonderfully made."

To our own mind, therefore, this single fact, in the character of man, is one of the most clear and satisfactory proofs of God-likeness. We commence with the earliest day's of man's knowledge; we know something of the processes by which he comes to know many things, which in the aggregate make up the sum of his knowledge. But we can none of us account for one of a thousand of our own ideas; much less can we affirm as to the various ways by which *others* acquire knowledge.

Take a single case; there is the child, which, when grown to manhood, we call "Sir Isaac Newton." His way from earliest life, is like that of most children; he is busy in the acquisition of knowledge, possibly, in some respects, in advance of others. By what means he acquires his intellectual strength we know not, but soon we perceive he is weighing the philosophy of the world as in a balance : the powers of his mind seem to have an almost superhuman energy. As if in search of something to know, and *after* he had learned what was to be found here, he passes to the very out-posts of the creation : there for a time he busys himself in brushing the dust from the stars that dimly twinkle upon the very confines of the creation ! Yet, the last item of knowledge he received was much more easily learned than the first.

Scarcely any view which we take of the human mind, that does not leave us impressed with a sense of the deep mystery that hangs around it. Who has not watched the operations of his own, when endeavoring to recall an incident or event, which appeared to have been, as we say, forgotten ? How faithfully memory will search for the key ! How diligently something within us, (I know not what to call it,) will turn over the pages of the past ! How busily all the members of that mysterious family, will bestir themselves, as if to assist each other in finding the thing that a kind of presiding agency there is in search of ! All seem to understand and to know perfectly well what is wanted, where to find it, or what will at last lead to the discovery of it. All seem to be animated with one and the same assurance, that whatsoever was once there, is there still, that nothing can be lost which had ever gained a residence, so to speak, in the mind.

(Seventhly.) Another point of this resemblance is seen in the power which the creature evidently possesses over that which we must call matter, in distinction from intelligence or mind. We feel constrained to use the word here in a kind of general or indefinite sense, though we are by no means satisfied with it in any sense whatsoever. We cannot fully suppress the feeling, that in some form or other, *the elements* of which matter is formed, or out of which things we now call matter were made, have been in existence from eternity. We know of no arguments, either from reason or Revelation, by which the eternity of matter can be disproved. We know not that it would add in the least, to the most sublime and elevated idea of God, for us to suppose he had existed from eternity, a lone and solitary spirit, without desire of companionship or matter for his infinite intelligence to act upon. Naturally and most earnestly do we shrink from any hypothesis on this subject, which is based on the recent origin of what we now look upon as the world of matter.

And if, to find relief from this painful position, we go back to unnumbered millions of years, we find no less difficulty in beginning then, than now. It is all dark, when we turn our eyes in the direction of the Infinite, whether of time or space, or God; not a *ray* of light from Revelation on this subject, has ever fallen upon our mind; and from the nature of the case, there cannot any.

Still, what we call matter, in its common or popular acceptation, is perhaps, well enough understood, to enable us to go on with the argument. We speak of matter in distinction from mind.

As there is no passage in the word of God, which says or even implies that the world in which we live was formed out of nothing, we are at liberty to assume that none of the various terms which are used to describe the work of creation involve that idea; God is said to have created man out of the dust of the earth. Here, certainly, the word create, or make, cannot be understood as implying a bringing of something into existence out of nothing. Why does not this passage inform us of the true meaning of ברא Bâ-râ, that it was to form or make from materials or elements already in being? ברא Bâ-râ signifies to create, cause to exist, create anew, etc., etc.

If this is so, it follows that, *man*, in a very important sense, *creates;* he provides himself with the requisite materials, and following out the suggestions of intelligence, actually brings into existence what was not there before, just as truly as his Creator, in the formation of man or the creation of a world.

What is done in this direction by a beast, a mere animal, is done in obedience to the law of instinct, by which we mean "a certain power or disposition, by which independent of all instruction or experience, without deliberation, without having any end in view, animals are unerringly directed to do spontaneously, whatsoever is necessary for the preservation of the individual or the continuance of the kind." The idea of *create* does not enter into this definition in any sense whatsoever. He that proposes to make a watch has a distinct end in view. He must needs shape all his plans in view of such end. That which is done by instinct, is done without plan, or even the remotest idea of an end.

The house in which man resides, whether it be a hovel or a palace, is the work of his hands; he has created, made it; it was the end he had in view. All his utensils of husbandry have been made by him. Every form or contrivance for navigating the sea, or traveling upon the land. All his garments, whether of fine or coarse texture, of whatsoever made or however prepared, have been by him created and made. The city in which he dwells, the Temple of God in which he worships, the food which he gathers from the earth or the seas, all is, in an important sense, the work of his hands. We are not to be understood as affirming, that he created these things in the sense in which we are to understand the Bible, when it affirms that God created the heaven and the earth; it is intended only, that he is their creator, in the following sense; his intelligence and agency were the sole causes of their existence, just as that same intelligence and moral agency are the legitimate and exclusive causes of his own moral acts.

(Eighthly.) But we have time to mention only one point more of resemblance between God and man. It is a point, however, which embraces almost all others. Man, like his Creator, is *a spiritual being.* God is also a spirit; infinite in all his perfections. The Pneuma, which God is said to have breathed into man, after which, " man became a living soul," is that in which consists the principal analogy between man and his Creator.

This Pneuma, like its author, is without any moral stain or bias. As it comes from the hands of God, it must be like all his other works, in itself good :—whatever there is of evil, therefore, whether in man or resulting from the freedom of his will, must be traced no further back than to the agency of the creature himself. The declaration that " Adam begat a son in *his* image, and after his own likeness," cannot be understood in any other sense than that which implies free agency, bound to personal responsibility. We cannot affirm that Adam's posterity, whether near or remote, are brought into existence *sinners,* any further than they are undeniably the work of man, in distinction from the work of God, *sin is character ;* but character cannot exist prior to the existence of that free agency of whom it is predicated, any more than we can affirm any thing else of a subject—while that subject itself is not yet in existence.

It has always been to us a matter of surprise,—that men should be in such haste, if I may so speak, to fix upon the first man as the guilty cause of sin. As a man, I feel afraid to go back of my own volition, either in man or in the angels that kept not their first estate ; lest I should be found attributing sin to the Author of my being. I am satisfied that Adam was—*by Divine appointment,* if you please, our federal head and representative ; if by this, you will understand me as admitting only, that *he was thus placed by the Almighty, in order that he might show how it would be in every instance with his posterity.* They were represented in him : i. e., he showed them, and us, just how it would be with any one of us, if left like him to stand or fall for ourselves. The utter powerlessness of penal considerations, to keep man back from sin, is another important lesson taught us in the experiment (if we may so call it,) which was made in Adam, or rather in his fall. Who has not had occasion to mark this in the utter failure of the arrangements of men, the severest penalties they can inflict, to keep men back from sin ? Murder is often committed, as it is said, under the gallows, while yet its victim is swinging ! There was no other way, so far as we can see, by which the Almighty could say to all his responsible creatures, what he has said to us in the fall of Adam. Placing him at the very head of the human family, at the head of his own race ; there, suffering him to disobey, or rather to do just as he should choose, in view of all the consequences, even to disobedience, it was but another method, and a most *effectual* method of saying to the human race, "there is the result whenever man shall feel no other influence than that of law; or whenever he shall consult only his own inclinations; or rely upon his own strength; or refuse to acknowledge his relations to his Creator: that is just as it will be with all his posterity; the first step which they shall take, which is of a moral nature, will be *a wrong* step; and so will be every subsequent one, till they yield to the saving influence of that plan, which, in the fulness of time, I shall introduce for their recovery from sin and its bitter consequences."

I cannot, of course, dwell upon this, as it is, in fact, only incidental to the subject under consideration. It forms no part of our present purpose, except so far as it may show, that whatever there is in man, that God has made, it is "as it was in the beginning, and ever shall be," all good; while it is *man* that "hath sought out many inventions."

I have already spoken of *the haste*, as it seems to me, which men have manifested in assigning *a casue* to the universal and deep depravity of man: that they should be anxious, if possible, to find it even antecedent to all volition; that is, antecedent to all responsible action in man, in a propensity to sin; or in a corrupt nature; or in a breach of covenant which God had made with Adam; or by imputing Adam's sin to all his posterity; or in something else. At any rate, a cause which effectually exculpates the sinner himself leaving the blame on whom?

Now, we do not deny: nay we admit, that there *was*

a most important connection between the sins of our first parent, and that of all his posterity : there is a most important connection between the sins of *every* parent and *his* posterity : a law which underlies all others, even that of example, by which we are led to expect, and are sure to *see* children in the image of their father. A cross, morose, vile parent may know of a surety, that the mark he will make upon his family will be distinctly legible even to the third and fourth generation. And since Adam was at the head of all mankind, it was fit that *his* act should be felt to the last individual who should belong to his family.

Yet no man in his senses ever thinks to hold a child responsible for his parent : or regard him as guilty of what his parent did, unless he shall be convicted of having *done* wickedly as his parent. Above all, no man ever dreams of *making* all the children guilty by *imputing* to them, what they never did, but what their father did, years and years before they had an existence.

We find a great many things in the history of the church, which greatly surprise us : but among them all *this* seems to us the more surprising ; that there should be such a fearful result, arising from the first transgression, and our Lord Jesus Christ, the Great Teacher, he whose office and mission it was to teach us the whole gospel, should not once allude to it ! The result of which I am speaking, is that which some *theories* advance or claim ; and not that I have admitted. Why, if it were indeed true, that God, by an act of his own sovereignty, constituted me a sinner six thousand years before I existed, and that too, in consequence of what Adam did, by taking his character, his guilt and making it mine, *why did not my Saviour*, in as much as it was his mission to explain all things, in regard to the way of life, why did he not on some occasion or other—mention it? It certainly was one of the most important acts of the Divine government: nothing that ever God did to me ever affected me more seriously than this, if it is so. Hence, I greatly desire to know.

Do you reply by affirming, "that it is of no consequence, whether Christ did or not, since *Paul* evidently did?" Are you quite sure of that? Paul is often quoted in support of the doctrine of *imputation*; but imputation in *his* mind was something very different from that which is thus named by St. Augustine, with whom the theory seems to have originated. Not once does Paul intimate, that God, in dispensing good or evil to man, took that which really belonged to one, and gave it to another. And if you fall back upon the declarations of the Old Testament, they are to the following effect:— "Blessed is *the man*, unto whom the Lord imputeth not iniquity." Abraham believed God, and it, (his faith) was imputed unto him, (Abraham,) not Isaac, nor Jacob, but Abraham, for righteousness.

But time would fail us, *has* failed us long ago. We have felt called upon to notice as far as we have those theories which have been formed for getting men into the world as the creatures of God, with a character, dark as depravity itself;—and that even, derived from Adam. The Bible, as it seems to us knows nothing of any such thing. Men become sinners now-a-days just as they did a thousand years ago; and a thousand years ago, just as Adam did, viz:—*by doing wrong*, disobeying God. *All* become sinners in this way; "there is none that doeth good; no, not one."

The meaning of the passage already quoted, " Adam

begat a son in his own image," evidently is, that he was, and was to be, the progenitor of a race that just like himself, should do wrong the first opportunity: the first time he should act upon his own responsibility. A statement that his son, Cain, took the earliest opportunity to verify. His posterity like himself, from that day to this, have sinned, in the first moral act, and in every subsequent act, just as Adam did, and for the same reasons; being left to the freedom of their own will; in other words, not being restrained, or prevented; and they have so continued to do till converted by the grace of God. This seems to be all there is of it; and certainly, it is enough.

There are many considerations, however, which lie along the line of our subject which we cannot even notice. It remains that we briefly recapitulate the several points of resemblance in man to his Maker, which we profess to have found, and be deeply penetrated with the fact, that these may all be without the slightest resemblance in respect to that holiness which we know is possessed by Him who made us and before whom we shall shortly stand. Man, like his Maker, then, determines the moral qualities of an act, from the relations known to exist; he resembles him too, in the power he possesses of exerting a moral influence over other moral beings; he is an intelligent being, so is his Creator; he is like God in respect to the influence of his own acts upon himself; he can, in a certain sense *foretell* those events or results, which notwithstanding, are dependent on the freest moral conduct of others; besides, there is a very marked analogy in respect to his capacity for knowledge: and in his power over matter; as well as his existence as a spiritual being. On this last is undoubtedly built his immortality, but of this it is not ours here to speak. From these considerations we find no difficulty in predicting for him, a fearful destiny, if by unrepented and unforgiven sin, he shall incur the displeasure of that being, whom he so much resembles, in all that is calculated to ennoble and purify. Let him beware of squandering his Lord's treasures, or burying his talent in the earth. And let him also, with profoundest reverence crave forgiveness, of his Maker, if in this comparison he hath said aught or claimed any thing which is presumptuous in him or derogatory to his Creator God.

CHAPTER V.

THE INEXORABLE ELEMENT IN LAW.

ARGUMENT UPON JAMES II. 10.

*" Whosoever shall keep the whole law, and yet offend in
one point, is guilty of all."*

See also Luke xvi. 10.

MANY who are among the most sincere and well meaning of the people of God, have been excedingly troubled
with both of these passages, but particularly with the
first.   It seems to them hard, if not unjust, to affirm,
that he who is guilty of one offense is guilty of all.   It
looks like taking away the last motive to reform, or to an
attempt at reform, in one who is guilty in having broken
the divine law, even in the smallest particular.   And
who has not done this?   Its language is that which
would seem to ignore all distinctions among men, making one man as bad as another, and *all*, however moral,
peaceable or amiable, guilty of the most flagrant sins!

In fact, the plain and literal import of either, is what
no man can believe, whatever the degree of sincerity
with which he receives the rest of the Bible; for there
are limits to a man's faith, as there are to his knowledge.
He cannot believe what he *knows* to be false, it being
quite as much as he can do to believe what he cannot

comprehend. But the statement here made, *if it must be understood literally*, any man knows cannot be so; and therefore, as we have said, its effect upon the mind of almost any one is exceedingly unhappy.

Very similar are the statements we should feel compelled to make, in respect to certain articles of faith in the Romish church, that, for instance, which teaches the real presence of Christ in the bread and wine of the Eucharist. No man can believe that. At any rate he cannot be an *intelligent* man that believes it. For every man must know, that in regard to such matters, we have no means of ascertaining whether it is so or not, but to refer the question directly to the senses. If the sense of taste shall testify that the communicant, as he is called, is eating truly and properly flesh, when he takes the wafer, and is drinking blood, instead of wine, when he takes the cup, he will be justified in inquiring into the matter, with a view to detect and expose the imposition, but not with the faintest expectation that he shall find it verified. So if his sight or smell, or any *other* sense shall testify to that effect, he will be justified in examining carefully to find how he has been imposed on, but nothing further. In all such cases, our corporeal senses are the last appeal.

Nor can any man believe, that the human race literally sinned in Adam and fell with him ; i. e., fell when *he* fell, however much, and *whatever* may be said in its favor. Those theories which are advanced with a view to explain such a notion, or defend it may seem satisfactory and conclusive. But no intelligent man, in the exercise, (the *right* exercise, I should say,) of those powers which distinguish him from his beast, can subscribe to any such notion.

If the man that asserts it, will go forward and explain it; if he will say, "I mean, only, that every individual of Adam's posterity, if placed in his condition would do as he did, and that any one of his race may, by looking to him, *see* just how it would fare with himself if placed there," if he will say, "this is what I mean and all I mean, in affirming that we all sinned in Adam and fell with him," we have no objection to the declaration, except that it is exceedingly liable to be misunderstood, and, that consequently it would be well to fix upon some other.

So of the passage in Luke, to which we have referred: —when correctly interpreted, it is not only perfectly clear and satisfactory, but a most important truth: " He that is faithful in that which is least, is faithful in much : and he that is *unjust* in the least, is unjust in much." If this is understood to mean that the man who rightly *uses* the smallest amount of means,—who properly employs the smallest amount of time, the smallest abilities, or talent, or—the smallest amount of wealth, or any thing else with which he may do good or evil, will furnish, in that very act, assurances, that if he had ever so much, he would do in like manner with it all,—why, then we have no difficulty in understanding it; nor in seeing in it, a most important principle.

This law, as any one may see, places the poorest man in the world on the same foundation with respect to his prospects or opportunity to secure eternal life with the richest. It makes his eternal salvation depend, under God, with what he *does* with what he has,—instead of depending on what he has not.

But the first passage, (that from James,) the one on which we propose to base our argument, presents a somewhat more intricate case. It is difficult understanding it as it is there expressed; though we are by no means sure that the sentiment it contains could be more clearly set forth in a smaller number of words. Its import, unquestionably, is not what it would seem to be; but on the contrary, it is the announcement of a general principle. The object of the inspired author is to affirm that he who commits *one* sin, as effectually closes the door of hope against himself on the ground of law, as if he had committed every sin of which he was capable: that though that sin be comparatively a small one, yet the influence upon the subsequent history or character of the sinner, so far as he is concerned, was as surely fatal as if he had committed the most flagrant one.

Statements are so frequently made similar to this, that we have become accustomed to them. Results of a most stupendous and overwhelming nature are said to have originated in those which were comparatively of little or no importance; yet we silently acquiesce. The universal depravity of man, and the consequent exposure of the whole race to final and endless perdition, are everywhere regarded as the result of a single act of disobedience; and that act, if we know anything of the comparative guilt or magnitude of different courses of conduct, must be regarded as a very small offense.

So, also, it is a very common thing, when speaking of those deeds or actions which are performed before conversion, to say—" they are all wrong; not one is right in the sight of God; they differ from other, and more flagrant acts of wickedness, only that they are what we may call ' amiable sins.' " It serves but very little to relieve us—to affirm—by way of defense or explanation, that *the motive* by which the doer is prompted, is not a good one in the sight of God. The individual who has planted himself upon this theory—seems to know all about the character of the motive, the view which God takes of those actions, and the degree of turpitude or hypocrisy, which each separate act contained; and we silently acquiesce in these decisions.

It is scarcely necessary for us to say, that these state-ments, in respect to those actions which are performed while men are in sin, as we say, greatly embarrass them: they appear to feel, as keenly as anybody, the lack of motive towards anything that is good : for, mark you, the statement is not, that those deeds which are performed by men in an unconverted state, are not *meritorious*; for this is a claim which we never set up in respect to any act, whether before or after conversion. But it is, that the identical acts which are performed *after* we are con-verted, and which are acknowledged as right in the sight of God, are wrong, wholly and totally wrong, if performed while man is in an unconverted state.

Then, again, if inquired of in respect to those actions which are performed *after* we are born of the spirit of God, if asked, what is their character; whether they are *perfect?* we unhesitatingly admit their imperfections: we feel compelled to affirm, that for some cause or other, when weighed in the balance of a just and holy law, they are every one of them found wanting.

How can these things be? and how shall we ever do anything in the sight of God acceptable, or perfect, if it cannot be said, we do it after our conversion ?

These are questions we propose to answer in the few paragraphs that follow. We shall confine our attention for the present to the consideration of those actions which are performed by men while in a state of impenitence or sin: and our object will be to ascertain, not only what is their true character, but *why* it is affirmed of them, that they (i. e. their actions) are wrong, wholly and totally wrong in the sight of God; but also, what are the relations they sustain to those actions which are performed *after* conversion and which are said to be right.

Where, then, in the scale of morals are we to place those actions which a man performs before conversion? In what sense are they wrong? Are they ever and in any sense right? Now, an act may be right in respect to an immediate, or a proximate object; and wrong in relation to the main, or ultimate one.

Let me illustrate my position by the following diagram, or Arithmetical problem. It is required to raise the number five to its fourth power. Now, we will suppose, that at the very out-set, a mistake is made; or, in other words the law by which we are to govern ourselves in all such calculations, and which, in more familiar language, is called the rule, is broken; that instead of saying, " five times five are twenty-five," we say " five times five are twenty-four;" the whole calculation, be it ever so long, is affected by that single mistake, or breach of " the rule." Thus, it will be seen, that in consequence of the misstatement, or breach of the rule, at the commencement, the third and fourth powers are both wrong, in relation to the main position or result; and both right, in relation to that which is undeniably wrong. Five times twenty-four are one hundred and twenty; and five times one hundred and twenty are six hundred. These statements are both true, and undeniable, whatever may depend on them; yet twenty-four is not the second power of five; nor is one hundred and twenty the *third* power; nor six hundred the fourth.

Let the calculation be extended now ever so far;

$$
\begin{array}{r}
5 \\
5 \\
\hline
25 \\
5 \\
\hline
125 \\
5 \\
\hline
625 \\
\\
5 \\
5 \\
\hline
24 \\
5 \\
\hline
120 \\
5 \\
\hline
600
\end{array}
$$

it is further and further from right: And what is more, it is just as sure to continue thus, as long as the calculation shall proceed. You might make millions of mistakes in the course of the calculation, without the faintest probability of returning to the right numbers, and of course, to the correct results. In fact, the worst thing that could be done, after the first error, would be to deviate from the exact rule, in such case made and provided.

Here, then, we have an instructive example of the nature of law: it makes no provision for mistakes, no arrangements for return. Its language being in all cases, "do and live; do not and die." The inexorable element is ever predominant; in truth, it is the animating principle, the very essence of law.

We know not that a more forcible illustration of the eternity of punishment, to those who die in sin, could be presented. Here the law is seen steadily and eternally yielding death to the transgressor. And though his deviations, at first may have been of the slightest character; yet the longer he lives, in that fearful relation, the surer is it that he will never leave it, inasmuch as no event can ever recall him; no blunder, or purpose ever throw him back upon the high-way of life.

In one of his defenses before the civil authority, the Apostle Paul made a statement which has embarrassed many. He affirmed, with his accustomed force and solemnity, that he " had lived in all good conscience before God unto that day." And yet this assertion covered two periods of his life, as utterly at war, one with the other, as those of any man that ever lived. If the Apostle, when under the guidance of Divine inspiration, could say that while he was persecuting the church of Christ, and as inspiration itself has expressed it, " was breathing

out threatenings and slaughter against them that called
upon the name of the Lord Jesus," was "acting in all
good conscience before God," what a fearful thing is a
man's conscience! and what has he to do to procure his
eternal ruin, but to follow the dictates of such a conscience! yet, under the circumstances was it his duty
to have done otherwise? should not a man always follow
the instructions of his conscience? If we mistake not, we
have in his case a most pertinent example of the matter
under consideration: he is wrong, evidently and fearfully wrong in all he does, with respect to the cause of
Christ; yet would it not have been suicidal for him to
have violated his conscience, and to have refused to follow
its instructions?

His error consisted in a false step at the first: he had
allowed himself to misconstrue the word of God, misinterpret the Prophecies concerning Christ, and of course,
be misled in respect to the act of obedience, or the question of submission to him. That ignorance and unbelief
which he pleads as the ground of his forgiveness with
God, are the results of his not having duly considered
the evidence in favor of the claims of Christ, or the
proofs of his Messiahship that were furnished by his miracles.

To return then, for a moment, to our recent illustration: it suggests in a most impressive manner, the nature
of that punishment which he will incur who dies in impenitence. As while in this world, however moral or
amiable he might have been, however much he may
have done in the line of benevolent effort, or for the support of the gospel, it was all done under the prestige of
a false position; it all originated in a wrong principle,
and of course was of no value in the sight of God. Had

the man been converted, and thus been brought to sustain the relation of a child in Christ, an heir of God, the same acts though not meritorious would have been sanctified by this near and intimate relation to Christ, and would have been an evidence in favor of his adoption.

Conversion, then, is the all important point with man; it places him back in the line of recovery; it expunges the errors which he had committed, and which he was living but to repeat. It introduces him into a new relation to God, a more near and intimate one than ever he had held before, and permits him to come forward and ask for favors at the hand of God which none but the dearest of his children can presume to inquire for.

Let the reader bear in mind, we are only aiming to account for the embarrassing fact, that an act, which *after* conversion is most praise-worthy and commendable; when performed at any other period of life, is not right in the sight of God, neither indeed, can be. And that not on account of any change in the intrinsic or the inherent character of the act, but by reason of that radical and important change which has taken place in the relations sustained by him who has performed the act. As seen in the diagram which we have introduced for our illustration, there is not a step after the Proton Pseudos, (the first error) which is right, or can be; so in respect to the character of those actions which are performed in unbelief, they cannot by any possible hypothesis be right, for they are all of them under the prestige or influence of unbelief.

We give another illustration. It is undoubtedly true, that we may find innumerable places, in this, as well as in other countries, where the thickness of a knife-blade will decide the destination of a drop of water or a flake of snow, in spite of all incumbrances or causes whatsoever. Go upon any height of land which divides the gathering waters of any of our rivers, and you may find innumerable localities, where you may place your finger or your knife, and the flake of snow which shall fall on the one side, when it shall have melted, shall start for the ocean under the self same cause which carries all waters there, and shall complete its journey by entering it thousands of miles from the place where another flake does; though this last, at its setting out, commenced *only on the other side of the blade!*

In a former place of our residence, as we passed over the ridge of land which divides the waters of the St. Lawrence from those that fall into the Gulf of Mexico, we were accustomed to notice a certain rock lying by the way side, on the highest inch of ground that formed that ridge. There, as one may see, you might place your finger where the drop of water which fell from the clouds and lighted upon one side of it, would slide off in the direction of those streams that went down the Niagara River, and thence into the ocean, at the Gulf of St. Lawrence, and that which fell on the other, would take the opposite direction and end its journey accordingly.

Let us now call these different routes by the names we so familiarly use when speaking of the different causes of human conduct or character, to wit, the one, obedience, the other that of disobedience; the one of salvation, the other of destruction; one, life, the other death. We will undertake to follow a drop, which has started for the ocean, among the waters that go down into the St. Lawrence, and thence into the sea. Its movements are at first slow, as it starts on its journey, though at an elevation of a thousand feet above its position when it shall have finished its course. It meets with innumerable obstacles, many of them at the beginning, so small, that were they to be met a little further on, would not be noticed. Yet it finds its way over, under, or around them, meeting other drops that have started on the same journey and under the same law, forming an alliance with them, contributing its full weight to hurry them forward, and receiving like influence and service from them. It soon helps to form a rill, then a brook, a stream, a river, which goes foaming and dashing on its way, leaping from the dizzy height into the dark cavern below, and finally meeting the accumulated waters of ten thousand streams, it moves along with resistless force towards the place of its final destination.

We have often, in our imagination, followed this drop from the place where it alighted, when it fell from the clouds, to its entrance into the sea. We have ever regarded it as strikingly emblematic of the journey of human life. Man, as he opens his eyes in early infancy, is that drop: he sets forward for the boundless ocean of eternity; having started, as we may assume, (and as we afterwards find to be true,) in a wrong direction. Its first excursions, as it goes laughing along in the brawling brook, are strikingly analogous to the days of noisy boyhood and frivolous bluster. We see it approach the headlong precipice of Niagara; careering along in sleepy unmindfulness of the approaching abyss. It arrives upon the brink, accompanied by millions that have been hurried forward by the same resistless laws; pauses a moment, as if to contemplate the fearful consequences, then plunges into the bottomless abyss below. I follow its journey a little further, while it hurries rapidly on as if frightened at the thought of its headlong and reck less leap, shut up in its narrow channel by a wall of adamant that rises on either hand to the very clouds,— as if some mighty power, in fear of an attempted escape —had thus attempted to cut off all hope, and shut up to perdition.

But it is perhaps unnecessary for us to follow our drop of water any further; we have only referred to it for the purpose of securing the light which it suggests. Who cannot see, not barely one of the human race, but millions of them ; yea, in a sense, all,—as they commence their journey for that boundless ocean which lies before us? They who have embraced the deadly sentiments of infidelity, are most strikingly represented by the rushing waters as they approach the roaring cataract. And what can be more expressive of the results which follow this rash and reckless step, this embracing of the fatal creed, than the dark and sullen flow of those agitated waters, as they hurry on between massive walls, from which there is evidently no escape? He must have been born and educated where reflection was prohibited by law, and where analogies were never thought of,—who sees nothing suggestive or deeply instructive in such scenes as these.

But this, as the reader must be aware, is not the object, or at any rate, the *main* object—for which we have introduced this illustration. We wish to speak of the fact, that from the commencement to the end of its journey, whichever way it turns, or whatever be its speed, it is, by supposition *constantly going wrong ;* and this— wholly in consequence of that fatal *first step.* Every thing which may be embraced in the vital interests of this enterprise, is made to depend on this first step ; it that is rightly taken, all will be well; if wrong, the bitter consequences are not less sure.

Another point in this analogy I must name. Our companion, on its way to the ocean, may be supposed to fall in with other waters which are taking the same journey—but which, like the river in its meanderings, flows on, now this, now that way; and in the course of a few miles, towards every point of the compass. Sometimes for whole leagues, it runs in precisely the direction in which it would have to flow to find exactly the opposite result. But its banks, on either hand, are risen high; large tracts of country, if not mountains, intervene to prevent it from forsaking its natural channel, and finding its way to the opposite ocean, if not—the opposite side of the globe.

Still, whatever be its course—whether it turn to or from the desired end, it is hasting away towards that ocean to which it was consigned by that eventful *first step*: only the thickness of the slender blade, at the outset, decides the whole! Vainly do we persuade ourselves, that a sedate, moral, blameless life is all that is required; vainly do we imagine, that because we do many things that are evidently as good as any body does—and perhaps in our estimation a little better—we are therefore sure of an interest in the Lord Jesus Christ! Our actions must all be classified—must be called after a specific name: there may be many of them that look well—quite as well as those of the saints of the Most High God, yet they may not be in the succession, as I may express it.

The explanation is, (if explanation be needed,) before conversion, man is on the wrong side of the line: he started for that eternity which is before us all, in the wrong direction; and though the law which he now obeys, or to which he is in subjection, be one which involves him in evil, yet the evil is inconceivably less, to the general interests, than if it were otherwise. The fault is not in the law, but in the abuse of it. A more serious evil could not happen to man than to be placed in circumstances where he would be just as likely to reap grapes from thorns as from vines—or in other words, derive good from evil-doing, or evil from good.

But this is a consideration to which I must attend further on; for the present, I have need to say, only, that many of the calamities that happen to us here, arise from the natural and unobstructed operations of laws which could not be repealed without ruin to man and dishonor to God. Nay, all the sore evils of life are to be traced in some way or other to the infraction of laws which are founded in infinite wisdom, and executed by infinite benevolence and mercy. Should God repeal them he would ruin the very sinners that complain of them; and that after all may not be saved by them.— The inexorable element, therefore, in the Divine law, is one of its greatest excellences; it cannot be altered but to be ruined.

But it is necessary that I should refer to another consideration—one which may be regarded both as an illustration, and as a matter to be defended: I refer to the condition in which the human family are placed through the influence of the first transgression. Many are accustomed to speak of this condition as one of the most calamitous and evil—while at the same time it is spoken of as resulting from an arrangement which is purely of God, and one that he might easily have avoided. Nay, I may confidently affirm, that in most cases where it is spoken of—in most if not all the Creeds where it is mentioned, the implication is, that it might have been otherwise, and no injury would ever have resulted to the government of God.

We are accustomed to regard the case now under consideration as one of the most perfect examples of the unyielding element, in the laws of God, of which we have any knowledge. Not the law of gravitation itself can be more so—in fact, it would seem that this was the lesson which the Creator designed to impress upon our minds, in calling us so frequently to the contemplation of that single feature in the laws of nature.

We allow ourselves to forget that one of the most serious evils which enter into a civil government, is the uncertainty, that even its best laws will be executed; to say nothing of those which are of a doubtful character. Why is not this to be regarded as God's method of intimating to man, that a chief excellence of his laws—is—that they will infallibly be executed? Why should we find our most serious cause of complaint against the laws of God, in that—which, if it could be affirmed of human legislation, would be its highest perfection?

But the reader is perhaps impatient to enter upon the consideration of this last illustration of our subject; to wit, the condition in which the first apostasy has placed the human family.

There is scarcely another subject in the whole range of theology, on which as much has been said and written, as upon that now under consideration. Yet it has never seemed to have occurred to those who have said most, that this method of tracing our unhappy condition back to Adam, is apparently unknown in the scriptures; particularly those of the Old Testament. The depravity of the human race, and their consequent lost condition, are subjects not wholly ignored in those writings which are evidently inspired, and which are anterior to the days of Jesus Christ.   But that this condition was a consequent, or a result of the first act of disobedience, in a sense that would make it to depend for its very existence upon that,—we are not only not informed, but we are not furnished with even an intimation of it. *Why,*—I pretend not to say; but so is the fact.

The most remarkable thing about it, however, is that Jesus Christ himself never once alluded to it : his instructions were very full and complete on almost every other subject connected with the character and destiny of man ; but upon the fact that he (man) comes into being with a fearful score already against him, and that this score is to be traced to the first man, and to *his* first sin, is a doctrine which was never so much as alluded to by Jesus Christ.   We are only stating a fact ; not that we attempt to explain it : for as we have said, it is a most mysterious one.

Still, the silence of our Lord Jesus Christ, on a subject of such vital importance, has led us to the conclusion, that these effects, or results arising from the sin of Adam are wholly destitute of the moral element.   We mean to say, that whatever the consequences of Adam's sin upon his posterity, we think they are not of a moral nature, or they would have been named by Him who came to bring life and immortality to light.   Our Great Physician, in his faithfulness to describe the malignant disease that he had come to remove, if it were true, that it originated with our first parents, would have informed us of this ; would have said, by way of accounting for its universality, " the virus or seminal principle of this disease you have inherited from your first parent; the disease which is unto death originated with him."

But he said no such thing; and therefore we are led to infer, that though there may have been *a certainty* as there undoubtedly was that in consequence of his sin, all his posterity would enter upon their responsible existence with just such a character as Adam had, or with just his experience, yet *that certainty* was not of a moral nature; neither did it of *necessity* (I mean a *moral* necessity) involve the moral destiny of man.

It seems to have been a principal object with him who was arranging these momentous interests, to place man in a position where he should work out the great and important problems of his existence as a responsible being, and leave the result, whatever it was, for future ages, to the end of time. One of these, was to determine what means to employ in *the government of man:* for he was not only the last of God's creative energy, but was evidently the chief. Every form or development of this energy, which had been previously seen, had been exercised in the creation of irresponsible beings: these, God could govern as he did any of the other works of creation by a purely physical force; for *instinct* is nothing more to the animal, than gravitation to the stone. But, how should he govern *man*, the being made in his own image after himself for a pattern? how should he control him whom he would govern, and yet leave perfectly free? here is a problem whose solution was never aimed at before; and for which none but the Omnipotent, Allwise God was sufficient.

To settle the first point; to demonstrate the first position, in this important problem; viz: that, man could not be governed by *coercion*, could not be controlled as all the *other* creatures of God—could be—could not be kept in purity and obedience by *force*, or *dread of penalty*, the Almighty places him where he is to feel no other influence restraining him than that of dreaded consequences, or penalty of broken law, to demonstrate to all his rational creatures the superiority of man even over the *angels ;* for they could not be restrained by this consideration alone. This, however, was but *one* object; the *main* one, undoubtedly was, as we have said, to demonstrate, that this exalted order of intelligences, this being in the likeness of God, could not be kept back from sin, and thus in constant readiness for heaven, through the influence of law only or dread of penalty: and by this means a first intimation of a remedial economy is introduced : indirect, we admit ; but not the less explicit or satisfactory.

Another point is also gained ; which is, that every one of the race may see himself in his father Adam ; may see just how he would certainly do if placed in like circumstances ; may regard himself as there having been on trial ; may contemplate himself as having yielded to the first temptation ; may see that in Adam, his father, he has thus sinned. Not that he *has*, by any means ; the declarations of creeds ten thousand, to the contrary notwithstanding. Man only sees how it would be or would have been *if in those circumstances :* and since he *is* and is to be in those circumstances, all the days of his probation ; and moreover, since it has been demonstrated just how he and all the race will certainly act when placed there, he may as well regard the matter as settled, he is a sinner, already a sinner, six, or ten thousand years before he is created, in the divine mind, as well as one year, or one day : so that our Confessions of Faith, in in this respect have not misrepresented any of us.

Here, then, the inexorable, or unyielding element in law, as well that of an all-merciful God, as that of inflexible justice in human affairs, or of irresistible consequences in the operations of nature, is distinctly seen. It has no *moral character* whatsoever; is neither praise nor blameworthy any more than the law of gravitation. The certainty, that men, in acting perfectly free will do wrong, is no more worthy of blame, than, that a stone will fall to the ground if unprevented. And the certainty that good men, when assisted by the spirit of God, will do good, will do right, is no more meritorious, than the falling of the rain on the thirsty earth.

The Apostasy of Adam, then, must not be regarded in any sense, as a cause of our degeneracy. It simply sets forth what *will* be or what would have been, instead of what *must* be. I have no more right to assign his defection as the cause of my depravity, than I have to represent my sin as having been caused by the defection of "Julian, the Apostate." It stands apart and by itself from every other act, or every law, except that which refers to the influence of example ; but example can never be relied on as a cause which shall produce such a certainty and uniformity of results. The fact, that I shall, or will decide a question in a certain way, provided I am permitted to do as I please, has nothing of a moral character in it. Example may be the occasion, but not the cause of sin.

"But," exclaims the reader, "is not this dwelling too long on an unimportant point?" Perhaps so: but we may not agree as to the question of importance here : the point upon which we have dwelt is far from an unimportant one, if we may judge of it by the tenacity with which a certain school in theology cling to it. It would seem almost incredible, that any man should ·be so bent on finding *a cause* for the universal defection of men, as to assign *this certainty* for it ; and in carrying out the theory maintain, that a certainty of such a character could not exist, except a moral virus had been imparted in the first transgression to the whole race. The smallest objection that we can think of, to such a theory, is that it renders it impossible for sin in any form ever to enter ; for, surely if in order to the existence of moral evil or sin, you must have a previously existing sinful state in the heart of the being who is to sin, it will not be easy, we think, to find an opportunity to introduce it at all. The theory which we are exposing was once in our hearing advanced in the following language. " You cannot have sin in the world without previously having a sinner." The *act of sinning* then, does not make the sinner ! The act of murder does not make the man a murderer ! but he is thus made by a previously existing murderous state of the heart !

Now, it cannot be denied that there is the shadow of a reason for such a declaration as this last, notwithstanding its obvious absurdity. Murder, in order to its being murder, must be a premeditated act : but, to be this, it must have existed in the mind, that is, must have been assented to by the heart, must have been deliberately determined on by the moral powers within ; *but all these are acts :* we are in search of something further back *antecedent* to these, and must have it, or we must abandon the theory which is based on it.

We shall, then, have to abandon the theory ; for it is obvious, we cannot have such an anomaly or monster, as a sinner before sin ; or as sin before we have a sinner.

They are undoubtedly *coetaneous ;* i. e. commencing their existence together. This is undeniably the fact with respect to the *first* sin, whether of Adam, or any of his posterity : if so, what becomes of the theory that a depraved, fallen nature, was bequeathed by Adam to his posterity, which is the cause, source and origin of all sin, and is itself sinful ? Every sin, this side of the first, is just like *the first,* or it is not a sin : if the moral powers of any of God's responsible creatures, have become so affected or marred by " the fall " as to be incapable of obeying God, why, then, they are obviously released from obligation to obey him. No man can justly require of him that is born without hands, that he perform the work of one who has both unimpaired : or that the lame and sick should discharge the duties of those who are in health.

The conclusion, then, to which we come, on this part of our subject, is not precisely like that with which the author of a certain book concludes his labors ; " a conclusion in which nothing is concluded ;" but it is just the one to which thousands have come before, who have thought long and patiently on this subject. Men become sinners now, just as Adam did *by sinning.* And the certainty, that all his posterity will do as he did, become sinners as soon as they are capable of sinning, is a *moral* certainty wholly ; and the result one that is invariable, because reached in accordance with the laws of moral agency. Man is what he is, becomes what he becomes by his own agency, either active or passive.

But it seems necessary before bringing my remarks to a close, that I should speak of another subject, one which is not wholly unconnected with that which forms tho burden of my argument: I refer to the character of those acts which are performed by man after he becomes a child of God. In conducting our reader, as we believe we have to the conclusion, that all our actions while in sin, or before conversion are wrong, and that this is the meaning of the passage at the beginning, if we have led him to conclude that all our actions *after* conversion are right, perfectly and invariably *right*, we have a task before us, in our attempts to correct this impression, of no very ordinary character. But it is a task we shall endeavor to perform in as few words as possible.

The reader will bear in mind, we clearly demonstrated that those actions (*works* I should call them,) which were performed before we become Christians were wrong not on account of an inherent character perhaps, but by reason of their relations to the specific character of him who performed them. Works of necessity partake of the character of him that performs them. The adversary of course can do only evil: not that he is deficient in respect to those powers with which a being must do good but that being an Enemy, and known through the Universe of God as such, his works must all be classed as those of an enemy, let them be what they will. Some of them may be far *more* vile than others; but all of them shockingly wrong.

So of him, and of his works, who has become a child of God; there is a sense in which it is true all he does in the sight of God is righteous and acceptable; not because it is perfect in itself, but because of the new relation which he sustains to God in Jesus Christ. A parent will regard with favor, that in his child, which he would view with deepest aversion in another; while perhaps the works of the former have done him far more injury than those of the latter. He knows, of course, that his child *intended* only good; while the other, only evil.

But possibly this supposition may not seem fair or just, as it implies an intention on the part of an unconverted man, which he as openly disavows as the devoted Christian does; the evidence of whose sincerity is furnished in the act.

Very well; let it be so understood, then : not that it is so, but that it *seems* so. We fall back upon the principle already laid down ; that the works, (the moral character of a Christian,) partake, in respect to their character, of the act which places him in a new relation to God. Relation here, as everywhere else, in morals, decides the moral character of whatsoever is done.

The truth of our position will be more apparent when we consider, the language, or import of the act which carries us over from the position of an enemy to that of a friend. Before conversion men are regarded as strangers, " aliens from the commonwealth of Israel;" but afterwards they are " members of the body of Christ," " heirs of the grace of God :" they have availed themselves of the advantages arising from that remedial system which God has provided in the gospel. By faith they have entered upon the large and rich inheritance, even in the present life ; and one of the benefits resulting from this, is the forbearance which God exercises towards them ; the allowance, (if I may change the term for a more expressive one,) with which their imperfections are viewed.

Still, they *are* imperfections,—in a certain sense, they are sins ; for they are a breach of that law which requires us to " love the Lord our God with all our heart, and our neighbor as ourself." And in every degree in which we fall short of this, if weighed in the balance of the sanctuary, we are found wanting. The principles upon which God comes forth for the salvation of man, under-lie all law and all authority: " they are near thee, even in thy heart, and in thy mouth, even the law of faith ;" or the system of salvation founded upon faith in Jesus Christ.

There is no such thing, therefore, as perfection to the Christian in this world. Still, he is accepted of God ; but it is on the ground of his relation to Another; One whom God heareth always. The inexorable element in the law, *now* is as much for his advantage as previously it was for his disadvantage. By it, his works, which are perhaps all of them imperfect, are now rendered accept-able to God,—are regarded as just and right; whereas —in the former relation, however good in themselves— they were not in this sense acceptable, they were per-formed in unbelief, and therefore were sinful.

Thus have we accomplished what we proposed ; we have set forth the principle upon which it is proper to say, that no work which is performed in unbelief, how-ever good in itself, is right in the sight of God; nor is any work performed in faith,—though imperfect, *unac-*ceptable in his sight, being sanctified by faith in the Lord Jesus Christ.

CHAPTER VI.

DID CHRIST PREACH THE WHOLE GOSPEL?

" What Christ does not teach is not apostolical, although Peter and Paul may teach it; again, what Christ teaches is apostolical, although Judas, Annas, Pilate and Herod should do the same." Luther.

The question we propose to discuss is that which we have placed above. Did Christ in his ministrations, advance all the doctrines which rightfully belong to the Gospel? May we expect to find in the instructions of the Lord Jesus, those principles and rules, which when combined, *make up the sum total* of doctrine and requiremement, which he has embodied in the plan of salvation?

This question we must answer in the affirmative, whatever becomes of church or state. Whenever it is understood, we are speaking of the mission of our Lord and Master, and the expectation is, that we say, *yea* or *nay* to the inquiry, " Did Christ declare the whole Gospel?" We unhesitatingly answer in the affirmative.

The consequences to any theory, however hoary with age, or reverend, are another consideration entirely. They who frame theories are to look after them; it is no part of his duty, whose business it is to run a straight line, to look after points which from their natural position lie not in the line.   Nor should he be concerned to take care of theories which obviously must be left out, though they belong to systems of theology, so called, which have occupied the attention of the Christian world, and employed the pen of the wisest and best of men.   We do, in effect, 'move the previous question,' cut off all debate, settle the matter forever of the legitimacy or illegitimacy of any principle which claims the remotest relation to the Gospel of Christ.

By saying that the Lord Jesus taught the whole Gospel, I do not affirm that every separate doctrine of it is taught by direct instruction, but, that *either* by this, or by fair deduction, every principle, or law, or duty is, insomuch, that if the law in question be not found in the instructions of Christ, or, at least its *germ*, so to speak, it matters not where else it be found, it is no part of the Gospel.

We cannot help it, if this principle should remove the foundation from under several important theories, the interests which are involved are such as to justify the movement in a direct line, till the legitimate consequences are reached.   What earthly hope or human thought can compare with the direct and appropriate action of unmixed truth?   The whole intelligent world is beginning to turn with aversion from that spurious form of Christianity, which proposes to eke out a system of salvation that Christ and his Apostles left quite incomplete; with tradition, or with so called revelation, given in these latter days.   Every friend of truth, as he crosses the line, which divides the known and acknowledged instructions of Christ, from those that are obviously derived from some other source, says within himself,

"Where am I to stop? where will that principle, which I am now following, lead me? What shall I do with the express injunction of Jesus Christ, "Call no man father upon the earth, neither be ye called Masters, for *one* is your Master, even Christ"?

To the candid, honest, sincere student of the Bible, no question is of greater importance than that which we are now considering. Having settled in his own mind the claims of the scriptures, having acknowledged that they are of God, he will be engaged all his life in referring any doctrine or practice, which may have been introduced to his notice, to this single test, "is it found in the Bible? Are there reasons to suppose that Christ taught it, either by inference or implication?"

The fact that it can boast the highest antiquity, is not enough; errors, too, are ancient. It was at the very cock-crowing of human history, that the Adversary advanced doctrines at war with God and subversive of the best interests of men. No age can render that which in itself is wrong, right, nor can any names, however honored or honorable, make that consistent and true, which is undeniably absurd and erroneous.

The sentiment which we have placed as a kind of motto, at the head of this chapter, requires a verbal alteration, in order to express the thought we wish to, and that which we suppose Luther himself, intended to express; we would say, then, "What Christ does not teach, is not *Gospel*, although Peter and Paul may teach it. Again, what Christ teaches is Gospel, though Judas, Annas, Pilate and Herod teach the same." The term "apostolic," he must have used as synonymous with gospel, or truth; for, of what importance is the question whether a doctrine be apostolic or not, if it be not a part of the Gospel?

This sentiment, thus expressed, whatever may have been the views of Luther, is one to which we are persuaded every man will subscribe in a moment who is himself a believer; or, in other words, who receives the instructions of our Lord Jesus Christ as a revelation from heaven, and the scriptures as the revealed will of God. What *other* errand had Christ, but to preach the gospel? What other object in coming into the world, but "to declare this greatest of all mysteries, how God can pardon sin?" What was his *mission*, but to lay down the only principles upon which God can be just, and the justifier of him that believeth?"

True; he must *close* his instructions by laying down his own life; since no arrangement or covenant with God, (in Hebrew Testament,) is of force, till the death of the victim which is to *seal* the transaction: but, it must have been a primary object with Christ, to explain and instruct; to advance sentiments in some way or other, that were embraced in the great plan of salvation, and to show how they were in harmony with the law of God, the will and mind of the Spirit, as revealed in the scriptures of truth. We are satisfied that the view which many entertain of the question, "Did Christ leave the point of *ecclesiastical polity* to be settled by the Apostles?" *is wrong.* It certainly could not have been an *unimportant* consideration; nor can it be fairly affirmed, that the various circumstances in which men were to be found—were such as to require this *discretionary* power to be vested in the Apostles. No other view of this matter can we regard as satisfactory, or as satisfactorily accounting for his supposed silence on the sub-

ject than—that which admits of the existence already—
of a body which he called his church—and which he intended should be regarded as his church to the end of
time. He evidently refers to an organization, *in his
day*, which he calls "*the church*," in a way that would
seem to intimate his firm belief, that he was not misap-
prehended in the least, nor in any danger of being. We
may add too, without fear of contradiction, that in accordance with all Ecclesiastical History, it was not till men
had become tired of the plain and direct instructions of
Christ—and had introduced innumerable amendments
to his laws and regulations; either by *tradition*, or by
pretended revelation, *that more than one form of church
organization was, or is to be found.* This is a fact of
mountain weight; and it is one with which every man
is familiar, who is himself "a scribe well instructed in
the things of the kingdom." He knows that up to the
middle of the third century, or later, you search in vain
for that, "lo, here; and lo, there!" which so distract the
modest inquirer after the school of Christ. The Bible
knows as much of the Grand Lama and his worship, as
it does of *diocesan episcopacy*, or that which has grown
out of it, Popedom. The thunders of gunpowder,—the
all but omnipotent energies of steam, and the process of
conveying intelligence by Magnetic Telegraph—are not
more unknown in the scriptures, that the doctrines and
offices of a great portion of the so called church of
Christ, as it exists at the present day.

We have no need, however, of occupying the reader's
time, or wearying his patience with this matter; there is
enough for us both at present, in the single declaration,
that Christ undoubtedly, either by express instruction,
or by fair implication, *taught the whole gospel.* He

need not be in haste to learn what use we intend to make of it; or what will be the consequences to his particular views of gospel truth, or of a gospel church. It is evident enough that these are questions which have nothing to do with the consideration of the subject before us. If the scriptures of the Old and New Testament " contain a perfect rule of faith and practice,"—if they who have them " are thoroughly furnished unto *every* good work,"—and if we are at present in possession of the instructions of Jesus Christ, as well as those of his inspired Apostles,—and the reader himself belongs to the true church of Christ, he need not be alarmed; *he will be able to find both himself and his church in the scriptures.* What could, *at any time*, be proved by the Bible, CAN BE NOW, or we have not the Bible. The Romanist recognizes *his* church, in some of its most distinctive features, in 1 Tim. iv. 1–3. He needs no Philip to tell him "of whom the Spirit speaketh here." He knows far better than is convenient or agreeable what church sat for that melancholy picture. You may place it before him to-day, and though you may safely affirm of him at the out set, that he has read his Bible as little as any man, yet he will show you in a moment that he knows something about that passage. The writer once opened to it, when conversing with a Romish priest, and asked him if he did not recognize himself there?" "What church," (was the question,) "what church sat for that picture?" To which he made no reply, but in a roar of laughter; utterly refusing to answer another question! And why? because, forsooth, his self-styled reverence discovered that the questions which were beginning to come were not the most comfortable, if they were the most *easy* to answer. It is by no means difficult, when conversing with this class of men, to see when they themselves are conscious of passing into territory which they know is wholly untenable, except by arguments drawn from other sources than the scrip-tures. If they are those whose strength is their igno-rance, or whose ignorance is their defense, they will not seem to *know* when they cross that line : the dogmas of " Mother church " are as sacred to them and as worthy of their credence as a revelation direct from heaven, attended by all the necessary vouchers for its authen-ticity : but if he be a man of intelligence, it will not be difficult to see that his risibles are somewhat disturbed, as soon as he attempts to bring forward arguments drawn from tradition only. There is a consciousness with him, as indeed there is with almost every body, that argu-ments in support of the Christian religion, which can not be found in the Bible, are worthy hardly to be laughed at.

Perhaps the reader has never reflected particularly upon the question under consideration; perhaps the declaration, that such and such doctrines are nowhere found in the instructions of Christ, may not at first strike him as a very important matter any way ; perhaps when he takes a particular doctrine, one which is found in his confession of faith, and runs over in his mind, the instruc-tions of Christ, he finds it nowhere among them, perhaps he does not at first see the bearing of that fact upon the doctrine in question. And, should he go for support to the instructions of the Apostles, and failing to find it there, should he be brought right up before the question, " is this, in fact, *against* my creed ?" it might be the first time in his life, that the question under considera-tion was regularly before him.

However, he would not fail to see at once, that *the silence* of our Lord, on any point, claiming to be a system of doctrines taught in the Bible, or any part of a system, would be, to say the least, a suspicious mark, or circumstance against it; and upon referring to the Epistles, should he find authority for it there, he would be likely to pause and inquire with more than ordinary anxiety, as to whether he could be mistaken or not in the construction that he had put upon these passages.

We do, therefore, take the position, that *the silence* of our Lord Jesus Christ, in regard to any doctrine, precept, practice, or ceremony, claiming to be a doctrine of the Gospel, a precept for the church of God, is a most valid, satisfactory and unanswerable argument *against* such precept or doctrine. *This is the great line which divides us from Romanism;* to every *Protestant* it is enough in respect to any doctrine, that it is no where found in the Bible. Say to him what you please, sustain your positions by the most formidable array of quotations from the so called "*fathers*," bring forward ever so much, from the writings or practices of the church, during the earliest ages of Christianity, and he has a question to propose at the close of the whole, because on this depends more than on all else. That question is, as I have said above, " what saith the Scriptures? Are they, or are they not, silent on the subject? If not, let us hear their testimony; if they *are*, we dismiss the doctrine or practice as lacking support forever."

And here it is in place to remark, no man by appealing to the scriptures, thinks it necessary to specify any part or portion of them, as maintaining doctrines which may not be found in any other portions of the Bible; it is ever felt by the friends of Protestant Christianity, that

the testimony of Paul on one and the same subject, is
that of Peter; and Peter's is that of James or John; and
all these together, agree with Christ; so much so, that
when any one of these writers sets forth a doctrine which
appears to conflict with that which has been advanced by
another, or by all the others, his testimony is at once set
aside.   Luther discovered, as he supposed, a discrepancy
between James and Paul, in respect to the ground of justification; and after striving long and ardently, to find a
harmony between them, and finding none, as he supposed, he proceeded to apply the exscinding scissors to
one of them.

If then, we feel justified in doing this, when it is discovered that one of the Apostles, as it seems to us, differs
from another, what must we say when we find one of
them differing from *all* the rest, and not only this, but
from our Lord Jesus Christ himself?   Should we not
examine those passages with the greatest care, which
seem to advance a doctrine that cannot be found elsewhere, to see if we understand them?   Ought we not to
bring the ripest knowledge of the language in which the
scriptures were written, to the consideration of every
part which can have a bearing upon the single question,
" is there here, in the case before us, a sentiment which
is advanced by no other inspired penman? and one,
especially not found in the instructions of Jesus
Christ?"

The reader is perhaps prepared to listen to what may
be required now, in explanation of what has been already
laid down or intimated in the questions we have proposed.   Where, then, do we find, in all the instructions
of Jesus Christ, the common notions of almost all Christendom, in regard to *the influence of the fall upon the*

family of man?   Where do we find a sentiment like that which is contained in our Confession of Faith ; "The covenant being made with Adam, as a public person, not for himself only, but for his posterity, all mankind, descending from him by ordinary generation, *sinned in him and fell with him in that first transgression?*"

Mark, we do not express a doubt as to the character of man, by nature, that it is unholy and opposed to God ; we are not finding a verdict against the doctrine of human depravity, any more than against that of human apostasy, but we ask for the chapter and verse where our Lord Jesus Christ assigned as *the cause* of man's depravity, the sin of our first parents?   Are we unreasonable in this demand?

The doctrine of man's depravity is clearly taught by the Savior, in many ways and on several occasions; his declarations to Nicodemus were equivalent to the assurance that "all have sinned and come short of the glory of God." But in no part of this interview does he advance the doctrine, that this *state* or condition, in which man *is* by nature, is one in which he was placed when Adam fell; "for that he sinned *in* him and fell with him." No where is it intimated that God, by an omnipotent decree has made our first parents a kind of universal agents or factors to do wickedness for us, and plunge us all into sin. The idea which is so great a favorite with some, and which is virtually endorsed by almost all the Calvinistic as well as Arminian churches of the land, viz : that "Adam was constituted our Federal Head and Representative," was evidently either unknown to our Lord Jesus Christ! or was considered by him one of those unimportant matters that he might safely leave untouched!

The reader may take which horn he pleases of this dilemma; if it seem easier to him to defend the position that Christ thought not best to *advance* that sentiment, we shall desire him to account for the fact some way or other; for he will undoubtedly take the ground that Paul has advanced it, (a ground which we have yet to examine in the course of this discussion.) But why did not "*The Great Teacher*" settle all these matters at once and with a single breath, as he did the necessity of the new birth? or the doctrine of his true divinity? Why did he not say, by way of explanation to Nicodemus, "ye must be born again, because the sin of your father Adam, is *your* sin, the state into which he fell is the state into which all his posterity are brought by his sin; *he*, ADAM, was your Federal Head and Representative, you sinned in him and fell with him," and *therefore*, "must be born again." This would have foreclosed all controversy with us.

We may possibly err in supposing that the silence of our Lord Jesus Christ on this subject is a matter of some importance; there is room for error almost anywhere. But why, if this was the case, if man is what he is, as an effect, while the apostasy is the cause, if he is a sinner "by nature," in consequence of a mysterious and inexplicable arrangement on the part of God, by which the character of Adam's posterity was involved in his first sin, why did not our Lord and Master see fit, *somewhere* in some part of his instructions to say so? He certainly advanced doctrines with great particularity, that would *seem* far less important than that which is under consideration; and, should we judge of the importance of any part of our creed, by the labor that has been laid out in its defense, we should surely regard that which we are now examining as second to none for its importance, and yet the mystery remains, that Christ in his ministrations and instructions never once referred to it ! His ministers here on the earth, show but very slight inclination to copy his example in this respect. The writer sat years under a ministry, during which he does not now recollect to have heard more than a few if any sermons, in which the dogma of Adam's federal relations to his posterity, was not, in some way or other introduced.

And this too when no man pretended to be able to explain it ! The very *thought* of inquiring into the connection between Adam's first sin, and that mournful condition of the human family into which the fall brought mankind, was preposterous in the extreme. " Come not here," (we used to be told,) " with your *reasoning*. Aim not to array this solemn and important doctrine before the bar of your *philosophy*. Seek not to square this mysterious arrangement by *your* notions of right and wrong." And the truth must be confessed, we dared not attempt an investigation. There was such a *halo of darkness*, (if you will permit the paradox,) around it, that we deemed it sin to inquire into it.

Nor have we been inattentive to the notice that others have seemed to bestow upon it : as we have passed over the history of the church, we have carefully noted the comparative interest which has been felt, or which *seemed* to have been felt by men in every age since this doctrine was first advanced in the church : for it is notorious, that it was not only unknown during the personal ministry of the Lord Jesus Christ, but it evidently came not into notice till the days of St. Augustine, or thereabouts. The end of the third or the beginning of the fourth century must be assigned as the period when

men began to explain the universality of human depravity by some sort of connection between Adam and his
posterity, which made it certain that if *he* had stood fast
in the integrity in which he was created, they also
would have remained firm and holy ; but if *he* fell—they
also, one and all—fell with him.

In this way the men of that generation endeavored to
account for the entire depravity of the race. That men
were depraved, seemed to be admitted on all hands ; that
as the Bible had said, they were "full of wounds and
bruises, and that there was no soundness in them," appeared to be established beyond a doubt ; yet—as to *the
cause* of this there was evident diversity of sentiment.
Novatius attributed it to to the influence of *matter over
mind ;* endeavoring to establish the dogma, that man
became corrupt as soon as he became a living soul.
Manes, on the contrary maintained, that—man was the
descendant of the devil ; that while a supreme deity
presided over all *good*, a no less supreme being originated all evil. Thus, the affairs of our world were managed by a kind of copartnership between two deities :
the author of all evil no less potent than he who originated all good !

The Manichæans evidently entertained notions on the
subject of evil in its relations to man, that were a deci-
ded improvement upon those which attributed it to the
influence of matter ; as this would involve the idea that
God, the only wise and good—was the author of it.
But the division of the Celestial Ruler into two person-
ages, each warring with, and against the other ; thus, destroying not only the unity of design in the works of
nature, but *the unity of the designer ;* giving to the
world in which we live, *two Gods*—instead of one.

This sentiment of course could not be embraced by any one who had any respect for the writings of Moses ; or in fact for any other part of the Bible ; the unity of the God-head being fundamental in the scriptures of the Old and New Testaments. Man must, therefore, make himself a Bible. Like Mahomet, he found it necessary to have a revelation specially for himself and his cause. This so called revelation very easily accounted for the universal depravity of man, as we have said, by making him a regular born diabolian: a son and heir of the devil—and nothing else.

Among all the multitude of notions, centering in this, there is only one which is particularly worthy of our notice at this time : the Manichœan theory fully accounts for the introduction of evil without involving the agency of God, or even his consent thereto. It introduces it in spite of him. He is made to stand by, as one that is' wholly impotent in the matter of preventing evil, and see his superior, (superior in this case, if no other,) work his own work, spread abroad his own influence, multiply his own agents indefinitely, if not to infinity, and not be able to restrain in the least.—The doctrine of a supreme duality removed every difficulty; however great the paradox.

Still, this theory had its thousands of adherents : it found its way into the church; gathered disciples there in great numbers ; made havoc of human happiness, as of human character; and involved the early ages of Christianity in darkness and in blood.

Augustine, a man ordained of God to a wide influence in the church of Christ,—during many years of his early responsibility *was a devoted Manichœan.* He believed, and taught, and practiced,—in accordance with the notion, that so far as there was any thing of evil here, it was—in spite of one of the supremes ; and therefore evil *only* because opposed to his particular will or interests or perhaps—caprice. Precisely the ground of a more modern infidelity.

Augustine lived in the unrestrained indulgence of all that a corrupt and depraved heart could desire, for the space of nine or ten years : at the expiration of which time, he professed to have been converted to Christianity.

It forms no part of our present purpose to inquire into the genuineness of his conversion, to discuss the question in any way as to his true submission to Christ, or his lack of it: he soon began to move in a wide sphere of influence, in the church of God, and to fill that sphere with evidences of his presence. With him originated the theory of original sin, as that doctrine is now preached by any school or denomination; and with him originated that exposition of the 7th of Romans, which is based on the hypothesis that the Apostle is describing *the religious exercises and experience of a Christian.* Strange as it may seem, it is nevertheless true, there were none of his predecessors,—none of the so called Fathers of the early church that regarded the Apostle as describing what he himself had experienced *as a Christian ;* nor did Augustine himself so understand it till he had been in the ministry many years, as is evident from several sermons still extant—and forming a part of his works, in which he took precisely the opposite ground ; or in other words,—the ground which had been taken by all the church from the days of Paul down to those of his own age : to wit, that Paul, in Romans vii. 13–25 is speaking of the feelings and views of a legalist.

Nor is this all; "it is no proof," inasmuch as it forms a part of the history of his controversy with Pelagius, that he took *that* ground *then*, only as a dernier, a last defence against the errors of Pelagius : errors—in which this formidable antagonist endeavored to maintain that man is *not* totally depraved.

This fact of itself, we apprehend, should lead us to pause before adopting the Augustinian view of that chapter ; not under the impression that Pelagius was right, or that the Apostle, in fact, said anything on the general subject of men's character by nature there any-way ;—but, to see the necessity of looking carefully at the circumstances in which a man is placed when he quotes a passage of scripture to support his positions,—or perhaps those circumstances in which he *had* been placed, from early life.—We do not know that the facts we have named affect others as they have us : we are not prepared to say, that the absence of all traces of, or allusions to—a doctrine like that of man's identity with Adam, so that *his* acts become ours,—or the total silence of Jesus Christ in respect to the common doctrine of a fall with our first parent, and a sin in him, will have any influence whatever, over the mind of those who receive these doctrines now : we can only say how this fact affects us, and how it always *has* affected us since we came to know it. For our part we think it a most rational hypothesis, that not only Augustine's contro-versy with Pelagius, but all his previous life, especially that part of it which passed while a disciple of the Manichœan school—had a most important bearing upon his religous creed : however absurd many of the notions he once entertained may be now regarded ; yet it is cer-tain—that early impressions will be likely to *tinge*, or if that is not strong enough—*stain* those which have been subsequently adopted even to the end of life. We very much question if any man—educated in infidelity, will—when converted—and truly converted too, have a mind as fully at rest on the great truths of Revelation, as he who has been brought up under the influence of piety. Dark suggestions, if not full grown doubts—like the obscene owl by day—will occasionally fly across the scene—and leave their possessor inquiring with some degree of solicitude as to whether he does in fact believe or not.

But, it is not only true, that our Lord and Saviour Jesus Christ,—neither in his public ministry nor in his more private instructions advanced anything upon the subject,—it is also true, that doctrine is not to be found in the Old Testament. There is the record of man's *apostasy*—carefully laid down ; in connection with which as it would seem to us—should have been, at least, some intimation,—if indeed it was so, that the character of Adam was to be that of his posterity: that they were indebted for their depravity to his first sin, inasmuch as God had been pleased to constitute him the Federal Head and Representative of the entire race: that there was to be an identity so to speak with Adam,—in respect to all his posterity, so that *his* sins would be *our* sins, in the same sense that those of early life, in a child, are truly and properly his, when he arrives at manhood or old age. True, there is one passage, (Gen. v. 3,) which would seem to imply, that the influence of Adam's sin *was* felt, at least, upon his *immediate* posterity : he is said to have " begotten a son in his own image." But if Seth, (who was the son referred to,) was in any respect different from Cain and Abel, in whose image, we would ask were *they* begotten? They were not born till after the fall : the effects of that melancholy event must have been felt in them, quite as much as in Seth : but the record would seem to imply, that *his* moral image was essentially different from theirs. The meaning undoubtedly is, that *the effects* of the Apostacy began to be more strikingly visible.

We are not saying any thing that would imply that his *immediate*, as well as remotest posterity, was not affected by his fall : it *was*, undoubtedly; so is that of every man, " to the third and fourth generation." But the thing that we affirm is, *the cause* of this change,—that which produces the sad and melancholy effect of human depravity, is never spoken of by our Lord Jesus Christ as the sin of Adam. Nor is there an intimation in all that he taught, that God had fore-ordained that we should stand in him and fall in him.

Perhaps we ought to say, before leaving this part of our subject, there *is* a sense in which the doctrines under consideration are undoubtedly true; it is true that all mankind sinned in Adam, and fell in him, by representation, so to speak, and that he is the representative, if not the federal head, of the whole human race, *i. e.* we can *see* ourselves in him.

With a view to explain what we have admitted—let us suppose, (and the supposition is not unworthy of notice,) that Adam's probation was in some important respects of a different nature from our own. *He was placed where he was, for the purpose of demonstrating the intrinsic weakness and impotency of penal considerations to deter men from sin.* It will not be denied that the trial, or experiment, in the case of Adam, was made under the most favorable circumstances ; that if a threatened penalty, in any case, could deter men from sin, it certainly would have done it in the case of Adam. The threatened evil, in case of disobedience, was one of the most fearful; "Dying, thou shalt die." Death was then, as now, " the king of terrors ;" especially, when we remember, that the death threatened, unquestionably involved the idea of an eternal separation from God, " which is the second death."

Let now the supposition be completed, by the requisition, that every intelligent creature of God shall look at Adam, and consider himself standing just where *he*, Adam stood ; surrounded with every thing to help him stand firm and unmoved in virtue, with the fearful threatening of death, in case of disobedience ; and let him see if he cannot perceive in the case of Adam, his *own* fall. It would not require a great stretch of the imagination for each individual of the human species, if at all intelligent, *to see himself there,*—and to come back from the melancholy spectacle with the feeling, that he himself, *sinned* there, and there fell. Let every man suppose that Adam was placed just there, in order that all mankind, *every one*, might see *himself ; see just how it would be with* HIM, *if left with no other support in the way of life and on the road to heaven, than the threatened evil of death or hell in case he should sin.*

When the gospel of Christ was introduced, it became necessary, as a first great lesson, to convince the whole race, ("the Jew first, and also the Greek,") that something more was requisite to sanctify and prepare man for heaven, than even "the law of Moses:" and—by this, I mean, that it required something more than *the influence of* even all his rites and ceremonies,—something more than the regulations of the Jewish service, or even the most faithful performance of those duties which had been enjoined on the nation by what Moses had received and taught. This is the great point which Paul sought first to settle, in his epistle to the Romans, —and also—in that to the Hebrews.

But there was a lesson, a most important one, for all mankind to learn, *previous* to this; which was, that something more than the influence of a threatened penalty was required to deter men from sin. To impress this truth upon the mind of man, to engrave it upon that of a world, was one important object of the arrangement we are contemplating. Accordingly, the first of the human race is placed in a position where the experiment is made, of keeping a soul in due allegiance to God—by the influence of law; or through that of penal enactments. And that every intelligent creature of God might be fully satisfied with the experiment, or rather its result, Adam is placed in circumstances altogether most favorable for a successful issue: the plan, though laughed at by infidels, was—like all the arrangements of God—the most perfect in every respect. No motives were permitted to bear upon our first parents, to urge them to disobedience—but those of simple authority. Had the command been "thou shalt not kill and eat thy first born," nature, itself, the natural affection of the parent would have prompted them to obey; and the question of their obedience to God,—as the supreme and rightful authority would have remained— to say the least—exceedingly doubtful.

It cannot be denied, then, that the principle of representation is fundamental in the true religion; it underlies the entire system: it forms a predominant element in the former, as in the latter dispensation. Consequently, the doctrine of the representative character of Adam, is *a correct* one, but not in the sense commonly understood. *He was not constituted, either by Divine decree, or by his own individual act, a universal factor or agent, to commit sin for his whole posterity.* It is utterly impossible, in the nature of the case, that he should sustain such a fearful relation to those who were not to live till after he was dead ; and not even then for thousands of years. There is one principle alone, upon which one man may commit sin for another,—and that is by delegation of authority by one to the other. " Qui facit per aliem, facit per se ;"—what a man does by another, he does by himself: but to do any thing by another, both the employer and the employee must be alive and doing ; the one appointing, the other performing.

Neither does the theory of imputation throw light upon the case, but rather darkness : it is no less difficult to take one man's character and bestow it upon another, making it truly and properly his, than it is to sin, or work righteousness for another ten thousand years before he exists. In fact this doctrine of imputation is only a modification of the *former* doctrine. It is sustained by essentially the same arguments ;—none of which, in either case, go back to the days of Christ. While we admit, that the doctrine of Adam's fall, and that he was accompanied in his defection by all his posterity, may be fairly traced to the age of Augustine, but not further, we are compelled to maintain, that the idea of imputation goes no further back than the days of Anselm, bishop of Canterbury,—or about 800 years ago!

This fact, we should think, must strike the advocates of this doctrine as being rather singular. That an arrangement, by which all men were made sinners, without even consulting them on the subject, should have been revealed in the Bible, but not discovered till about eight hundred years ago, must we think, strike any one as exceedingly strange. It surely cannot be urged, in the way of explanation or defense, that it was because the dogma was comparatively a *small*, or trifling matter : nor can it be said, that it was on account of the inability of the ancients to understand the word of God. They were unable, of course, to understand, or rather *to find*, in the Bible, what never had been written there : an inability which would have been a blessing to their descendants, some of them, had they possessed it and faithfully used it. Blessed are they who understand *only* what is revealed!

We know not how a man must feel, who, upon becoming well acquainted with the history of the church, its doctrines and practices, is compelled to convict his creed of the sin of pretending to be built on the testimony of God, while in fact, it has for its foundation, only the traditions of men. We have no power in fact, to sympathize with those who have labored all their life to propagate and defend a doctrine, and then have the mortification to learn, that it was not only unknown to the ancients, but absolutely ignored by the Lord Jesus Christ, himself: a doctrine too, which, for astounding importance is not even surpassed by that which teaches us "that Christ must needs suffer and die and be raised from the dead." A man must feel, that he is treading a very slippery path, when he is endeavoring to trace out and defend, yea explain and *apply* a doctrine that professes to have been revealed, yet was not discovered ill within the last hundred years! Pio Nino, must have felt the need of an extra amount of gravity, when he an-

nounced the famous dogma of "the immaculate conception of the mother of Jesus." There must be some, even
among his followers, who will occasionally look out from
under lowering eye-lashes and inquire how these things
can be? How a mystery of that stupendous nature
should have remained undiscovered, lo! these five thous-
and years, to be revealed in these latter days? It would
seem as if every intelligent man on earth, to whom the
fact should be made known, would utterly despise it for
that reason, if no other; yet what is the difference
between the year 1854, and 1,000, in the age of a doctrine? or, rather, wherein is that foundation, which was
discovered some ten centuries this side of the days of Jesus
Christ to be preferred to one that remained unknown
till within the memory of a child?

The reader may be anxious to know if the doctrines
of which we have been speaking *were* really unknown
till so late a period? He may not have had his attention directed to this subject once in all his life; yet, if he
will seriously reflect upon it a moment, he will feel
something more than curiosity prompting him to ask why
this fact has been kept concealed till so late a period in
the history of the world? And if he be a protestant, as
he probably is, he will undoubtedly inquire wherein they
are on a better foundation who believe that all men are
sinners because of *the imputed* guilt of Adam's sin, than
they who believe in the immaculate conception because
the present pope has affirmed it?

But let us address ourselves to the consideration of
this question, "is the doctrine, that we sinned in Adam
and fell in him," found in the Bible? or is it not? And is
its twin brother, though born some eight hundred years
later, that we are all sinners because God *imputes* unto

us the sins of Adam, is this a doctrine of revelation? or
is it not?

Before we proceed to the direct proof, that neither is
found in the Bible, we will quote at some length, the
remarks of the late Professor Stuart on this subject. His
words are : " I would put the question to all who thus
magnify the matter of imputed sin, and ask them in the
most serious, respectful, and fraternal manner, whether
the Bible actually treats this subject as one of such commanding importance ? Excepting the account of the fall
of our primitive ancestors, as recorded in Genesis, *not
one sentence*, or even *word* is to be found respecting this
event itself, or *the imputation* of any one's sin to another,
in all the Old Testament. Once only (Hosea 6, 7,) is the
fact of Adam's sin even adverted to; and there the case
is doubtful, inasmuch as our English version has rendered it. " But they, like men, (כְּאָדָם che-â-dâm,) have
transgressed the covenant. (בְּרִית che-re-im.)" " It
seems more probable to me," adds the Professor, " that
we should here render (כְּאָדָם che-â-dâm) by the words,
like Adam: and as to the *covenant*, (בְּרִית che-re-im,)
it is the usual appellation in the Old Testament, for *commandments*, or *directory precepts*. For example ; this
appellation is often given to the Ten Commandments. Even
in the account which is given of the *fall*, in the book of
Genesis, *not a word is said of the effects it would produce on the posterity of Adam !* How much our primitive parents knew concerning this, it is impossible for us
to say ; inasmuch as we must merely make it out by
conjecture. All that is said in the account of the fall
and the sequel of it, is, that " the seed of the woman
should bruise the serpent's head." Surely this does not

afford ground, on which we can build the dogma, that Adam's sin was imputed to all his posterity.

"Now, what is here said of the Old Testament, on the subject of imputation, is not the result of party spirit; nor is it said with a view to sustain a particular *creed :* it is all of it plain matter of *fact :* it is, therefore, what any man may find, if he will read. Any one who is desirous to see how much, or how little *support* the doctrine of Adam's sin, imputed to his posterity, is found in the Old Testament, can, by searching, find. The appeal is, therefore, to the scriptures: if the advocates of the doctrine are *right*, they can gainsay and overthrow this argument. But we confess we know not how. And if an appeal to the Bible be fatal to their cause, then it is true, we have here a most clear and satisfactory example of the *manner*, in which *God* has treated this subject: and what, kind reader, *is that manner?* Has God *ignored* it? or is the whole record evidently just what it *would* have been, had he known nothing about it? The Old Testament was given to enlighten the ancient church, and guide them till the coming of Him who was "to bear our griefs and carry our sorrows;" and on whom was to be laid, according to the doctrine of imputation, the iniquity of only the elect; yet, not a solitary passage is found which seems to know anything of such an arrangement.

"In the New Testament there are two passages, and only two, which are claimed by the friends of imputation, as bringing to view that doctrine; or as declaring in *any* way, that the consequences of Adam's sin were visited upon his posterity. These are, Romans v. 12, 19; and 1st Cor. xv. 22. In the latter passage it is stated that "all died in Adam;" or in consequence of Adam; or *through* Adam, as a cause. The whole passage reads thus: "As in Adam all die, even so in Christ shall all be made alive." The import of which is: that as Adam caused the death of all mankind, so, in consequence of what Christ has done, all shall be raised from the dead: in John xi. 25, and in several other passages, the Lord Jesus Christ *claims*, that it is through him, that the dead are raised. But as death comes in consequence of sin, and as all have sinned, we are to look for death as resulting to every one who has laid the foundation of it, or introduced its cause independent of anything else as a cause. If the sin, which caused the death of all mankind, was only the sin that was *imputed*; then, the *resurrection*, which all mankind are to experience results from the imputation of Christ's righteousness to them. But *all* are raised from the dead; are all blessed with Christ's imputed righteousness? It is a part, and we believe a very *essential* part of the theory we are examining, that the righteousness of Jesus Christ is imputed only to the elect: do none but the elect rise? And what becomes of the *non*-elect? Are they annihilated? Do they not come with you and me to judgment? A candid answer here will decide much.

"We are therefore compelled to fall back upon the import of this passage which we have already given, viz: That the death of all mankind was the result of Adam's sin; the temporal, *literal* death: and accordingly the resurrection of all from the dead would result from the labors of Jesus Christ. As one, by sin, introduced or occasioned death; so the other by his meritorious righteousness, became the remedy of sin in every form, and in every sense in which a remedy is felt. This construction is apposite, in the place where it is used: the Apostle was proving the resurrection from the dead. This was his aim, when he alluded to the influence or consequences of Adam's sin upon his posterity. And he was under the guidance or direction of the Spirit of Inspiration, when he did it : we cannot, therefore, suppose or admit, that he turns aside from the object he had in view, to sustain, or attempt to sustain a doctrine wholly unconnected with that of the resurrection of all mankind, which was to be brought about by the Lord Jesus Christ.

"In the former passage, (Romans v. 12–19,) it is affirmed, that "death entered the world, and passed upon all men," and that "all were made sinners by the offence of Adam." The import of which is plainly the same with that of the one we have just explained. It simply speaks of the consequences resulting to the human family from the sin of Adam ; and, on the other hand, those which arise from the labors, sufferings and death of Christ to the same class.

"The amount of what we have found on this subject, from searching the scriptures, is, that Paul, when setting forth the glorious effects of Christ's redemption, *twice compares* it to, or with the disastrous effects of Adam's sin, in order, as is evident, *to heighten the picture by contrast.* Here is the great central idea, and object of the comparison.

"I now ask, and I shall insist on a definite answer. I urge the question on all who by their very creed profess to receive the scriptures as the only and sufficient rule of faith and practice, whether a doctrine thus treated, (?) no, thus *ignored,* by inspired men, thus wholly unnoticed by our Lord Jesus Christ, if not unknown to him, a doctrine never produced in the Bible, should be erected into an "articulis stantis vel cadentis ecclesiæ ?" I cannot force my mind to believe that such a view of the subject can be justified either in theory or practice. If it can, then adieu, forever to all efforts in the church of God, to make any distinctions between articuli fundamentales, et non fundamentales."

" It must be ever," adds the Professor, and we think with good reason, " unspeakably more important to know and feel, that we are poor, wretched, ruined, corrupt and utterly depraved sinners ; and our only hope of salvation is, what Christ has done and suffered, and that in him there is abundant ground for hope, unspeakably more important, than it ever can be to know *how* we became sinners, and what influence this or that temptation or allurement has had in corrupting us. The bare statement of the case is a sufficient proof of the allegation."

The reader is by this time prepared for the astounding declaration, that not a single passage in the Old Testament can be found, which either asserts or implies that, one man's sins or his righteousness, is ever placed to the account of another. The term *impute* is used, I am happy to admit, but in every instance as in that where it is *first* used, where good or evil is *imputed*, it is imputed to the individual himself, who has done the thing, on account of which such good or evil is imputed. Thus in Genesis xv. 6, "And he (Abraham,) believed in the Lord ; and the Lord counted it to him for righteousness." The simple act of believing what God had promised him, in respect to the number of his posterity, Jehovah *counted* to, or, which is the same, *imputed* to Abraham as *his* righteousness. The reader will be careful to observe that it was Abraham's own *personal belief*, which was counted to him for righteousness, and not that of another · in other words, it was his own *personal act*

which was placed to his own personal account; and that
is all there is of it. It is just what God does, or is ready
to do, for both the author and his readers, one and all,
when we *believe* in the Lord Jesus Christ he will place
that act to our benefit, and not to another's, nor another's to ours.

Also, Lev. vii. 18. " If the flesh of his peace offering
be eaten at all on the third day, it, (that is, the offering)
shall not be imputed to him ;" to wit, the offerer. The
meaning of it is, it shall not be accepted as his proper
offering, because his conduct was not proper on the
occasion. Lev. xvii. 4, " He who killeth an ox, and
bringeth it not to the door of the tabernacle, blood shall
be imputed to that man." That is, as is plain to any
one, his own misconduct shall be reckoned to him, or
placed to his account in such a light, as that he shall be
regarded or treated as one that has shed blood. 2d Sam.
xix. 19, " Let not my Lord *impute* iniquity to me."
Here is not a prayer, that his iniquity should be imputed
to any other one. Psalm xxxii. 2, " Blessed is the man
to whom the Lord imputeth not iniquity ;" i. e. to whose
account the Lord does not reckon iniquity, in such a
sense as to proceed to its punishment, but *pardons it.*
Psalm cvi. 31, " Then stood up Phineas, and executed
judgment, and that was counted unto him for righteousness unto all generations ;" that is, as before, what
Phineas himself *did*, was placed to his account as righteousness, and to no one's else. Just as in the case of
Abraham's *belief*, because he " executed judgment," he
was counted a righteous man. Abraham *believed*, and
Abraham, not Isaac nor Jacob, was counted righteous
on that account. Among all the cases which can be
found in the Old Testament, *there is not one* where the

imputation of sin or righteousness is in the sense of a transfer of character, or placing that to the account of another which properly belonged to him who had done the deed on account of which was the act of imputation. Therefore, it is, that we reaffirm our former position; the Old Testament Scriptures speak directly of one's own sin, or righteousness being imputed to himself; but never, in a single instance of its being imputed to another.

Now we are sorry for a theory that falls to pieces as easily as this does: and we are sorry for the men that have built on it; but as we shall not be likely to have any great amount of righteousness "*imputed*" to us, by the friends of this theory, on account of our sorrow for either it or them, we shall not indulge in this kind of remark any further at the present. It would seem difficult of belief, however, that a dogma as extensively received as is that we are examining, when compelled to fall back for its support on the scriptures, should be found without even the shadow of a foundation: but such is the fact. The Testaments, both old and new, may be searched "as with the candle of the Lord," and the doctrine will not be found there; there is no form of expression that *implies* it: there is not a passage, which, if it were thought to contain such a sentiment, would not undergo a review that would certainly result in its rejection as of human, instead of Divine authority.

Were we not conscious that we are dealing with men and with theories, that are not much frightened at *absurdities*, or even impossibilities, we would say something in reference to the utter impossibility of the thing, which is here claimed, to wit: the taking of one man's character and transferring it to another! The very *thought* is absurd.   But men, who have that kind of courage which enables them to march right up to *any* absurdity, without flinching, will not, of course, flinch at the idea of building their favorite theory upon an absurdity or even an impossibility, if need be: we plead guilty, however, to the simplicity of having thought it *possible*, that even these men, when they come to search the scriptures, and find that not a single passage can be even tortured into the service of saying or implying, that God had taken the sin of Adam and imputed it to all his posterity, in such a sense, that nations yet unborn are sinners, and worthy of an eternal hell, would fall back for a moment and consider.   For, it does not seem to affect the question of man's sinfulness anyway, materially, *whether he was ever born or not!*   This terrible process of dooming a man to hell, by taking his neighbor's? no, his *ancestor's* sins, even the sins of those who have been dead a hundred generations, and placing them to his account so as to make them truly and properly his, needs not to wait for a man to be born; he can be just as easily damned before he sins, as sin before he is born.   This whole matter of convicting a man of sin, and of dooming him therefor to endless punishment, on the theory of imputation, may all be gone through with, or (to speak more in accordance with the principles of that theory,) *might* have been transacted the day after Adam fell, as well as to wait till the judgment!

But, as we have already expressed it, we have no very flattering prospect of success in this direction: the absurdity or utter impossibility of a thing, is no great embarrasment to councils such as that of Constance or the synod of Dort.   Nor are they much in the way of men, who like Augustine or Anselm, are bound to complete *a the-*

ory, when once it has been commenced, cost what it may. The fact, that the Bible knows nothing of it, and that the Lord Jesus Christ never saw fit to mention it, is a secondary consideration, altogether, with them.

But, it will be asked, are we to believe, that "The Assembly of Divines," at Westminster, who have given us the Assembly's Catechism; which catechism they have put forth as a system of doctrines, *taught in the Holy Scriptures*, have advanced the doctrine under consideration, without a single passage, either in the Old or New Testament for its support? Are we to understand the writer as affirming that these men have sent forth what they would have us receive as an epitome of all that God has revealed for the conversion of men, or the sanctification of those who are converted, and yet, after professing to sustain all their doctrines by the word of God, have advanced here the astounding assertion, that "they," (meaning Adam and Eve) "being the root of all mankind, the guilt of this, their first sin was imputed to all their posterity, and the same death in sin and corrupted nature conveyed to all, descending to them by ordinary generation," without scripture, either in the Old or New Testament for their support?

Our answer will consist in a reference to, or rather, a quotation of the passages at full length—on which, it seems—the said doctrine is supposed to be based. Acts xvii. 26. " And hath made of one blood, all nations of men, for to dwell on the face of the earth, and hath determined the times before appointed, and the bounds of their habitation." Gen. ii. 16, 17, " And the Lord God commanded the man, saying,—of every tree of the garden thou mayest freely eat : but of the tree of knowledge of good and evil, thou shalt not eat of it ; for in the day that thou eatest thereof, thou shalt surely die," or,—as it is in the margin, which is supposed to be more in accordance with the original, "*Dying*, thou shalt die." Romans v. 12, 15, 16, 17, 18, 19, and 1st Cor. xv. 21, 22, 45, 49, "For since by man *came* death, by man came also the resurrection from the dead." That is, *in consequence*, or *as* a consequence of Adam's sin, all die, (temporal death, of course, is meant, or the doctrine of universal salvation follows) "so—as a consequence of the labors, sufferings and death of Jesus Christ, all are raised from the dead. "For as in, (through, by reason of,) Adam all die, even so in Christ shall all be made alive." And, as it is written, "the first man, Adam was made a living soul; the last Adam, a quickening spirit. And as we have borne the image of the earthy, we shall also bear the image of the heavenly."

In respect to these passages, it will be sufficient to say, that from Acts has not the slightest reference to either the sin of Adam; or its extent; or its consequences. Nothing more is asserted than the original identity, or unity of the race: and that this race was created for the purpose of replenishing the earth with inhabitants. In addition to which is the doctrine that God's determinations in respect to man extend to their lives as well as "the bounds of their habitations;" whatever that may mean. In that which is found in Romans; the Apostle is comparing the consequences of, or the effects of Adam's sin upon his posterity, to the effects of Christ's labors, sufferings, or death upon all mankind. If now we understand the Apostle as saying, that by *imputation*, or in any other way, even if such a thing were possible, the sin of Adam was so placed to the account of all mankind as to result in the death of all;

in other words—men *die* because the sin of Adam is *imputed* to them: then, it follows, that they who are *raised*—are raised in consequence of the fact, that Christ's righteousness is imputed to them: in other words, *all* will be raised from the dead, because the righteousness of Jesus Christ is imputed to all! Are the friends of this doctrine prepared to subscribe to this? "I trow not:" it is with them a standing dogma, that the righteousness of Jesus Christ is imputed to none but the elect, See chap. xi. sec. 1st, Confession of Faith. As to the other passage, (1st Cor. xv. etc. etc.) The Apostle, as we have said in a former part of the argument, is endeavoring to prove the resurrection of the dead. There is not, in all that he has said, the most distant allusion to such an idea, as that for which the passage is cited. The doctrine is advanced that as death came in consequence of Adam, so the resurrection from the dead—was the result, or was to come in consequence of what Christ had done.

We have no fears that any but the believer in universal salvation will understand the term *death* as embracing the idea of spiritual death ; a *state* of death in sin: and even *he* must ignore the fact—that in both passages, especially that of Cor, the Apostle is speaking only of the resurrection. We are compelled to admit that the doctrine of the final, eternal, and complete recovery of our race from the evils of sin—does not *do* as great violence to these passages as that for which they are quoted in our confession of faith. But as no reasonable man will attempt to establish this doctrine, by citing these passages especially, we may safely dismiss the subject here.

The sum of what we have said is plainly this: there

is not the shadow of a foundation in any part of the Bible in any passage, either by direct assertion or by implication, for the dogma of imputation: we are satisfied, that had they, with whom this doctrine originated, lived a few hundred years later in the history of the church or the age of the world—that doctrine would never have been thought of. We are evidently indebted for it to the "thick darkness that covered the people," during the dark ages, and that was not removed by the morning of the reformation. They who are satisfied with the dogmas of men, (uninspired, of course,) may be satisfied with the common notions on this point: but, for our part, possessing as we do,—that "more sure word," we prefer for ourselves to draw from "the wells of salvation,"—and have that for our foundation which is furnished by the Bible.

Do we indeed judge harshly when we thus speak? What milder terms than those we have used can be found? The facts in the case are plainly as we have said. Neither the Old nor the New Testament, *the Bible* in no part, appears to know anything of this plan for making men sinners, or for making them righteous, any more than it does of the arrangements of Romanism for man's salvation, those which provide a Purgatory, where the sinner, dying impenitent is furnished with a *red hot gospel*, for his special benefit. And what is more, the Lord Jesus Christ, in no part of his instructions, either by direct precept, or by implication, advanced any such sentiment. He taught the native and universal depravity of man, the necessity of his being born again, and of the agency of the Spirit of God in the work of conversion. He taught the necessity of repentance towards God, and faith towards *him*, as our Lord and Savior; he left the world in no doubt as to his relations to God the Father. His instructions as to man's ability, are plain enough, we think, to need no explanation, or argument. The doctrine of election, at least that view of it which throws the blame of non-election *upon* the non-elect themselves, is fully brought out in his instructions.

Indeed, we cannot go farther in this direction; no reasonable man will suppose that, in order to show that Christ did *not* teach the doctrine under consideration, we are going to copy or quote all he did teach : we are willing to risk all that may be involved in the assertion that there is not an allusion, in any of his instructions, to the doctrine in debate. If any man will point us, or any of our neighbors, to a passage, either in the Old Testament or the New, in the gospels or the epistles, where the idea is fairly advanced, that men become sinners in any other way than by personally sinning, and that too, *after* being fairly born into the world, we lose the argument.

Nor is the declaration in Romans v. 19, to be construed in opposition to this last remark. "For as by one man's disobedience many were made sinners," can never be understood by any one with fairness as meaning only, that they were so *putatively*, or hypothetically; there is not a passage in any part of this epistle where men are spoken of as sinners in any other sense than that of *personal* sinfulness. The fact, that it was "by one man's disobedience many were made sinners," stands before us as a FACT, a matter of revelation that cannot be disputed and will not be by any one that has a proper regard for the truth, yet in what way, or in what sense is *not* revealed. Nevertheless, be the way what it will, *the result is, that men are sinners, fully and truly sinners, just as any one is, who sins, and for the same reason, viz : they have personally sinned, every one.*

If now you assume the horn of modern orthodoxy, and with a view to avoid difficulty, say that men were made sinners by an omnipotent decree of Heaven, and that the fact that God had so decreed, was sufficient to satisfy any one that it was right, right in God to do so, and that sin was sin, nevertheless, and man was the only sinner in the firm, we have only to say the thing is not only impossible, but absurd, not only impossible and absurd, but it is what never was revealed, and that it never was revealed because it was never true.   In addition to all this, the solemn, the unbroken silence of our Lord Jesus Christ, is not only accounted for, by the hypothesis that no such thing was ever known, either in heaven or on earth, but it is abundantly evident, if it were so, there *would* be unrighteousness with God.

We say again it must not be forgotten, the sinner of Romans v., *was a veritable sinner.*   If the offense of Adam had any effect upon him, in this direction, it was to *make* him an ungodly man ; he became something more than a hypothetical transgressor.   It will do to talk of " hypothetical baptism," and possibly of " hypothetical conversion," if conversion means only " a change of mind," but a " hypothetical sinner," or a " hypothetical christian," are rather supposititious things.   It is far safer to suppose, that the expression, " by the offence of one many were made sinners," refers to a fact as a result, rather than the existence of a cause.   It may have been the design of Inspiration to express this idea, " the offense of Adam placed his posterity in circumstances, where it was certain that they would be sinners as soon as they became responsible beings."   Man is said to have made his family most wretched and vile, when, by his own disgraceful and villainous course he has only placed them in circumstances where they will act, each for himself *freely* in the way their father has acted.

God is said to have hardened the heart of Pharaoh, and then, again, Pharaoh is said to have hardened his *own* heart. Now, it is not likely there were separate agencies here meant, or separate *causes;* no one supposes that in one case, *God* was the efficient cause of the hardness of Pharaoh's heart, and in the other, that Pharaoh, himself was. This passage, together with one or two more in the scriptures, on this subject, may be fairly explained without supposing that God had any other agency in bringing about such a result, than that he was the author of that system which might lead to such a result, and which, in fact, in accordance with the laws of free agency, and only because man is free, *has* led to such a result. In this case it is proper to say, as it is said, "God hardened the heart of Pharaoh," simply because he suffered him to do just as he *chose* to; in the same way, it is proper to say, Pharaoh hardened his own heart, because he acted freely and of choice, notwithstanding the Divine mandate.

When an event takes place, which is properly and legitimately *the result* of a system or plan, whether that result was the intended one or not, it is proper to speak of it as having originated with him who originated the plan or system, even though the result be one against which the author of such plan endeavored to guard his system to the utmost. In this way, and by this principle alone, can Romans ix. 18 be explained, so as to remove from the Divine government, even the appearance of having caused the sinfulness of man. "Therefore hath he mercy on whom he will, and whom he will he hardeneth." That is, he originated that system, which we call a moral system, because it embraces *moral beings* and all their actions: though many of these actions were not what he desired. But moral beings must be *free*, free to choose life or death: God can use a certain degree of influence to persuade one and all—to become the subjects of his grace, yet he is under no obligation to in either case: now it is easy to see that if in the one case he uses that influence so as to cause it to result in the salvation of him who is the subject of it, and in the other *withholds* the necessary influence to produce such a result, it is perfectly proper to say as is said: "He hath mercy on whom he will, and whom he will he hardeneth. That system which *results* in the sinner's harding his own heart originated with God.

But there is one passage further to which we must refer before we leave this subject. Romans v. 13, ἁμαρτία δὲ οὐκ ἐλλογεῖται μὴ ὄντος νόμου, is translated by some as in our common version, "sin is not imputed where there is no law." But Calvin, who seems to have seen nothing of this theory of imputation in this passage if any where else, but to have aimed more at finding the true import of the passage itself, feels compelled to translate it, "sin is not made account of where there is no law:" that is, "where there is no positive law there is but little thought of sin ; *any* sin, however great." Where men have no Bible there is not much account made of sin. It will not be denied that this is the fact everywhere : men who have not been favored with revelation, or having it, have not obeyed it, are habitually inclined to make light of sin. "Fools," as the scriptures have it, (not idiots but open despisers of the word,) " fools make a mock at sin ;" regard it as a trifle or something unworthy of notice.

But suppose it shall be insisted, that its true rendering is as in the textus receptus, the received version before us ; what disposal do the friends of imputation make of it? what *can* they? The turn they give to it is this : " If men's own sins are not imputed to them, and yet they actually came under the sentence of death, then it must follow that the sin of Adam is imputed to them, and that for this reason, or on this account, they are condemned." But where, we may ask, where are we to look for men that have no sins of their own ? insomuch, that in order to make them worthy of death, God must needs take the sins of their ancestors and place them to their account? The Apostle avers that sin was in the world before the law, (v. 14,) in other words, that it was not necessary for a man to have the written law, in order to be placed in circumstances where he could become a sinner; a personal veritable sinner. If anything is to be learned from the Epistle to the Romans, it is, that all men are sinners ; not putatively, hypothetically or by mere supposition ; but in truth and in fact.—Now where *are* those men, where *were* they whose own sins were not, and who, for that reason, as we are to infer, were never to die, and therefore, must be *made* sinners by an omnipotent—arbitrary decree of God, so that there could be some show of justice in killing them ? What a theory ! Men by this supposition were not personal sinners, even in the days of the flood ! The old world was drowned, not because of its own sins, but by reason of the sins of Adam ! and *these* had been imputed to it that God might seem just in destroying it.

Verily, we need not be surprised that such a doctrine

as this was not found in the instructions of Jesus Christ; nor in any part of the Bible: every step we have taken in this investigation has served to confirm and establish us in the belief, that there is not a passage in the Bible where it is either declared or implied, that the sin or righteousness of one man was ever imputed to another. Abraham believed, and his faith was imputed to *him*, not to Isaac or Ishmael, for righteousness. So it is in the reader's own case, if he is a believer, *his* belief is accepted as a personal righteousness; in other words, if he has faith in Christ—he is treated—by reason of what Christ has done for him and for all mankind just as *if* he were righteous. This is the whole theory of justification by faith; and this is intelligible.

No intelligent man reads the fifth chapter of Romans and *understands* what he reads, without perceiving, that the Apostle is there comparing *the influence*, or the effects of Adam's sin upon his posterity, to, or with—the influence of Christ's life and death upon the whole human race; showing an analogy in several important respects, and carefully pointing out several in which that analogy fails. One of these is, that in both .cases this influence was without a personal act on the part of man in that direction. That is, as *in consequence of Adam's sin* all die spiritually as well as literally, *so in consequence of what Christ has done all are placed in a salvable state*, as it is said: are thus recovered from a spiritual death as they will in the end be literally raised from the dead. And, to a certain extent, or in a certain sense, both these effects are independent of the belief or disbelief of man.

But the intelligent reader will not fail to perceive that in both cases these effects were *real:* they were something more, as we have several times said, than supposititious, putative, imaginary. The life, labors and death of the Lord Jesus Christ, did not so affect the condition of man as to restore to him that *holiness* which his father, Adam had lost; but simply placed him on another and a more favorable platform of trial: it gave him the benefit of a new arrangement; one based on the stipulated condition of faith in Christ: a protracted day of trial.

One point, (and we mention only one,) where this parallelism fails; a point referred to in the expression, " but not as the offence, so also the free gift;"—*the evils*—evil effects, or consequences of Adam's sin, come drifting over all his posterity, without a personal act on their part as the procuring cause; while in respect to the benefits resulting from that which Christ had done, reached no man to the extent of removing the evils of the first transgression, except as a consequence of his obedience unto the faith. In order to make what Christ has done effectual, or perhaps available to his salvation, man must believe, obey, and repent: in other words, must comply with the terms of life; but *nothing* was required of him, to secure his full share in the evils arising from the first transgression: as soon as he began to exist he began to *feel* the bitter consequences of what had been done by another.

This is evidently all the imputation that *Paul* knew, and all that we should be able to find were we satisfied to let scripture speak for itself and theory take care of its own affairs.

We will say further, while on this point, the advocates of universalism are heartily welcome to all they can find in the way of support to their doctrine, in the passage under review, or in that kind of imputation we have here admitted : but, as to that view of that doctrine which we reject, we not only deny that it can be found here, but we affirm most confidently, that if it could, either here or any where else in the scriptures, the doctrine of the infallible salvation of all the race would be found there too and in the same passages. For if *sin* is imputed to all mankind, irrespective of their acts, *holiness* (by the condition of the parallelism) must be imputed to the same extent. There is a sense in which it is true, *the benefits* of what Christ has done flow to all the race of man; but that sense we have several times given, as simply making the salvation of all mankind *possible*, possible on certain stipulated and oft repeated conditions: whereas, in respect to "the curse," there were *no* conditions whatever. And this is difference enough.

"But," says the advocate of the dogma we are opposing, "I *mean* by imputation that God has so transferred the character of Adam, his *guilt*, if you please, to his posterity as to make it certain, that each individual of the entire species, as soon as he exists or acts upon his own responsibility, *will himself sin*, and that most certainly or irresistibly." But this is just no imputation at all; it is simply *an omnipotent decree*, that every man shall be a sinner, whether he will or not; it is simply saying, on the part of God, "I am determined that the great majority of men shall be sent to hell; and since I would do it with some show of justice on my side, I will arrange the affairs of my government so that every man shall infallibly and irresistibly sin not only as soon as he is capable of sinning, but before, so that after all, those who perish shall perish for their own sin. To the rest I will impute *a good* which they never did, but yet, on account of which, or because they possess it, I will save them."

It is with great reluctance, we allow ourselves to speak of such a theory as this; it borders so hard on blasphemy. We fear " it is that sin which hath no forgiveness; neither in this world nor in that which is to come."

What should we say of a man, *a father*, who should be desirous to see all but one or two of his sons inmates of a state prison for life; and, for the purpose of bringing that about, should arrange that as soon as one was capable of committing the necessary sin, he should be where he could do it—yes, in circumstances where *he could not choose but to do it ?*

But, if by this type of imputation is meant only, that God has ordained that every one of his responsible creatures shall be placed in circumstances where he shall be permitted to do just as he pleases, even when it is well known to him, that every man will do wrong, with a previous purpose on his part to appoint to eternal life all that can consistently be brought to obey the Lord Jesus Christ, why, then we say as before, there is nothing of imputation here; *it is truth ;* it is right.

If, finally, it is meant that God has ordained that every one of his responsible creatures shall be free, free to choose life or refuse it, and at the same time has appointed such a connection between cause and effect as to make the sin of one man the *cause* of the sins of another ; if God has ordained as a law of moral beings, that he who does evil will most certainly cause *others* to do evil, and that the *strength* or *power* of this cause shall depend on *the relation* which the one sustains to the other, why then, as before, we say, there is nothing here of imputation ; it is what he does every day we live, and in respect to every *man* that lives, without an attempt at the transferring of character.

Every man throughout the sphere of his influence, and to the full extent of it, if that influence is evil, helps to involve his fellow men in evil. Just so far as his life affects the destiny of others, it is in the direction of death. This is true, especially of parents, in reference to their children. Who feels that any injustice, any wrong is done to a family that is involved in evil, in consequence of the wickedness of the parent? Who does not *know* that they who are born of vile and profligate parentage are most sure to be themselves most vile on this account? That while no man however pious, can hope to see a sinless offspring, as coming from himself, they who are nearest in character to our Lord Jesus Christ, and they alone, have the promise of children proportionally nearer the kingdom of Heaven? Who has not observed a thousand times, that bad example, whether in a parent or in another, has that mysterious power of making it certain in proportion to its strength, that they shall be evil who feel that influence? And who is he that thinks to arraign the justice of God on that account? It is only the same law which makes it the more certain that they who feel the influence of a pious example, will be more likely themselves to be pious. This is in fact a law of all moral beings ; who shall find fault with it? " Thou wilt say then, why doth he yet find fault, for who hath resisted his will? Nay, but who art thou, O, man, that repliest against God ?" They who will complain of the arrangement we are contemplating, will complain of the fact that God has linked our destiny, one with another; but what would be the condition of the race could not the wise and prudent, especially the parent, hope to use an influence that would render it morally certain, that they who should *feel* that influence would be, by far most likely to be themselves wise and good? The *more* certain the better, in the direction of good, why not in the direction of evil? · It will thus serve the more soundly, and the more solemnly to caution man to beware of the influence he shall exert; would not that be well? In fact it is but one and the same law; that which makes it certain that holiness or piety in one, shall be likely to be followed with piety in others, is the same arrangement with that which makes it certain that *im*piety will be followed by the same, impiety.

Nor am I speaking of the influence of *example*, merely, example is only one development of this law. There is a fearful certainty, that he who does evil *once*, will do it again, and that *if* he do it a second time, he will most certainly go on in that direction. We cannot of course talk of a man's being influenced by his *own* example. We refer to a law, an unwritten law, an arrangement on the part of God, which makes it certain, that he who *begins* wrong will, if left to himself, end wrong. We speak of a certainty, that if a man in early life, commits a sin, its effects will follow him in an evil direction till a remedy is introduced by the special grace of God, and that in proportion to the magnitude of that offence will be the certainty that evil will follow.

The same is true of this law, with respect to that which is good; there is a joyous certainty, that he who begins right will end well; a mysterious arrangement by which it is most certain, that he who does right even *once*, will do right again, and that since "a three-fold cord is not easily broken," he who has done right habitually and publicly will be most certain to see, that a mysterious but strong cord is drawing others into the habit of doing good too.

I must again assure the reader I am speaking of something beyond example; it seems to underlie almost everything else in *a moral system.* It is a law which needs no explanation, and no defense ; we all understand that if *a judge,* for instance, in a single case takes a bribe, its effects will follow him all the days of his life. He will never be able to feel towards himself, as he did before he took it ; he will never respect himself after wards as he did before; nor will anybody else respect him or think of him as before. He may do what he can to repair the evil ; he may do all the law requires of him, in the way of reparation, it will make but little difference, the evil which he has done is in its nature and in a very important sense, irreparable. ·

So with a man in any sphere, or at any period of life ; whatever he does is stamped with an immutability, an eternity. He may outlive his name and place, but he cannot outlive his actions. He may *forget,* as it is said, (though we cannot, strictly speaking, forget anything we have once known,) man may forget his name and that of his dearest friends, one and all, *yet he cannot forget his sins ;* nor can he, if Christ has ever been revealed to him as the heaven-appointed, heaven-annointed expiation of his sins, ever forget Christ. He may experience that, through faith in Jesus Christ, which will assure him that his sins will never be remembered in condemnation against him : that is all, that is enough, this side of the day of final and eternal adjudication.

I wish the reader to direct his attention once more to the consideration of that which I have several times called a law, which underlies motive, influence, example, threat or penalty, and which makes it certain that he who has done either right or wrong, *even once*, will feel the influence, or *the effects* of what he has done on himself, and most certainly see them on others; that the influence or power of this law will ever be in proportion to the comparative magnitude of the act, and this will often be determined by the *position* of him who performed it. He who is highest in authority can do that which will most deeply affect the interests of those over whom he bears rule. If he does a *benevolent* act, one which at once commands the admiration, the hearty approval of every intelligent being, its power to influence others in a similar way is in proportion to the dignity, the exalted character and position of the being that has done it.

The reader can now see the absurdity of that doctrine which is beginning to obtain some favor, especially in New England, which teaches that the Atonement consisted in *the example* of our Lord Jesus Christ. But as this is incidental to the present discussion, I pass it, with a single remark. Beyond all reasonable doubt the Atonement derives its value, as an arrangement for the forgiveness of sins, *from the dignity and elevated position or character of our Lord Jesus Christ*. If so, it is easy to see the application of the principle of which we have just spoken.

The supposition then, is not an improbable one, that this law of which we have spoken, is at the bottom of that arrangement which connects the sins of Adam's posterity in some way or other with his own. Not by the absurd plan of imputation, but by an arrangement which makes subsequent results to depend for their character upon a first or fundamental principle, and that a law which makes them the results of free and deliberate agency in the subordinate or dependent.

The reason, then, why Christ, in the course of his instructions, said nothing of imputation, would seem to be obvious; *there is no such thing; there never was.* The Bible being the source of all information in respect to theology we must give it up. There is *the word* there we admit, in the translation; but in every instance where it is used, the context and the circumstances, expressly show, that it implies only a bestowment of something upon a man, in consequence, or as a reward for acts or services that he himself had done. Not a single case is there from the beginning to the end of the sacred volume where it is said or even implied, that either good or evil is bestowed upon a man, which good or evil belonged of right to some body else. Those cases in which the believer is said to receive the benefits of Christ's labors are numerous and explicit; but they in no wise imply that his *righteousness* is, or becomes the believer's : for if it does, then it will inevitably follow, that the believer is *as* righteous as Christ was : an assumption which some do make, we admit; but who are they? To an intelligent, well-balanced mind, a man who knows himself and is not altogether ignorant of others, the bare announcement of such a thought is shocking in the extreme.

There are undoubtedly many, who, in their devotions make frequent and earnest use of *the name* of Christ; repeating the assurance over and again, that they have asked all in his name; but who, if asked at the close to say what they *meant* by such an expression would find themselves in difficulty. Thousands who seem to think they have done so beyond the possibility of mistake, because they have used that formula. They forget that "all are not Israel that are of Israel;" all do not *pray*, who use the words of prayer; all do not *believe* who affirm in the most solemn manner, " we believe in God the Father;" etc.

The question then returns; what is it to ask "in the name of Christ?" What does an intelligent Christian mean by such an expression: " we want to know," says the reader, " whether we have ever asked aright or not." Our first answer, and our last, (as we might almost say,) is *we must be in Christ*, in order to be able to ask in him: that is, we must sustain the relation of children to God, by reason of our faith in his son, Jesus Christ. We must ever have a clear and vivid impression, or knowledge I might say, of the love which God the Father cherishes towards his son. Then when we approach him in prayer, using the formula under consideration, when we say as Christ has taught us, " all we ask is in the name of Jesus Christ, thy son," *we ask it on account of the relation we sustain to God in Christ his Son.* We ask not the slightest favor on account of ourselves, or by reason of what we have done; but on account of a new and gracious relation that we sustain to God, through faith in his Son.

The case is similar to this: we are summoned to the door to see an individual who has asked an interview with us; he is clothed in the vestments of a beggar: he describes his needy condition in as few words as possible, then proceeds to ask of us favors of no very ordinary value. We at once make up our mind to refuse him, and begin to shape our conversation in that way, when he adds as a last consideration, " I am the son of your friend, A. B., whom you love with more than a brother's affection, who said to me on leaving home, if I came to want, I should only need to mention *his name* to you, and *prove my relation to him*, and whatsoever I needed would be granted." My door is of course thrown open, my stores and treasures are at his disposal, so far as his wants are ascertained in proportion to my love for him *in whose name* he comes, is my desire to meet and remove his wants.

Let not the reader forget; the point for the applicant first of all—to establish, is—his *relation* to the individual in whose name he asks: everything depends on this. Its application is obvious :—we must be "heirs of God, and *joint* heirs with his Son, Jesus Christ," before we can plead the promise referred to. This settled, and we may ask what we will, *in the name of Christ*, (that is, in accordance with the arrangement of which Christ is the foundation,) and it will be done for us. All the principles involved in this arrangement, *all the conditions*, upon which the promised answer depends, must be complied with: then we may ask and we shall surely receive.

Before we close we must be permitted to address a word of expostulation, or advice—if you prefer that term, to the friends of that theory which we have attacked: what is gained, what advantage to the cause of truth can possibly arise from the use of such a dogma as this? How does it in any way, or to any extent—contribute to the Christian's growth in grace or add to his confidence in God—for him to struggle thus with conscience and with common sense, and last of all—with the plain and obvious interpretation of scripture, with a view to compel himself to say—he believes such a doctrine as this? He meets at the outset the astounding difficulty, that the thing is impossible; at the next step he sees its absurdity: but when these Alpine difficulties are both surmounted, " there come two woes hereafter;" the *cruelty*, the injustice of the thing, and the final, eternal condemnation to which it leads and in which it ends.

The child that comes into existence, loaded with *the constitutional infirmities—or diseases—*of its parent, even when these refer only to evils in his physical system, *proclivities* to disease, regards himself as most deeply afflicted; and that he is: but what is his calamity compared with that of every man, on the supposition that he comes into existence with a soul, *saturated*, so to speak: with *inherent* sin—as a *punishment* for *imputed* or *supposititious* sin? This is the distinguishing, or essential feature of the system of imputation: man is born with a great core of moral bitterness in the very center of his moral being which becomes the *"causa causans"* that is—the substantial and fundamental grounds of every subsequent act and making every act sinful!

For my own part, I find no difficulty in accounting for the fact, a fact which I have so often mentioned with pleasure, that our Lord Jesus Christ never once hinted such a dogma as this. And when I subject the writings of the Apostle Paul to a faithful and careful investigation, I find no such doctrine there. Nor is there in any part of the Bible, the shadow of such a thought. Yet we have men in great numbers, in every part of the only evangelical church on earth, who appear to feel, that this doctrine, as we have above defined it, is the great central principle in the gospel. They do not seem to think, that they have preached a gospel sermon, unless they have fairly stated, and fully sustained the idea, or position, that Adam's sin is imputed to all his posterity, becoming *the causa causans* of *original*, inherent sin, and of all actual sins that follow!

It will possibly avail little if anything towards persuading them to review their decisions on this subject, to remind them of this *to us* important fact they will affirm, that *many* things are taught us by the Apostles which are not found in the instructions of the Savior; and that these instructions are just as authoritative as if they had been specifically announced by our Lord Jesus Christ.

We deny utterly and most explicitly, that any doctrine is advanced by the Apostles, which cannot be found, either by fair inference, or implication, or direct statement, in the instructions of Christ : either the very thing, in terms most explicit and unequivocal, *or its germ* is found in the doctrines or inculcations of Jesus Christ. Else, why should Paul take such unwearied pains to sustain his positions, those that *seemed* to be at variance with, or more correctly *beyond* the explicit instructions of Christ, by referring to the fact, that " thus spake the Lord ?"   In every case (a single one excepted, 1st Cor. vii. 6—et 12,) he falls back on the assurance that he has the mind of Christ : and at *the close* of the instructions referred to, he expresses it as the conviction of his own mind, that he is sustained in what he has said by the concurrent testimony of the spirit of God. v. 40.

One thought further, and I have done : if the doctrine in question be in truth and verity a part of the system of doctrines which are furnished us in the scriptures, if the sins of Adam are imputed to all his posterity, and the sins of all believers to the Lord Jesus Christ, it will then follow, that Adam was the smallest (in the sense of least guilty) sinner, that ever lived, and Jesus Christ, (I tremble to write it,) was the greatest! We once heard that sentiment sung in a professed hymn of praise to God! but it was by a man who was known to be deranged. But look at the premises from which it is deduced. "Christ bears our sins in his own body on the tree:" "that is"—says the imputationist, "our sins were all imputed to him; became *his*." *Therefore* (let some other hand write the conclusion, not mine.) Adam had only his personal, *actual* sin, none by imputation; therefore he had less than the *least* of his posterity! Yea: there is one inference further, and undeniable, however severe: if there is no sin but that which accords with the theory of imputation, (an act which is itself sinful *originating* in a sinful state of the heart,) then Adam was just no sinner at all! "Let him that readeth understand." Adam the only *sinless* being that ever lived; and yet the *originator* of all the evils that ever were introduced by sin! These are the legitimate, the undeniable results of the theory of imputation.

Can a system which involves such consequences as these be a part, even *any* part of the system of divine truth, revealed and published for the salvation of man? Can I close my eyes to those undeniable results, and for the sake of theory, or with a view to sustain a so called system of theology, say, "*I believe?*" Never; no; *never.* I must be unmade, as to my moral constitution, made over and made up after a pattern not showed to Moses in the Mount, nor to me in the valley, before I can subscribe to anything of the kind. The laws of my being require it: the laws of God demand it. These I must and will obey; so help me, my God and Saviour! whatever becomes of theories or creeds.

CHAPTER VII.

ON THE STANDING STILL OF THE SUN AND MOON,

AS RECORDED IN JOSH. X. 12, 15

PART I.

In the Biblical Repository for October 1833, an article will be found " on the standing still of the sun and moon, at the command of Joshua," supposed by the editor to have come from the pen of Prof. Hengstenberg of Berlin ; which takes the ground, that the above passage is only a quotation from a book, or a volume of poems, therein cited ; and that consquently, the so-called miracle of arresting the sun and moon never took place. The author, whoever he may have been, expresses the wish, at the close of his essay, that what he had done might lead others to a deeper investigation of the subject ; and, if his views were wrong, correct them ; if right, confirm and develop them. Whether the following article shall do either of these, is left for others to determine. No one we think can read that article, which, in a certain sense originated this, without feeling that it is too short, and that it leaves in an unfinished state a subject of vast importance, the investigation of which had been happily commenced. This was the feeling of our mind when we read it ten years ago, and it has remained unchanged in this respect ever since.

The ground which we have taken, and that which we shall endeavor to sustain, is, that Joshua x. 12–15, is an extract, or quotation, from a work to which it refers; and that, consequently, it forms no part whatever of the Sacred Record. The main point in which we shall differ from the writer referred to above, will be, in supposing that the passage under consideration found its way into the text, at a period much later than that which is fixed upon by the learned Professor, in the context. This, of course, denies that any miracle like that of stopping the sun and moon, as represented in the extract, ever occurred.

The passage reads as follows: " Then spake Joshua to the Lord, in the day when the Lord delivered up the Amorites before the children of Israel, and he said in the sight of Israel, Sun, stand thou still upon Gïbeon, and thou, Moon, in the valley of Ajalon. And the sun stood still, and the moon stayed, until the people had avenged themselves upon their enemies. Is not this written in the book of Jasher? So the sun stood still in the midst of heaven, and hasted not to go down a whole day. And there was no day like that before it or after it, that the Lord hearkened to the voice of a man. For the Lord fought for Israel. And Joshua returned, and all Israel with him, unto the camp to Gilgal."—Joshua x. 12–15.

The following, therefore, is the only question with which we are concerned: Is this passage any part of the Sacred Record? Is it written by him who wrote the book of Joshua? Or is it a paragraph introduced by some one who, perhaps, was engaged in transcribing the

sacred writings, who, having a copy of the book of
Jasher before him, and recollecting the manner in which
the writer of that book notices the victories of Joshua,
saw fit to insert it in the words of the author, taking special care to inform the reader where he obtained it, and
where it might be found?   We think, as we have already
intimated, that it is the latter.   But if the former, if the
passage be truly a part of those writings which compose
the book of Joshua, and which record the wonderful success that attended the arms of Israel, when God wrought
with them to empty the land of their enemies, and to
establish them in it, then do we most cheerfully receive
it as the word of God, and verily believe that " the sun
and moon stood still at the command of Joshua, and
hasted not to go down about a whole day."

Before we present the argument, however, in favor
of our position, we shall take the liberty to introduce
some

PRELIMINARY REMARKS.

The passage under consideration has evidently been
regarded with very great interest, both by the friends
and the enemies of revelation.   The frequency with
which it has been brought forward with a view to *disprove* the authenticity of the whole Bible, has led the
friends of revelation, perhaps, to be more determined
in their defence of it than they otherwise would have
been.   They have seemed to act under the impression,
that to give it up was virtually to surrender the truth of
the scriptures.   There can be no doubt, we think,
that I. John v. 7, has been defended in this way,
until, by the great majority of those who receive the
Bible as the word of God, it has come to be regarded as

genuine.   And yet, the proofs against that passage amount almost to a demonstration.   The same may be said of Ecclesiastes xii. 8–14, and of some others.   The object in endeavoring to retain these passages cannot have been exclusively, or even principally, *the doctrines* which they are thought to contain, for, so far as these passages seem capable of being understood, they declare no other doctrines than those which are abundantly sustained by other passages of scripture, whose genuineness has never been attacked by any who would not attack the whole Bible.

The doctrine of the Trinity is undeniably in the word of God, whatever becomes of 1st John v. 7, and that of a future state of retribution can be found there, without a reference to the dubious verses in Ecclesiastes, especially verses 11 and 12, which seem wholly without meaning.   It is evident that the cause of truth needs no false supports.   We ought, perhaps, to say with Dr. Chalmers, it can have none, for, if we introduce into the foundation of a superstructure any material which is not substantial, anything which contains in itself all the elements of decay, we virtually endanger the whole fabric, because when that which was true and of permanent value comes to receive the additional weight, which for a time rests securely on the false, but which, by reason of the decay, has been thrown upon the good, it is crushed beneath it, as if it were itself spurious like the other, and the fabric perishes.   We render, therefore, very dubious service to the cause of revelation, when we persist in defending and retaining that which we ought at once to give up.   We do not intend to be understood as saying or even admitting, that we are to surrender a passage *merely* because unbelief or temerity has attacked it, but only that we are not to *depend* on those passages which, to say the least, are somewhat doubtful, since we may thus be understood as risking the defence of our whole cause upon them.   This is a rule to which we desire to adhere.

These remarks apply with great force to the passage under consideration.   We need it not in support of the doctrine of a particular overruling and special Providence.   We can show without difficulty, that he sustained the prophets and apostles, by giving them power to perform those works which no other man could, and which were, perhaps, the best credentials that the nature of the case admitted, in favor of the truth of their message.   There is enough of clear and indisputable Scripture in support of this, without the so-called miracle of arresting the sun and moon.

But it is distinctly admitted, that this consideration should not influence us to reject the passage in Joshua. *It may be true.*   The thing which it asserts is not more difficult for a wonder-working God than any of the well attested miracles that he wrought.   The plagues of Egypt, the passage of the Red Sea, the giving of the Law, the supplying of the people with bread from heaven, or any of the miracles recorded in the New Testament, are as marked exhibitions of Divine power, as the stopping of the sun and moon.   And even if it were not so; if the miracle we are considering were one that evidently demanded a much *greater* effort, in our estimation, on the part of God, we ought not to be influenced by this consideration, in making up our mind as to whether we should believe or not.   How can we determine the comparative degree of power which the Almighty must put forth in any given case?   How can men say which is the greater or the less work for Him to perform, " who giveth no account of any of his matters," and " who worketh all things after the counsel of his own will?" No matter how great the miracle, no matter how stupendous the work, if indeed it is what God has wrought, and he has caused a record to be made of it, we are to receive it. But the question before us is, did he perform it? Did he, in answer to the request of Joshua, cause the sun and moon to stand still, that his people might avenge themselves of their enemies? This is the whole question which concerns us. It will not be regarded, we believe, as irrelevant or improper for us, in this place, to remark, that no one who has attempted to explain this passage, or who has advanced a theory in regard to it, seems satisfied with his own work when executed. He turns away with evident discomfort, as if to say, " there, I have given the best account of it in my power, and I hope you will be satisfied with it." Even the enemies of revelation, as they have attacked it, with a view to destroy the argument from miracles, seem not to regard themselves as having done any thing toward the accomplishment of their object, in destroying the credibility of the Scriptures, when they have swept the passage away.

It may also be well enough, in passing, to advert to the circumstance which first directed our attention to the question of the genuineness or inspiration of this text, viz., the astounding fact that a miracle of this magnitude was never once referred to in the writings of the prophets, apostles, or evangelists, or even the instructions of Jesus Christ. By no one who preached or prophesied, at a period subsequent to the conquest of Canaan, though he may have mentioned, and repeatedly

too, most of the mighty works which were done for
Israel, is the stopping of the sun and moon alluded to,
even once !   We shall undoubtedly here be told, that
the prophet Habakkuk has referred to it.   But they who
undertake to maintain this will find it quite as difficult
a task as to defend the passage in dispute ; all which
will be made to appear in its proper place.

*We shall now give a few of the principal theories in-
vented to explain the passage :*

1. There are those who understand it *literally ;* who
suppose that in obedience to the command of Joshua,
the sun and moon stood still in the midst of heaven,
and hasted not to go down about the space of a whole
day.   We speak, of course, the language of every day
and of every age, in reference to this matter, without
regard to the philosophy of the thing, or the more rigid
principles of astronomy; this is the language used in the
text.

They who embrace the literal view, suppose, of course,
that the diurnal motion of the earth was arrested for the
space of about twelve hours, that the waters of the sea
were prevented from rushing out upon the land, by the
same Almighty hand which had made all things, and
which had been thus stretched out to work this important miracle ; that all things found upon the surface of
the earth, which otherwise would have been piled into
a mountain of ruins, by the sudden cessation of the
earth's motion, were prevented from doing so by the
same hand : in short; that every thing took place as
here recorded, without figure, metaphor, or poetry, just
as it would appear to an intelligent inhabitant of the
earth, with all the necessary means before him for
measuring time, and with the sun and moon passing

through the heavens. And this is the view to be taken, if it be determined that the passage before us is an inspired portion of the word of God. *The difficulties we may feel are no greater than those felt in connexion with any well-authenticated miracle recorded in the Scriptures.* And we know not that we feel any difficulties whatever in respect to those which are well attested. We suppose that He who has established the laws of nature, has power to alter those laws whenever it shall seem good in his sight; and that he can arrest or reverse them when he pleases.

The literal interpretation of this passage is found as far back as the days of Jesus Siracides, the author of the book of Ecclesiasticus, about 150 or 160 B. C., and. is referred to in chapter forty-six, in the following words: "Was not one day as long as two?" And so late a writer as Budè Guilloumè, (or Buddeus,) born at Paris, 1467, founds an argument against the Copernican Philosophy on the literal interpretation of it. Gallileo and Columbus met with it in the mouth of the bigoted monk and ignorant priest, who were opposed to their philosophy. In a word, it has been *the general* view taken of it by those who have received the Scriptures as a revelation from God, from the earliest notices of it. This circumstance may have some bearing on determining the true character of the passage.

2. Another opinion is, that the Almighty so far arrested or altered the ordinary course of things, as to cause *an extraordinary refraction of the solar and lunar rays,* without stopping the sun, moon, or earth, in its course; but only causing things to appear to the inhabitants of the earth just as they would, were the sun and moon to be made to pause in their journey through the heavens.

This is the ground taken by Mr. Taylor in his edition of Calmet's Dictionary. It supposes that the event transpired at midsummer, when the sun was in his highest northern position; that it was near the full moon, just at the setting of the sun, and of course as the moon was rising. At Gibeon, then, (latitude 35 deg. 30 min.) the longest day is fifteen hours. If now we add one hour and a half of twilight, morning and evening, we shall have eighteen hours of daylight, so that the rays of light have to be bent from their natural direction only long enough to make up the remainder of twenty-four hours, at which time the sun would reappear, which would fully answer, in his estimation, the purposes of the miracle. And with this view of the subject Professor Stuart seems to accord. In a letter to the writer of this article, he says that "it was only κατ ὄψιν," i. e., in, or according to appearance.

This, it is thought, will obviate all the difficulties which are felt by the advocates of a literal interpretation; will make the Sacred Record consistent with itself, and leave our confidence in it altogether undisturbed. We shall in this way avoid, as it is said, all serious objections against the miracle, such as the following: "It disturbed the whole course of nature; made a double day for one hemisphere, and a double night for the other; made the month on which it occurred longer than any other, and the next shorter; held the tides standing, so that where it was high tide there was an inundation, and where low, the extreme reverse; saved the houses and mountains upon the earth's surface from being shaken out of their places, and crushed in one common ruin."

But we have great difficulty in embracing this view

of the subject. It proceeds on the ground that the Jewish leader uttered the command about the rising of the sun, whereas the passage itself evidently indicates that it was nearer the close of the day; and the circumstances which are hereafter to be considered, will abundantly show that Joshua, and all Israel with him, were at Makkedah, somewhere about the hour of three or four in the afternoon. A more serious difficulty, however, is, that it supposes the rays of the setting sun to have been so bent out of their natural course as to have enabled the inhabitants of Judea to see the sun in the west till he should reappear in the east, *which would give some two days and a half of daylight*; and that is more than we know what to do with!

But these are difficulties to which the attention of the reader will be called more particularly in the subsequent part of the article.

All that we have now said proceeds on the ground that the phenomena of nature are described just as they appear to the eyes of the beholder. This mode of speaking is perfectly correct and proper, and the Scriptures, if they are to be understood at all, must use language in accordance with the common modes of speaking, not regarding philosophic distinctions. Were it otherwise, they would mislead a great majority of their readers, and prove an endless source of confusion, instead of their being, as they are now, "a light to our feet and a lamp to our path."

3. Others have supposed that unusual atmospheric phenomena appeared near the close of the day, which performed the office of the sun and moon, by shedding such a light upon the path, both of the conquered and the conqueror, as to prevent the escape of the one, and

inspire the courage of the other, and that, in accordance with "poetic license," these phenomena are said to be the sun and moon, pausing at the command of Joshua, when he had asked in general terms, only for light enough to enable him to complete the work which had been so auspiciously commenced. The great objection to this view is, that it bears a marked family likeness to that kind of exposition of the Sacred Record, or to those rules of exegesis which generally invoke the aid of an earthquake or a thunder storm, whenever anything supernatural or above the ordinary course of nature is to be explained. Every miracle on record, no matter how well attested, has by this method been explained away, or worse; since, to represent men who are divinely inspired, as stating that for truth which is but the result of their own fear, or the creature of a diseased imagination, is infinitely worse than to have no miraculous works whatever to which to appeal. Besides, one man has as good a right to draw upon the resources of imagination as another. The field is illimitable and open to all, and when once entered is rarely left, until the mind is incurably secured to the interests of unbelief.

4. Some there are who regard the whole as an example of highly wrought, figurative, poetic description of a most signal victory, achieved over the enemies of God *in a single day;* and to be classed with many other descriptions of fact found in the Bible. According to this view, Joshua asks of God time enough to make an end of the five confederate kings and their forces; and in answer to his prayer he is so far assisted by the co-operation of God as to accomplish in one day the work of at least two, when left without these special manifestations of Divine power. Vatablus, Professor at Paris,

one of the number that embraces this theory, thus para-phrases it, and virtually makes it a prayer: "Lord, let not the light of the sun and moon fail us, till we have vanquished all these thine enemies. Enable us this day to complete their utter overthrow."

We have less objection to this view than to any yet considered. No doubt our ignorance of the bold and imaginative language of oriental poetry, together with our prepossession in favor of grave prose, would lead us to reject many things which are indisputably true. Look, for example, at the eighteenth Psalm, where David is but describing his victory over the enemies of the theocracy. He introduces the tempest and the earth-quake, and many other manifestations of Divine power; so that this signal victory is plainly attributed to these, whilst his own labors and those of his adherents are lost sight of. Compare also the song of the children of Israel, after their passage of the Red Sea, Ex. Chap. xv. and the triumphal song of Deborah, Judges Chap. v., in which we have this remarkable declaration, "The stars in their courses fought against Sisera." The whole prophecy of Habakkuk may be cited in illustration of the remarks we have just made.

But we cannot adopt any of the theories to which we have adverted, for reasons that follow. We cannot receive the third, in any of its modifications; for, if we assume that the passage in dispute is from the pen of the writer of the *book* of Joshua, we must understand every-thing literally, just as it is represented in the text. Though expressed in poetic language, (as we shall here-after see,) it is nevertheless plain, simple, and perfectly intelligible; nothing of ornament or exaggeration in it; every term used is evidently to be understood in the

most common and easy sense. We feel bound, moreover, to reject every theory which is built upon the
hypothesis that the author of the book, in this instance,
forgot himself, and spoke of an event as having taken
place which was only so in appearance, or in imagination. Nor can we admit that, in simply declaring his
wonderful success for a day, he has made use of a language that few, if any, can understand. We prefer to
understand and explain the passage literally; and, as
such, to receive, what it declares as truth, unless we show
positively, and beyond all doubt, that it is no part whatever of the Sacred Scriptures. We cannot admit that
Joshua was so ignorant of natural phenomena as to mistake a halo around the sun, or the lingering fragment
of one, for the sun itself. A child would not have been
thus deceived.

5. We come, therefore, to the theory or explanation
which we suppose to be the correct one. It supposes
the passage to be a quotation, or an extract, from a book
which was known at the time as "the book of Jasher,"
which was probably a collection of poems, descriptive
of some important events, having truth for their basis,
but fiction for their dress. Inasmuch, however, as all
turns on the single question, whether the passage properly belongs to the sacred scriptures or not, we shall
proceed to consider the arguments which, to our mind,
seem obviously opposed to it. They are arguments too,
of which every reader can judge, both in respect to their
pertinence and their weight.

1 Joshua x. 12–15, is evidently an interruption of the
narrative, and an interruption which, when considered
with reference to its own statement at the close, destroys
the credibility of the whole passage. For the sake of

perspicuity, we shall divide this argument into two parts; first considering the evident interruption of the narrative. The reader has only to turn to the chapter itself, and leaving this passage out, read the remainder. He will there find a well connected account of a series of events, which are in themselves natural, orderly, and perfectly consistent one with another. Joshua and his army leave Gilgal at nightfall, or soon after, travel all night, and arrive probably at daybreak, or very early in the morning, before Gibeon, beleaguered by the five con-federate kings. He routs them with great slaughter, and then pursues them along the way that goeth up to Beth-horan, thence to Azekah, and thence to Makkedah. Here it is told Joshua that the five kings are hid in a cave. He gives orders to secure them by rolling a great stone to the mouth of the cavern, and then to pursue the fugitive enemy in order to follow up the advantages secured. After accomplishing their overthrow, or chasing them till they seek refuge in their fenced cities, the army of Israel returns to Joshua, who, as it seems, is still at Makkedah; probably to prevent the escape of the five kings. These are then led forth and slain, and the narrative goes on to inform the reader, that those cities to which the dispersed armies had fled, are next attacked and overthrown, and his conquest pushed into the far south, *after* which, (verse 43,) Joshua returns and all Israel with him, unto the camp at Gilgal. Now, this is perfectly natural and consistent with itself; and no inter-ruption of any kind ; the events are recorded just as we should expect they would occur, in connection with the knowledge of the success which had attended the arms of Joshua in the campaign.

But what shall we do with the fifteenth verse? A most serious and insurmountable difficulty this, indeed! "Joshua returns and all Israel with him unto the camp at Gilgal." Returns from Makkedah, immediately after the sun and moon had paused in obedience to his command, till the people had avenged themselves on their enemies, returns to Gilgal, distant some thirty-three or thirty-five miles, returned, as it would seem, that night! "But these five kings fled and hid themselves in a cave at Makkedah. And it was told Joshua, saying, The five kings are found in a cave at Makkedah. And Joshua said, Roll great stones upon the mouth of the cave, and set men by it to keep them, and stay ye not, but pursue ye after your enemies, and smite the hindmost of them." So, then, we perceive that neither Joshua nor Israel *has* returned to the camp at Gilgal, but all are at Makkedah, whatever becomes of verse 15th, or anything connected with it.

2. The passage under consideration *claims* to be just what we have regarded it—a quotation, or an extract, and nothing more. The question which occurs in verse 13, "Is not this written in the book of Jasher?" is proof abundant that he who introduced it, either intended to inform his readers where he found it, and consequently that he wished to be understood as quoting, and nothing more, or *appealed* to a contemporaneous work, or record in proof of what he then asserted. For our own part, we consider it of little importance which ground is taken; the one is just about as fatal as the other to the passage. A third supposition is not possible, the question is either a declaration, though indirect, that the author *intends* it as a quotation, or he would support himself in the assertion that the sun and moon stood still in obedience

to the command of Joshua, by appealing to another author and another record. We shall consider this last view of it more at large in a subsequent section of this article (See 5.)

If then, the ground be taken that it is a quotation, and the author, whoever he may have been, paused in the midst of it, *in order that he might guard the reader against supposing that he would be understood as declaring that this ever took place,* the point is settled. There seems to be at least an effort on the part of the writer, to prevent misunderstanding. His question is equivalent to this : Do you not find what I am now recording in the book of Jasher? Or perhaps in accordance with his true meaning, Do you not find the victory that Joshua achieved over the enemies of God, *noticed or referred to in the book of Jasher, in the words here inserted?* And this, as the reader must carefully remark, is the language which might have been used at any age since the book of Joshua was written.

3. There are some considerations connected with the well-known references to " the book of Jasher," which seem to bear somewhat heavily on the main question, and which we may as well notice here as at a subsequent part of the argument. These references are only two; one is under consideration, and the other is found in 2 Sam. i. 18.

Josephus supposes "the book of Jasher" was composed of certain records, and was kept in a safe place in the Temple *at the time* to which these two notices of it refer ! and that it contained an account of what happened to the Jews from year to year. So that the book was not ranked among inspired writings, but only regarded as correct ; so much so that the author obtained the name of Jasher, or the Just!*   Bp. Lowth thinks it was a poetical book, or a volume of poems, extant at a period *long before* it is referred to by the author of the book of Joshua and of Samuel!   *An uninspired man referring to events that did not take place till long after he wrote!*

Suppose, then, we take the ground that the book of Jasher was extant at the time of the conquest of Canaan. *When could it have been written, in order to have contained a notice of the standing still of the sun and moon?* That is, upon the supposition that Joshua, or the writer of the book of Joshua, made a record of this miracle as soon as it was wrought, when could the book of Jasher have been written, to have contained a notice of an event which must have been recorded immediately after it transpired, to have been *referred* to by this very book, in the record which is therein made to the same event?

It must be carefully borne in mind that, if Joshua is the writer of the book which bears his name, he is the author of chap. 10, 12, 15, i. e., if the statement here is true: how, then, can we account for this reference to a book which is said to have contained a notice of the same event, when, beyond controversy, Joshua made a record of it as soon as it transpired?

The book of Jasher, then, must have been extant *before* the conquest of Canaan, and must have referred to an event which did not transpire *till during the wars of this conquest!* or the writer of the book of Joshua must have neglected to notice a most signal event, till Jasher had had time to speak of it in a poem, so that he could

---

* Josephus Antiq. Jud. lib. 5. cap. 2.

cite this poem in confirmation of his own statement; or the whole of the passage in dispute has been foisted into the text at a period long subsequent to the occurrence of the event which it proposed to record.

But we are met by a more serious difficulty still, in the other notice of this book; that found in 2 Samuel i. 18. David here bemoans the death of Saul and Jonathan in a poem, at the commencement of which there is a reference to the book of Jasher, similar to the one before us: "Behold, it is written in the book of Jasher." What is written there? That poem? Is this found recorded in the book of Jasher? If so, we have a difficulty of no ordinary kind to be removed here. The death of Saul and Jonathan took place at least four hundred years *after the conquest of Canaan* by Joshua; Calmet makes it four hundred and thirty. Did Jasher live and write during the whole period of four hundred and thirty years? *And if this was so*, when, and how, and where did he get the poem which David had made on the death of his friends, so as to be able to insert it in *his* book *before* the writer of the book of Samuel had inserted it there? The author of "the book of Jasher" has the poem which David made, and inserts it in his book before David has made it! We set up the plea of ignorance here. We know of no means of removing these difficulties, so as to save the disputed passage from the doom that seems to await it. Nor can we give any other explanation of its being found here than that already offered in regard to the passage under discussion in this article.

But further remark seems necessary in respect to the last passage cited. What, then, does the writer say is written in the book of Jasher? The *poem*, which immediately follows? Or does he declare that the circum-stance of David's giving him command that the children of Judah should be "taught the use of the bow" is there? We are not unprepared to answer the latter question. The words "*the use of*" are supplied by translators; remove them, and a serious difficulty in the way of correctly understanding the passage itself is re-moved. "Also he [David] bade them teach the chil-dren of Judah the bow;" that is, *the poem*, so called by reason of one of its leading terms, or first words. It was then, as at the present day, the practice to designate a piece set to music from some one or more of its first words; e. g. "Lord of all power and might," etc., etc.

Books were so designated by the Hebrews. Thus the book of Genesis was called Bereshith, the Beginning; the book of Numbers, Bemidbar. Sometimes they in-troduce a poem with this formula: "az-Jasher," i. e., "then sang;" "az-Jasher Mosheh," "then sang Moses." Ex. xv. 1. The Samaritan Pentateuch reads, "Jasher vè-jasher Deborah," "then sang Deborah."

"The book of Jasher," therefore, was probably a col-lection of sacred songs, composed on various occasions, and thus named because many of its pieces commenced with the above formula: "ve-Jasher."*

One of its pieces undoubtedly was that recorded in 2 Sam. chap. 1, in which David gives vent to the swell-ings of his heart at the death of Saul and Jonathan. The notice of it found in the eighteenth verse bears evi-dent marks of violence in its introduction. There is nothing natural, easy, or in accordance with the subject matter of the context. What possible harmony between

---

* Compare Bishop Lowth. Prael. pp. 306, 307, notes. And Dr. Gregory Trans-lation, vol. ii. pp. 152, 153, notes.

the announcement, that orders had been given to instruct the children of Judah in the use of the bow, and
the elegiac strains that follow?   Would a poet of such
ineffable skill as David possessed, pause at the commencement of a poem, so perfect in all its parts as the
one before us, and give command concerning the train-
ing of youth in the arts of war and blood-shed?   Were
the fires of vengeance burning so deep in his soul, that
his hands refused to touch the moaning wires, until he
had laid the proper plans for avenging himself at some
distant period on those that had slain his friends?   It is
not possible; the whole verse is spurious, beyond a
doubt; a bungling interpolation by some one, years after
the death of Saul occurred, or after David noticed it in
the melancholy strains, which he or some one else duly
inspired, has recorded.   Remove the interpolation, and
the passage reads easily and naturally ; retain it, and all
is unnatural and contradictory.

4. There are other, and most serious difficulties in the
way of receiving the disputed passage as a part of the
records of truth.   The one which now follows, we regard
as of some importance.   While all the surrounding text
is, for the best of reasons, the gravest prose, *the passage
itself is poetry*.   It forms three perfect distiches: thus—

> " Sun, stand thou still upon Gibeon,
> And thou Moon, in the valley of Ajalon.
> And the Sun stood still, and the Moon stayed her course,
> Until the people were avenged of their enemies.
> And the Sun tarried in the midst of the heavens,
> And hasted not to go down in a whole day."

This, in connection with the beginning of the twelfth
verse, we regard as comprising probably the original
extract; and the remainder of the passage as having

come from the pen of him to whom we are indebted for the interpolation.

But it will perhaps be replied, what if it be poetry? Is there any thing uncommon in a writer's thus breaking off from prose and introducing poetry, with a view to give effect, or force, to a magnificent work which he wished to record? We are disposed to regard it a very uncommon thing. We can see no reasons whatever for introducing poetry here, in the middle of a narrative, which required only a plain unvarnished statement of the facts just as they occurred. Was not the event in question one which required in the narrator great plainness and precision?

5. The passage itself contains the elements of its own destruction, in respect to several statements which it makes. We are persuaded, no one can read it, with these distinctly before his mind, without having his confidence in it utterly destroyed.

One of these we have already considered at some length, in our remarks upon verse fifteenth, "Joshua returned and all Israel with him," etc. But we feel inclined to introduce to the reader's notice the views which some others have taken of this passage. Calvin and Massius declare the fifteenth verse spurious.

They have no authority, however, for so doing, except that which arises from the character of its own statements; they see the utter impossibility of reconciling these to the well known and rational averments of the context. It appears to them quite clear, (as indeed to whom does it not?) that Joshua and all Israel with him, could not have returned to the camp at Gilgal, and at the same time remained at Makkedah, engaged in the summary process, therein described, of punishing their enemies. The fifteenth verse is omitted in the Septuagint, at least in the older MSS. The Alexandrine and the Vatican also want it, but all this proves only, that the ancient transcriber, like the modern interpreter, met with a difficulty in it which he could in no way surmount, and therefore chose to *cut* the knot which he found himself unable to untie. Others, as Buddeus, have endeavored to obviate the difficulty by slightly varying the translation. Instead of reading as now, "Joshua returned," they propose to read it, "And Joshua *purposed* to return," etc. That is, as they say, he was on the *point* of doing this, but having been informed that the five kings were found secreted in a cave, he changed his purpose, and remained to push his advantages to the end.

But we cannot concur. Such a purpose is altogether inadmissible, even if we were fairly over the difficulty arising from the consideration that it is all supposition. Joshua was not the man, by a precipitous retreat, to lose the advantages which he had that day gained over his enemies. Is it likely, that he would thus throw away the fruits of a most signal victory, which God had evidently given him, and let slip an opportunity of completely vanquishing his combined enemies? And further, what occasion had he for such haste in getting back to his camp? He had nowhere been beaten, nor in all the land was there a Blücher to come pouring his dark masses down upon him just at nightfall, to snatch from his brow the priceless laurels of an unquestionable victory, and utterly extinguish his hope and his fame. No, he had nothing to fear, God had been his defence, and there were not the least signs of his withdrawing this protection.

Besides it must be borne in mind, that any defense of the fifteenth verse will ruin the 43d, where the same words are literally repeated, and where they *seem* evidently to be in place. The proposed amendment, therefore, instead of freeing the passage from one embarrassment, actually involves the whole in more.

Another consideration, which seems to subvert all confidence in it, is the astounding assertion that " there was no day like that, before it, or after it." In what respect? we are here compelled to inquire. Was this said with reference to its *length*, or to something else? Certainly he might have averred that, in respect to every *preceding* day of time, there had been none like it, if it was, as the passage declares, a day wherein they had the light of two ; but whether he could have assured the world that there was never to be another like it in this respect, is somewhat questionable. How could *he* say whether God would not, in the course of his wars with wicked nations, employ another Joshua, and, as he had done in the case before us, (that is, upon the supposition the thing recorded is true,) so do again, give him authority not only over the treasuries of hail, but over the sun and moon, nay, over time itself?

But the reader must carefully bear in mind that the record claims nothing remarkable for the day, *with respect to its length.* On the contrary, the writer specifies the particular respect in which that day was unlike any one that had been or ever *was* to be ; and what was it? Anything in regard to its length? Certainly not, but it was " *that the Lord hearkened unto the voice of a man !*" Now we respectfully inquire, if this *was* the first time " that the Lord hearkened to the voice of a man?" Or was it the last? Did he not hearken to

Moses? How many times? Did not the Most High hearken to the voice of a man when he emptied the treasures of his wrath upon Pharaoh and his land? And how many times did the half-subdued king of Egypt beseech the servant of God to intercede for him, and prevail? How was it at the Red Sea, and at the waters of Meribah; at Rephidim, and at Sinai, and at Jericho? And how has it been since? Has there been no intercourse kept up between heaven and earth, during the last three thousand years? Now, we are assured in the passage before us, that there is to be no day like that to the end of time. If, then, we suppose that day to have been unlike any one that had been, or *was* to be, in this respect, that the Lord heard and answered the prayer of man, what shall we say of the following declaration? " Elias was a man subject to like passions as we are, and he prayed earnestly that it might not rain, and it rained not on the earth by the space of three years and six months. And he prayed again, and the heaven gave rain, and the earth brought forth her fruit." And was this the *only* instance in which God hearkened to the voice of man? Nay, verily; he heareth prayer to-day.

But it may, perhaps, be said, the meaning of the declaration is, that God had never hearkened to the voice of a man *in this particular sense*, or in so remarkable a manner, and never would again. In reply, we need only say, there is no end to suppositions. If we regard the sense of the passage, as it stands, incomplete, and on that ground proceed to furnish the supplement, · we enter an illimitable field, and shall be likely to find, in the end, that every one has the same right to introduce hypotheses as ourselves.

Neither can the ground be taken, that the point, or the particular, in which that day was unlike any that had been or that would be, was, that the Lord fought for Israel: for this would contradict almost the entire history of his dealings with his people. How was it with his people at Rephidim? And did not the Lord fight for Israel, when he overthrew Og, king of Bashan? And have there been no instances since? What is the historical part of the Bible but one continuous record of his marvellous works to maintain and defend his people? This hypothesis, therefore, must be given up.

Nor should we fail to remark in this place, that to maintain any of the above suppositions surrenders the main point in debate: for if the writer of the disputed passage, in his declaration that there had been no day like that, and there would be none like it again, referred either to the circumstance, that the Lord hearkened to the voice of a man, or that he fought for Israel, he did *not* refer to the standing still of the sun and moon, *and this is the point in dispute.*

We can easily conceive that a heathen poet, one who knew little of the wondrous works of God, and who scarcely believed the little he had heard, who allowed himself almost any license in his art should make the assertion we have been contemplating. But that a man acquainted with the history of Israel, his escape from Egyptian bondage, his passage of the Red Sea, his journey through the wilderness, his overthrow of Jericho, and destruction of Ai, to say nothing of the numerous instances remaining; that such a one should declare that this was the first and the last time in which God would take it upon himself to defend his people, we cannot believe; especially when we take into consideration that he was at the same time divinely inspired.   We are, therefore, compelled to regard these considerations as the elements of utter destruction to the credibility of the passage which contains them.

6. It seems, moreover, not a little remarkable, that an event of such stupendous grandeur as this which we are contemplating, (the sun and the moon arrested in their journey through the heavens, and compelled to remain stationary about a whole day,) should have perished from the memory of the whole world.   Why do we not find some notice of it in the traditions of other nations? Would not the world have been likely to remember it, if such an event had ever occurred?   For, to all who should have been then living in that hemisphere where the event is said to have taken place, there would have been the same or similiar phenomena, the day as long again as an ordinary one ; and to those who inhabited the other parts of the globe, the *night* would have been equally prolonged.   Why do we not find some scrap of history, some vague tradition, to say the least, of such a day and such a night?

The deluge, confessedly of little if of any more importance, has left its history, not only engraved upon the rocks of our highest mountains and deepest valleys, but also ploughed deep into the mind of every nation and every people on the earth.   In fact so strong is the argument drawn from this source, that were we not to find the history of the flood in the Scriptures, we should feel compelled to admit its existence.   But why should this event be so carefully registered in the memory of earth's population, and nothing be known of a certain day some three thousand five hundred years ago as long as two days?   There are many and strong reasons for believing, that the deluge would have been unknown in the traditions and histories of nations, while the miracle in question would have been carefully remembered had it ever taken place. By the flood, the earth was swept of its inhabitants; there were none left, save the family of Noah, to make a record of that catastrophe. But in regard to the matter we are considering, *all* its population remained. They were eye witnesses, either of an unusual day, or of an exceedingly singular night. Why do they not remember it?

We must notice another circumstance here: the tradition or other record, whatever it might be would have varied according to the different situation of the nation or people where that tradition was found. The earth, was then, as now, a globe; and consequently this circumstance *must have* given a peculiar shape, or charac ter to the tradition. Thus, as we have already intimated, among some there would have been the recollection of one day as long as two; with others a night of equal length. With those living in India, China, and Japan, it would have run thus: " thousands of years ago, the sun lodged on some of the western mountains, and remained stationary about the space of a whole day." With others, those living far west of the land of Palestine, it would have been. "The sun once found it impossible to ascend the eastern skies, and remained fixed in his chariot some twelve or fourteen hours." We find however, nothing of the kind, not a shred of a record; not the faintest traces of a tradition of any such event; a silence for which we find it difficult to account, except upon the above ground, that no such event ever occurred.

And yet, it will not be denied that our expectation of

this tradition is altogether natural and just. What could have been more difficult for the world to forget, than the day of which we speak? Were such an event to occur at the present moment, with what deep interest would earth's population stand and measure the flight of time, and record the growing anxieties which would be uttered in respect to the result! And how many speculations, and how many theories, how many causes would be assigned for the remarkable occurrence! The preachers of a bewildering fanaticism, which marks the present age, might gratify their vanity by recording the conversion of thousands, nay, millions in a day.

But we shall probably be told, that all we are here requiring has really taken place. Herodotus, as Mr. Horne informs us in his "Introduction to the Critical Study and Knowledge of the Holy Scriptures," Herodotus has found among the Egyptians the very tradition in question. In conversation with the priests, he had learned that in a very remote age the sun had four times departed from his regular course; having twice set where he ought to have risen, and twice risen where he ought to have set." Mr. Horne admits, however, that the circumstances are not the same in all respects, in the one record, that they are in the other. Yet he seems to think that, since we cannot tell to what *else* the Egyptian tradition referred, it is proper to regard it as referring to the day when "the sun stood still on Gibeon, and the moon in the valley of Ajalon!" Thus, in the first place, assuming the truth of the thing to be proved in order to account for this tradition, and then bringing forward the tradition to prove the truth of the thing assumed! A fair example of arguing in a circle.

But, if Mr. Horne has furnished us with the data upon which his mind is made up, we are compelled to say our faith can never span an arch like this! And we do most deeply regret that a man so generally correct in his conclusions as the author in question, should have allowed himself to be influenced in this matter by considerations of no weight whatever, and utterly irrelevant to the matter in hand, even if they lacked not weight. He might with equal propriety, have selected anything else as well as this. The famous Zodiac of Dendera, or Esneh, would have laid the foundation for a much more plausible theory than the record we have found in Herodotus. However, the thing, as it is, is not wholly without its use; since it evidently shows, in the first place, that the expectation of some tradition, or history of such an event, in case it had ever occured, is altogether natural and reasonable; and in the second, that no tradition worthy of a moment's consideration can be found, or it would have been brought forward in place of the one we have been considering. That Mr. Horne should have consented to bring out this, is proof, we think, that he felt the imperious demand for something of the kind; and also, that he could find no better, else he would have brought it forward. If so, we are sorry it did not occur to him that the difficulty lay in the thing to be proved; the event itself had never taken place.

We are disposed, therefore, to move confidently forward in the line of our argument, under the healthful influence of the feeling, that we have judged correctly in supposing that *an event like this should have left some traces of its existence in the memory of the world before whose eyes it must have taken place.* The period

of time is not so far back as to give any one the shadow
of a defence on the ground that the tradition had perished.   Most of the marvellous works which God performed in connection with his people, when he took
them by the hand to lead them out of Egypt, and which
were wrought before they were settled in Palestine, are
carefully treasured up in the traditions of those nations
which lived in the immediate neighborhood of the localities where these events are said to have taken place.
A place (whether the true one or not affects not the
argument) where Israel passed the Sea is readily pointed
out to the modern traveller, as much so as if the event
had occurred but yesterday, and with the apparent feeling that the interests of a world are suspended on the
truth of the testimony.   The rock, out of which Moses
is said to have brought water for the thousands of Israel
just as we read in the Scriptures, is shown with as much
precision as if your guide had been present when it was
done.   We do not, of course, wish to be understood as
saying, *that rock is* indisputably *the true one ;* but what
seems especially worthy of remark is, this tradition is so
vivid, and lies so deep in the mind of the people, as to
compel them to fix upon a certain rock as the identical
one referred to in the Bible.   They can forget the locality, but not the event.

But, let us suppose that some may be so destitute of
foresight as to assign as a reason for this tradition, not
the actual occurrence of the thing specified, but the
record is made of them in the Scriptures.   Well! is not
the passage we are examining found there also?   And
has it not been there for at least two thousand years, and
if true, as long as any part of the Bible?   Why has
it not given rise to a tradition as well as the other

events which have been recorded? Why would not an individual, who should have repaired to the Jewish Scriptures one, two, or three thousand years ago, to read the record of an event there found, that should have given rise to a tradition which was destined to travel down to the present day, why should he not have fixed upon the record made, i. e. Joshua x. 12–15, if it had been there? And without controversy it *was* there, as soon as any of the book, on the supposition that such an event took place. Besides, we are disposed to inquire what an argument of this kind would be worth? Let us suppose a tradition of the deluge to exist among the nations of the earth, and it is asserted that this tradition originated in the record found in Genesis: How, then, would we ask, can it be a proof of the deluge? A tradition, in order to be of any weight whatever in proving an event, must have originated in the actual occurrence of the event, and not in the record which had been made of it. It must have had a separate and independent existence, or it is worth nothing as proof. That which is found among all nations respecting the Flood is directly in point.

Moreover, a tradition which should have for its origin a record in the Scriptures, or any where else, must, from the nature of the case, be limited to a portion only of the human family; whereas, in regard to Joshua x. 12–15, we feel justified in asking, nay, *demanding* a universal one. *Can it be found?*

We feel, therefore, justified in declaring that the death-like silence which obtains among the numerous traditions of men, respecting the stopping of the sun and moon, is stubborn proof that no such event ever occurred.

7. We find, also, from a careful examination of the passage in connection with the whole chapter, some serious diffi~ulties arising from *the position* which it assigns to Joshua, considered in relation to the sun and moon; and also from the position given to several cities and other localities at the time.

Where *is* Joshua, when he is said to have issued the command, "Sun, stand thou still upon Gibeon," etc. ? Both the true record and that which we regard as false, place him at Makkedah. (See verse 16.) The battle commences at Gibeon, early in the morning: and Joshua, after routing his enemy, pursues them along the way that goeth up to Beth-horon, and smote them to Azekah and unto Makkedah. But, at what *time* in the day is he at Makkedah?

He leaves the encampment at Gilgal in the evening, (verse 9,) and marches all night. Now, as Gibeon is distant from Gilgal at least twenty-four or twenty-five miles,* he could not have reached the former place, where the battle commences, until sunrise, or after, the next morning. Whether the enemy fled at the first sight of Joshua, or whether they remained, we are not so particularly informed; but the latter is more probable, since we are told (verse 10) there was a great slaughter of them at Gibeon. On any ground, therefore, it is most certain they could not have arrived at Beth-horon before he middle of the day. Here, as they were passing from the upper to the nether Beth-horon, the Lord attacks them with hail; and as they are now at least ten miles from Gibeon, where the battle commenced, they have to pass to Azekah and thence to Makkedah, which is the locality of Joshua when he is said to have uttered the

* See map of Palestine, by Edward Robinson.

command. But, since Makkeda is at least eighteen, if not twenty miles from Gibeon, where the attack commenced, it must have been as late as four o'clock P. M. when they reached the place. Let us now look at the order particularly: "Sun, stand thou still upon Gibeon; and thou Moon, in the valley of Ajalon." But where *is* Gibeon from Makkedah? *Nearly due east*, at least eighteen, if not twenty miles. And what is the hour of the day? At least four P. M. And where would the sun be to a person standing at Makkedah, at four o'clock in the afternoon? Over Gibeon? Nay, verily; the sun could have been over Gibeon only in the morning; and at that time, Joshua and all Israel with him were at *Gibeon*. Instead, therefore, of lodging upon Gibeon, at that hour of the day, the sun must have been west or southwest from Makkedah; and the moon, to have been visible at that hour, must have been just rising in the east instead of being in the valley of Ajalon, which is south-east from Makkedah. Where is there escape from this entanglement but in the supposition, that the passage itself neither belongs here nor anywhere else in the Bible? Remove it altogether, and the difficulty vanishes; the record will then remain free, connected, and natural; but as it is, we freely confess, there seems to be no defence for it. Especially is this true, when it is considered in connection with verse fifteen, to which we propose soon to give further attention.

On the supposition that the record here made is true, and the miraculous event which it records, a matter of fact, we cannot understand why it is not once referred to in all the subsequent Scriptures. It certainly could not have been on account of its comparative unimportance; it was a miracle, as we have already remarked,

which, if true, would fall little short of that stupendous
event which destroyed the whole world. Why, then,
is it nowhere noticed? Why is it not once alluded to
by those who so often and so faithfully reminded Israel
of the great and mighty works which God wrought for
their deliverance and their defence?

Undoubtedly we shall be told that it is referred to in
Hab. iii. 11, "The sun and moon stood still in their
habitation." This, in truth, would *seem* a very clear
case. If so, it will undoubtedly *remain* clear after a
faithful examination. We shall not quarrel with the
translation, nor invoke the aid of an earthquake, in order
to explain it away; but shall cheerfully admit that, after
due investigation had, if the passage turn out to be a
reference to Joshua x. 12–15, we have no further difficulty with it, whatever becomes of the considerations
already offered, each of which seems clear and conclusive. A single case of obvious reference to this event,
whether by prophet, apostle, evangelist, or any one else,
" who spake as he was moved by the Holy Spirit," will
end all debate, by placing it, so far as the writer is concerned, beyond dispute for ever. To the investigation,
then, let us proceed.

Habbakkuk iii. 11 must certainly be explained by the
same general rules which apply to the rest of the chapter. Consequently, if this passage, " the sun and moon
stood still in their habitation," is a reference to an event
which at any time literally occurred, we shall demand
the same of all the rest. God is therein represented as
" coming from Teman, or the South, his glory covering
the heavens, his brightness as the light; with horns
coming out of his hands; as preceded by the pestilence;
walking upon glowing coals of fire; standing and meas-

uring the earth; pausing, casting a look upon the na·
tions and driving them asunder; scattering the moun·
tains, *and causing the perpetual hills to bow.*"   When
did all these things occur?   And where is the record of
them?   Again: " the tents of Cushan are in affliction,
the curtains of the land of Midian tremble."   When
was this, and where recorded?   The prophet next inquires if " the Lord were displeased with the rivers, if
the Most High were exercising his wrath against the
sea?"   To what event are we referred here?   And
what is meant when God is represented as riding upon
his horses and in his chariot of salvation?   His bow, we
are told, is made quite naked.   Then the mountains are
said to have seen God, and trembled.   The deep utters
its voice, and lifts imploring hands on high; the sun and
moon stand still in their habitation; next they move
forward at the light of God's arrows, and at the shining
of His glittering spear.   Jehovah is there represented
as moving through the land, and threshing the heathen
in his anger, walking through the sea with his horses,
etc., etc.

Again we ask, when, where did these things occur?
*We shall insist on stretching one and the same line of
interpretation on the passage under present examination,
that we use for measuring the rest of the chapter.*   If we
must admit that the eleventh verse is a reference to an
occurrence which had a literal and matter-of-fact existence, we shall contend, to the end of the chapter, that
the remaining assertions are also references to true and
real transactions.   We demand that it be understood
that the God of heaven, in a bodily visible form, at some
time previous to the record here made, was seen coming
from the south, with horns springing out of his hands,

literally bearing a bow and arrow, walking on glowing coals, scattering the mountains, riding on horses, driving his chariot, compelling the sea to lift up its hands and voice for mercy or something else.

But how does it happen that verse 11 should be thought to have had a reference to an event which actually took place, while no one supposes for a moment that a single one of the remaining declarations ever referred to a transaction which at any time literally occurred? Why does no one show us when and where "the perpetual hills did bow?" The answer is undoubtedly, The assertion in verse 11th, is nearly, if not entirely, literal, as a reference to what is recorded in the disputed passage, and what is thought to have occurred. But there is a better reason to be assigned than this. The marked and unquestionable similarity between the two passages (Joshua x. 12–15, and Hab. iii. 11,) is proof abundant, that *one* must have originated in the other. Either Hab. iii. 11, is a reference to the one in Joshua, or that in Joshua is to Habakkuk. Let the ground then be taken, that the author of the book of Jasher, at what time soever he may have written, finds the glowing description in Habakkuk of the conquest of Canaan, and selecting the startling declaration in verse 11, clothes it in his own language, and makes it a theme of a short poem. Afterward a transcriber of the sacred volume, or of the book of Joshua, when he arrives at the place in the narrative where we find the extract, takes the liberty to introduce the whole passage from the book of Jasher, taking special pains to inform us where he found it. This hypothesis possesses several qualifications which are of great weight. In the first, and least important place, it is a plausible one; in the next, it fully accounts for the fact

that the event is not once referred to by the writers of the
Sacred Scriptures.   Neither by prophets, nor by apostles, nor by the Lord Jesus Christ, is there the slightest,
the remotest allusion to anything of the kind, while every
considerable well authenticated miracle is again and
again referred to in the most explicit and unequivocal
terms.   Scarce a page of the Bible do we peruse, without
having our mind directed to some one, or more, of those
magnificent works which God had wrought in the beginning, and which he continued to work for the defence
of his people, and the exhibition of his power in the sight
of his enemies.   Let the reader compare, at his leisure,
Psalms 105, 6 and 7, where we have a summary of the
mighty works of God, and which are left on record to be
made known to the people; yet, a record of the arrest
of the sun and moon is not found there, is not even
alluded to in this " summing up," if we may so speak of
the whole of God's dealings with his people.

And the author of the epistle to the Hebrews, where,
in chap xi., he is almost wholly employed in citing
examples of faith and its mighty works, and where he
even notices the case of Rahab, and the conduct of
Moses' parents in secreting him, and the directions of
Joseph respecting his bones, etc., etc., never refers to the
standing still of the sun and moon, at the command of
Joshua !   And yet, there is not an event referred to in
either of the passages named, which for grandeur and
sublimity, and the manifestation of power from on high,
and the still more important exhibition of the power of
faith, will compare at all with the so-called miracle
whose record we are considering.   It is, therefore, impossible for us to believe, without *some evidence*, (and while
considerations of undeniable weight are pressing so hard

against it,) that any event like that which is recorded in the passage under examination, ever occurred

9. We shall add only one consideration more. The passage in question is evidently no part of the word of God, since it leaves in spite of every effort, a false or wrong impression upon the mind of the reader, an impression which is directly at war with the connected and true narrative of the campaign. We have already alluded to the fact that when these verses are wholly omitted, and the record read as if they never had had existence, there is no obscurity, no difficulty, no embarrasment whatever. The mind is not tortured with the assertions in verse 15, " And Joshua returned and all Israel with him, unto the camp at Gilgal," followed immediately with this, (verses 16 and 17,) " But these five kings fled and hid themselves in a cave at Makkedah ; and it was told Joshua, etc., etc." Why should these five kings have fled in such terrible affright, after their pursuers had " returned to the camp at Gilgal ?" And what additional security could the cave at Makkedah have furnished them, when once their pursuers were all gone? And how shall we contrive to get Joshua *back*, " and all Israel with him," to Makkedah to hear the intelligence that " these five kings are found hid in a cave," and to give instructions, that great stones should be rolled upon the mouth of the cave, and men stationed to watch, lest these kingly subterranean prisoners should make their escape.

Mr. Horne proposes here to cut the knot, by rejecting verse fifteen altogether, and retaining the rest of the passage. He says, " verse fifteen is apparently contradicted by verse forty-three." (He might have said, by all the chapter except verse forty-three. Though *this*, even, would still be a contradiction.) He adds, " In the former place he (Joshua) is said to have returned and all Israel with him unto the camp at Gilgal; which he certainly did not do until the end of the expedition, (verse forty-three,) where this declaration is properly introduced. It (verse fifteen) is therefore either an interpolation, or must signify, that Joshua *intended* to return, but changed his mind on hearing that the five kings had hid themselves in a cave at Makkedah."*

With respect to this *intending*, or *purposing* to return, we have already said enough under our fifth argument, to which the reader is referred. We wish only a word further in this place, on the false impression which the passage unavoidably leaves on the mind of the reader. It is, that the whole work of completely vanquishing, or subduing the confederate kings, was accomplished in one day, and at an hour early enough to enable the conqueror and his victorious army to return to their place of general encampment at Gilgal, that night; whereas it is abundantly evident from the whole record, and also from the nature of the case, that the undertaking must have occupied *weeks*. Let us look at this matter. Makkedah, as we have seen, is at least forty if not forty-two miles, in an almost due west direction, from Gilgal. Here we suppose, and the record evidently demands it, that Joshua and all Israel with him, pass the first night of the campaign. The work of leading forth these five kings and slaying them is probably performed in the evening, after the return of those who had pursued the enemy until they had shut themselves up in their "fenced cities." We think no one will contend for a greater day's work, than Joshua and his people must

---

* See Introduction to Crit. Study of Sacred Scripture, vol. 1, p. 643–44, Lond. ed.

have performed by the time we have supposed; we think no one will demand that they should have done more, in the course of twenty-four hours, than to travel some forty miles, fifteen or twenty of which must have been passed in hard fighting.   And there is a large number of *cities* named in the subsequent part of the record, which were overthrown by Joshua and his army, during this expedition; for doing of which we must have some *time*, BEFORE "Joshua returns and all Israel with him unto the camp at Gilgal."

Joshua passes from Makkedah unto Libnah, which, with its king, is delivered into his hands; and he does to it as he had done unto Jericho and its king.   From Libnah, he passes and all Israel with him unto Lachish, which surrendered to him *on the second day;* and to which he did as he had done unto Libnah.   From Lachish he passes to Eglon, and overthrew that.   From Eglon, to Hebron, and conquers that with all its cities. Next he passes to Debir; and as he had done to Hebron, so he did unto Debir.   From this place he makes an excursion into all the hill-country, thence into the south; thence into the country of the vale, and of the springs, and destroyed all their kings; "he left none remaining, but utterly destroyed all that breathed, as the Lord God of Israel commanded."   And, after smiting Kadesh-Barnea, even unto Gaza, and all the country of Goshen, even unto Gibeon with all its kings, "he returns and Israel with him unto the camp at Gilgal."

Let any one, now, take a map of Palestine, one on which these different cities are laid down, and after examining their relative positions, and determining their proper distances one from another, let him follow Joshua to the end of his expedition, and say if he would regard it as an enterprise of only one day. Let him say, if he thinks any mode of conveyance, known at that time, or any means of travelling employed, even at the present, in that country, would have enabled a man, *without* stopping to demolish cities or behead kings, to pass over that tract of country and return to Gilgal, I will not say in one day, but in one week. We leave, therefore these difficulties on the mind of the reader ; satisfied that he cannot regard them in any other light than insurmountable, and directly subversive of the passage, which evidently cannot be retained as a part of God's word.

But before we leave this part of the discussion, there are a few considerations to which we will return for a moment.

We believe most fully in doing a thing effectually ; if it be done at all. And especially if it be of the nature of this before us. We think no man should be called upon to record his vote either for or against our argument, till he has carefully looked at all sides, weighed our argument, picked every flaw in it he can, provided himself with an answer if one can be found.

In like manner, in respect to our defense of this position :—We ought not to lay down our pen, however weary, so long as there remains a single good thought which may be advanced, one that will add to the force of those already brought forward. The undertaking in which we have been engaged, is not a small one : there is much depending upon the results or conclusions to which we profess to have come. Thousands and tens of thousands have read the passage, again and again, without a suspicion of its unsoundness ; have had no more doubt of its genuineness and authenticity, than they have of that which relates to the passage of the Red

Sea, or to anything else which is admitted as a miracle.
If their attention has never been called to it particularly
they were startled at the announcement of a proposal to
show that it was no part of the word of God, and that no
such event ever occurred as that which it professes to
record. References to it as a true and veritable occurrence may be found in all ages of the Christian church.
And as we have already seen, it was referred to by those
who lived antecedent to the Christian era. Following
the course of time, or the direction of events, from the
days of Christ down to the present, we find but few who
dissent from the general impression, that it is a record
of a true and most important work of God. Even within
the last twelve months we have seen it referred to in a discourse before one of the most intelligent audiences of
our land, in a way that did not admit of a doubt, that he
who referred to it, *believed* it ; and not only so, he did
not seem to have had a doubt that his audience believed
it too ! And yet, the strangest part remains to be told ;
this same man was heard to say, a short time before, he
had not a doubt of its spuriousness ; that he should as
soon think of using any other monkish fables as that in
the services of the house of God !

After carefully reviewing the argument which we are
about closing, we have felt that one of its strongest
points should be pressed a little further: we refer to
that which is based upon *the other* reference to the
book of Jasher, that which is found in 2 Samuel i. 18.
I see not how an intelligent reader of the Bible can pass
that passage without pausing to inquire into the matter
somewhat faithfully. Not that it is at all important
which ground is taken ; whether that, David is said to
have commanded them to instruct the children of Judah

in the use of the bow, or that the *Poem* was thus named, which is the more probable case: but it is the circumstance, that the book of Jasher is referred to at all: for certainly, if such a book was in existence at the period when Joshua is represented as having referred to it, then surely its author could have known nothing of what David was to do, who was not to be born till full 400 years afterwards! And, should the ground be taken that Jasher lived and wrote in the days of Joshua, there is no small difficulty in accounting for his noticing such an event as that of the standing still of the sun and moon before Joshua did even if that event occurred.

The case is this: here are two events, (or are *said* to be:) beyond all reasonable doubt as to time they are more than 400 years apart: and here is a book which professes to notice *both* of them! Now then, we are compelled to admit, or rather to affirm, that if that book knew anything about the *first* event, the standing still of the sun and moon, it certainly could not know anything about that *other* event, the death of Saul and Jonathan. Moreover, if it knew anything about this *last* it could *not* know anything about the first; that is,—in the way which is implied: For, in respect to both, the book is referred to as having made mention of the events. We confess, with what of sincerity we can, to a conscious inability to see how these things can be. There is, in our estimation but one explanation; both references are indisputably spurious, the work of a much later age. Some lazy bigot, in his zeal for a religion that he could love, because it allowed him to hate every other being in the universe, except himself, knew not how else to employ his tedious moments: and accordingly sat down to the task of weaving this sleezy medly of nonsense, profaneness and dreams: then, to secure for it a foot hold or place in the confidence of men, he contrives in this absurd way to show that there was some sort of recognition of it in the oracles of God! Magnificent foundation this, surely!

There is, in fact, but small room for mistake, in attempting to account for the existence of such a work as that of the book of Jasher. It is the product of evil-minded, ignorant men; those who have such a cordial dislike for truth and righteousness that they imagine themselves called of God, and so freighted with special revelations as to need no watch or care as to what they say or write; the world will not dare to inquire into either their credentials, their qualifications or their works.

Perhaps we cannot better conclude the present essay on the general subject, than to relate an incident or two connected with our first knowledge of the so-called Book of Jasher. We had long been familiar with *notices* of such a book; meeting them in the course of our studies; but nowhere had we been able to obtain a view of its luminous pages, or its brilliant display of ancient lore. Those who referred to it were generally compelled to admit, that what they knew of it was not from any personal knowledge of it, not having themselves ever seen a copy of it. This was the amount of our knowledge of it, when we sat down to the preparation of an article for one of our literary Quarterlies, the Biblical Repository. Our reflections upon these two references to the book, Joshua x. 12–15, and 2 Samuel i. 18, were sufficient to lay the foundation of an argument against the so-called miracle of Joshua, which is found in the foregoing pages, and which we ventured to close with a kind of *challenge,* as some would call it, to any one who would undertake its defence.

We were soon served with a notice in one of the papers of the day, that a certain Professor in one of our Colleges proposed to *accept* the so-called challenge, and bring our adventurous logic to a careful account. Either the said Professor regarded the undertaking so easy, the task so light, as to *require* but little thought on his part, or care—as to the manner in which that little was presented. Certain it is, as will be seen in the following essay, his defense of the marvellous exploit, said to have been performed by Joshua, and carefully referred to as having been noticed in the book of Jasher, was a most lame and silly thing, evidently to be classed with the "spread eagle" genus. We take no manner of praise to ourselves, be it understood, for having demolished that defense at a blow: a child could have done the same. We found it a far more difficult task to comfort and soothe the redoubtable professor, under the mortification arising from his sad discomfiture. We tried faithfully; so did the editor of the Repository, the work in which his calamitous overthrow was duly chronicled; but all to no purpose: the lapse of some fifteen years, if we may judge from an epistle we have just received from him, in answer to a request that we might publish his essay between these two articles, that the reader might enjoy the benefit of that learned production,—has served to molify and heal his lacerated feelings but little. His heart was evidently made to bleed, at the thought of the manifest injustice which was done him: and yet he could not consent to have *his* essay republished, that *others*, as well as himself, might see what great injustice he had received at the hand of the writer and the editor of the work in which *our* essay was published.

After reading with some degree of surprise the essay of the Professor, and reflecting upon its weak points, or more correctly, its utter *want* of point, and while gathering up the views with which we were intending to " answer him according to his folly," we had occasion to step into a gentleman's library, in search of a work that we desired to look into, when the true and veritable " book of Jasher" stood before us!   Surely, thought we, here is a God-send.   We hastily seized it, and craving the loan of it for a little time, conveyed it to our study for further investigation.

The reader may well suppose that we went in search of the two famous passages ;—that in Joshua, and that in 2 Samuel.   These, of course, were our great concern.   We soon succeeded in finding the first ; but the other, we could not so readily fall upon.   Accordingly we at once sat down to a perusal of the whole volume.   The results of this examination we have given in chap. viii. so far as was necessary for the accomplishment of our object.   We found the desired passage ; accompanied by references to circumstances and events, and in the midst of statements which had about as much reference to the death of Saul and Jonathan, or to the Elegy which David is said to have prepared in commemoration of this event, as it had to the Newtonian philosophy, or the variations of the magnetic needle !   Not one grain of truth is there in the whole volume, except what is contained in garbled extracts from the sacred writings ; and these are combined with fabulous and silly statements in about the proportion of the infinitessimal of truth to the balance of absurdity.

These circumstances we have just named may seem irrelevant and unnecessary; but if the reader will take the trouble to seek the book itself, then sit down to a patient perusal of it, he will see how utterly without foundation is any thing that must depend for its support upon statements which are properly its own. In the absence of this, he should be furnished with at least a suggestion, or intimation of the character of a book, which our common Bible represents Joshua as quoting with a view to sustain himself in an assertion which he appeared to think would not be believed! This is undeniably the view you must take of the passage, kind reader, or you must come with us to the conclusion, that it is indeed, an awkward and profane attempt to pass off for inspired, a story which never had any foundation, except in the bewildered imagination of one whose proper sphere and home was the mad house.

CHAPTER VIII.

ON THE STANDING STILL OF THE SUN AND MOON,

AS RECORDED IN JOSH. X. 12, 15.

THIS chapter, like the preceding, first appeared in the Biblical Repository, some years since, in answer to an article in the Methodist Quarterly Review, attacking that; it was by Prof. H. M. Johnson, now of Dickenson College, Carlisle, Pa.

It is proper for me say, that I have written to Mr. Johnson, with a view to obtain permission to print his article, in immediate connection with that which precedes this; which is the one that it professes to overthrow: but have not succeeded in obtaining leave to do so. My object was to set forth, so far as I could, the arguments and considerations which may be advanced in opposition to the view which *I* have taken of the main question. The Prof. complains in his letter to me, that I have misquoted him. It would seem an easy matter for him to have proved it, if it was so, by just allowing *his* article to be published between these of mine: but, he has declined, and I have no alternative but to publish mine as it appeared in answer to his, and leave it for the candid reader to judge for himself, as to what is proven and what is not.

The Reviewer, (Mr. Johnson,) introduces himself to the reader in the following strain of purest fustian: "The Biblical Repository for Jan. 1845, presents us with a full-grown, and perhaps timely delivery, of a German embryo idea, in the shape of a profound doubt of the genuineness of the passage in Joshua; giving account, that the sun and moon stood still; which doubt grows in the mind of the writer into a certainty of disbelief, duly compacted with a ligamentous evidence, authority and criticism; and arrayed withal in the necessary argumental investments. We wish to unfold the wrappages of this new-born, before its strength shall have become consolidated; to dissect its members and prove whether there be in it a life which may not die."

By the time we had concluded this, we entertained sound fears, that it was all over with us, we had even settled upon an epitaph: "*Alas, poor Yorick!*" Because, having seen that our " embryo idea " was threatened with " dissection," we thought it possible, that a like fate awaited ourselves: on more mature reflection, however, we have been led to regard what is past on the part of the Reviewer, only a " timely," and as we would fondly hope, " *safe delivery* " of a vast amount of wind.

Finding ourselves, therefore, still in the land of the living, we shall endeavor to show to the satisfaction of every reasonable man, that " this new-born " does, in fact, " contain in it a life which may not die."

At the very outset of his enterprise, the Reviewer seeks to secure a verdict in his favor, and to make all necessary provision against prospective defeat, by representing, that all such speculations as this, which he is about to " dissect " are the legitimate offspring of German Rationalism.   How easy thus to overthrow an antagonist !   Who can entertain a doubt after this, that the sun and moon stood still, according to " The book of Jasher ?"

Homer has somewhere related that a snail, on looking out of his shell, saw a frog leaping by ; and being seized with a desire to leap in like manner, forthwith crept out for that purpose ; but on making trial of his leaping powers, soon found that he must first build himself a stool.   Here we have, if we are not utterly deceived, the veritable and main object of all such manœuvres.   In order to enable the reader to see clearly and judge correctly in this matter, he must look through glasses smoked with slanderous suspicion !   There is not a candid man on earth, one, over whose intellect the smell of thought ever passed, who would discover, on reading the Examination, *the faintest traces of that form of Infidelity.*

" Success " says Johnson, (the Dr., not the Professor,) " inspires courage :" and having met with no insurmountable obstacles in getting through with an introduction, the reviewer girds up the energies of his pen to the task of meeting the arguments brought forward in support of the doctrine of the Examination.   We shall endeavor to accompany him, at an humble distance, if possible, to learn the fate of our unhappy idea ; and if it is slain, " be in at the death."   He condescends to shed a ray of hope upon our prospects, by admitting the first argument in all its force : the argument (see Biblical Repository for January, 1845, p. 107) is, " Joshua x. 12–15, is evidently an interruption of the narrative ; an interruption, which, when, considered with reference to its own statement at the close, destroys the credibility of the passage." It is there added in explanation, " the reader has only to leave it out, and he will find a well connected account of a series of events, in all parts perfectly consistent with itself." "True," says the Reviewer,—" and the same may be said of any paragraph in any narrative of events occurring successively, and not necessarily dependant on one another." But we ask if these statements are *not* so dependant one on the other, that the credibility of v. 15, "and Joshua returned and all Israel with him unto the camp at Gilgal," is hopelessly lost, if the *rest* of the narrative (v. 16 et. seq.) be true? How can Joshua and all Israel with him, return from Makkedah to Gilgal, a distance of some thirty-three or thirty-four miles, the evening of the day on which they had achieved so signal a victory, and yet *be* at Makkedah (see v. 16) to bring out the five kings to slay them? If Joshua and all Israel with him, have retured to Gilgal, they are not at Makkedah as is stated in the subjoined text: which now of these two conflicting statements must we give up?

In order to escape, if possible, from this difficulty, the Reviewer endeavors to separate verse 15 from the rest of the suspicious passage. He admits that all commentators have found a difficulty in it, which they knew not what to do with; and that the statement therein made is not reconcilable with the surrounding text. (See Methodist Quarterly Review for 1846, pp. 507, 508.) But his labors to save the remainder, when he has given up verse 15, amount to but little, as we shall soon see. With what a grace, the complaint of cutting knots instead of untying them, comes from a man that finds it necessary so soon to introduce the knife! Especially is this the case, when, in the course of his efforts to defend the rest of the passage, he becomes so thoroughly convinced of the hopelessness of his cause as to express a willingness to give up all after the appeal in verse 13, "Is not this written?" etc. (Review, p. 508.)

The controversy then would seem to be narrowed down to a very small compass; but no, we go for the whole, and nothing less. There is such a marked family likeness in all the parts as to force upon us the belief, that they belong together; and since we are favored with a sight at the Book from which the whole appears to have been taken, we shall prefer to present "an extract," a larger one than the disputed passage, yet one that embraces it, to satisfy the reader we have judged correctly in deciding, that inasmuch as in life they have been most firmly united, in death they should not be parted.

The reader will allow himself to smile at the idea just advanced, yet it is most true. "The Book of Jasher" is now lying before me; the veritable ספר הישר "Sepher Hajasher," (literally, "correct record,") with its chapters and verses and with the passage in dispute, is at hand! We shall quote it in its English dress, presuming the Reviewer will be satisfied with the assurance, that it claims to have been originally written in Rabbinical Hebrew, to have been discovered in Jerusalem, when the city was taken by Titus, and to have been first printed in Venice, A. D. 1613. So much for its authentic antiquity! What could be more satisfactory?

If there is anything of the ridiculous and absurd in this representation, it belongs neither to us nor our cause. Our Professor must share it, for aught we see, with no one,—since it is exclusively his. He maintains, as we shall soon see, that it was altogether "reasonable to suppose, that a poetic account of this great miracle

was actually in circulation, " *before* history, with a graver
pen, enacted the imperishable record !" (Review, p. 509)
A book containing the famous extract, a volume as large
as the entire Pentateuch, written and put in circulation,
after the miracle of stopping the sun had been performed
and *before* that miracle had been recorded by the sacred
historian ; a flying scroll which has been sailing through
the heavens, lo ! these thirty-five hundred years, has
finally lighted upon our table, here before us ! *credat qui
potest ; non ego.*   He who can receive this, ought surely
never to be accused of not believing enough.

The reader, it is presumed, and possibly the Reviewer,
will be glad to see the entire passage from which the
verses in dispute are thought to have been taken.   He
can then determine for himself, whether there be any
good reason for stopping at the appeal in the midst of
verse thirteen,—as suggested by the Professor,—regarding that which precedes it as a true record of an event
which actually took place, and that which follows, to
the end of verse thirteen, the original extract.

BOOK OF JASHER, Chapter lxxxviii 63.

" And when they were smiting, the day was declining towards evening, and
Joshua said in the sight of all the people,
  Sun, stand thou still upon Gibeon,
  And thou, moon, in the valley of Ajalon,
  Until the nation shall have avenged itself upon its enemies.
  And the Lord hearkened to the voice of Joshua,
  And the sun stood still in the midst of the heavens,
  And it stood still six-and-thirty יֹמִים (yom-im,) times, or moments, or
    days !
  And the moon also stood still
  And hasted not to go down a whole day.
  And there was no day like that before it or after
  That the Lord hearkened to the voice of a man,
  For the Lord fought for Israel."

CHAPTER lxxxix.

(1.) " Then spake Joshua this song, on the day that the Lord had given the Amorites into the hand of Joshua, and the children of Israel, and he said in the sight of
all Israel :
  (2) Thou hast done mighty things, O Lord,
     Thou hast performed great deeds,
     Who is like unto thee ?
     My lips shall sing to thy name.
  (3) My goodness, my fortress, my high tower,
     I will sing a new song unto thee,

THE PASSAGE CONTAINING THE DISPUTED ONE.

Thou art the strength of my salvation.
(4) All the kings of the earth shall praise thee,
The princes of the world shall sing to thee,
The children of Israel shall rejoice in thy salvation,
They shall sing and praise thy power.
(5) To thee, O Lord, did we confide ;
We said, thou art our God,
For thou wast our shelter
And strong tower against our enemies.
(6) To thee we cried and were not ashamed,
In thee we trusted and were delivered.
When we cried unto thee thou didst hear our voice,
Thou didst deliver our souls from the sword,
Thou didst show unto us thy grace,
Thou didst give unto us thy salvation,
Thou didst rejoice our hearts with thy strength.
(7) Thou didst go forth for our salvation,
With thine arm thou didst redeem thy people,
Thou didst answer us from the heavens of thy holiness,
Thou didst save us from ten thousands of people.
(8) The sun and moon stood still in heaven. (see Hab. iii. 11)
And thou didst stand in thy wrath against our oppressors,
And didst command thy judgments over them.
(9) All the princes of the earth stood up,
The kings of the nations had gathered themselves together,
They were not moved at thy presence.
They desired thy battles.
(10) Thou didst rise against them in thine anger,
And didst bring down thy wrath upon them ;
Thou didst destroy them in thine anger,
And cut them off in thine heart.
(11) Nations have been consumed with thy fury,
Kingdoms have declined because of thy wrath,
Thou didst wound kings in the day of thine anger.
(12) Thou didst pour out thy fury upon them,
Thy wrathful anger took hold of them,
Thou didst turn their iniquity upon them,
And didst cut them off in their wickedness.
(13) They did spread a trap, they fell therein, (Ps. vii. 15 : lvii. 6)
In the net they hid, their foot was caught.
(14) Thine hand was ready for all thine enemies,
Who said. through their sword. they possessed the land,
Through their arm they dwelt in the city ;
Thou didst fill their faces with shame,
Thou didst bring their horns down to the ground,
Thou didst terrify them in thy wrath,
And didst destroy them in thine anger.
(15) The earth trembled and shook,
At the sound of thy storm over them.
Thou didst not withhold their souls from death,
And didst bring down their life to the grave.
(16) Thou didst pursue them in thy storm.
Thou didst consume them in thy whirlwind,
Thou didst turn their rain into hail,
They fell in deep pits so that they could not rise.
(17) Their carcases were like rubbish
Cast out in the middle of the streets.
(18) They were consumed and destroyed in thine anger,
Thou didst save thy people with thy might.
(19) Therefore our hearts rejoice in thee,
Our souls exult in thy salvation.
(20) Our tongues shall relate thy might,
We will sing and praise thy wondrous works.
(21) For thou didst save us from our enemies,
Thou didst deliver us from those who rose up against us,
Thou didst destroy them from before us,
And depress them beneath our feet.
(22) Thus shall all thine enemies perish, O Lord,
And the wicked shall be like chaff driven by the wind,
And thy beloved shall be like trees planted by the waters.

(23) So Joshua returned, and all Israel with him, unto the camp at Gilgal, after having smitten all the kings, so that not a remnant was left of them.

(24) And the five kings fled alone on foot from battle, and hid themselves in a cave," [all this, kind reader, after they had all been smitten, so that not a remnant was left,] " And Joshua sought for them in the field of battle, and did not find them.

(25) And it was afterwards told to Joshua, saying, the kings are found, and behold, they are hidden in a cave," etc. etc. (See Josh. x. 16, et seq—Almost word for word !)

Here are the facts in the case ; and here the " song," which Joshua sung, if we may credit the book of Jasher, when the Lord had given up the Amorites into the hand of Israel !   But this song, which claims to have been written immediately on the occurrence of the events which it recounts, is made up, as any one may see, of detached sentences from the Psalms of David, the writings of Solomon and of the Prophets.   In the midst of it, (verse 8,) we have the passage which undoubtedly originated the story of the sun and moon standing still ; a passage either quoted from Hab. iii. 11, or Hab. iii. 11 is a quotation from that.   The reader may have his choice here between the two suppositions : the Reviewer it seems has already made his election.   It is, in his estimation, far more reasonable to suppose that " the poetic effusion (the song by Jasher) should be antecedent to the prose record ;" and as no one believes that Habakkuk was written before the book of Joshua, it follows, that Habakkuk is a literal quotation from the book of Jasher ! At the close of the whole, we have the famous passage which terminates the extract as we find it in Joshua : " And Joshua returned and all Israel with him unto the camp at Gilgal."

We submit now, whether the theory, which, in the opinion of our Reviewer, smells so rank of German Rationalism, and which he seems to think would look very foolish even to its author, if he would bestow ten years more of study upon it, is not a plausible one ?

Nay more, is it not the *only* one which an intelligent, careful reader will regard as worthy of any confidence?*

Devoutly were it to be wished, that this so called "poetic effusion" had never seen the light, or that no one had ever thought to illuminate the sacred record by introducing extracts from it. We feel bound to say of it as a whole, something as a clear-minded, sound-hearted old man once said of a sermon from a Universalist. "The scripture that he quoted, and quoted *right*, was good." So of the self-styled "Sepher Hajasher," or " correct record;" that which it contains, which is scripture, is well enough; unless so combined with the fancy and conceit of him who has gathered it up, as to pervert utterly its meaning; which is the case before us.

The reader, we think, will sympathize with us in our disgust for this book, when we assure him that among all the Apocryphal writings now extant, there are few, if any, more replete with absurdities, vain and inconsistent surmises, or more deeply imbued throughout with the smut and moonshine of monkish superstition and folly. It commences with the history of the creation of man; it claims (as indeed it must) to have been extant when Joshua was written, in order to be quoted. And yet, (O consistency, thou art a jewel!) near the close, and immediately after the record of Joshua's exploits, it speaks of the conquest of Britain by the Latins! Chap-

* We think the supposition a most reasonable one, that he who had the temerity to introduce the passage where we find it in Joshua, tenth chapter, saw the evident inconsistency of quoting the book of Jasher as a book that was extant when that of Joshua was written. Hence the appeal, verse thirteen, " Is not this written?" etc. These words we regard as his *own:* while *all* the rest is from the book Jasher. The *song*, too, which had been gathered up, as we have proved, from all parts of the Old Testament, was too long to be inserted entire ; therefore, we have only the beginning and the end of it. Hence the astounding absurdity involved in it: " And Joshua returned and all Israel with him unto the camp at Gilgal ;" since verse sixteen of Joshua x., and verse twenty-four of the song before us, are a plain contradiction of it.

ters three and four are occupied with an account of Enoch; he is represented by the writer as having been a king, a *great king, a king of kings !*   Query, where could he have obtained subjects at this age of the world ? Next, that we might be thoroughly penetr ated with the exaltation and renown of Enoch, the historian represents him as passing most of his time in retirement; thus modestly intimating or suggesting that Enoch was *a monk !* A circumstance which indicates the age of the document itself.   But the writer, in order to lend a finishing touch to the exalted character of Enoch, after having spoken of him in the language of the Bible, as walking with God here below, sends him to heaven on a pacing horse! Was not this the original of our Reviewer's " winged Pegasus ?"   Jasher's account of Nimrod's hatred of Abraham, is but a garbled reiteration of Matthew's record of Herod attempting to destroy Christ.   The star which he represents as making its appearance at the birth of Abraham, needs no explanation.   He describes Babel with great particularity.   It was a tower ten miles in diameter, and thirty miles round ; was carried up to such a height, that when a brick started at the bottom early in the morning, being tossed from man to man, one directly over the other, it would arrive at the top late in the evening !   Moreover, as those on the top amused themselves with shooting arrows directly up, they perceived on the descent of these arrows, they were covered with blood : by which they inferred, says the writer, that they had mortally wounded many in heaven ! And at the dispersion, he is careful to name all the countries colonized and settled by the various tribes which were scattered abroad.   Among them we have an account of the settlement of France and of Italia !

The only shadow of a misgiving in the mind of the writer as to the consistency of these things, manifests itself in an awkward attempt to furnish the name "Roman," and that of the river "Tiber," with Hebrew terminations.

Still, we maintain that this book, in order to have been referred to in Joshua, must have been extant when the book of Joshua was written. Our heroic Reviewer felt this, and manfully girded himself to the task of making all appear smooth and credible. He says, (Review p. 509,) " we claim it as the more reasonable to suppose, that the poetic effusion," (the poem by Jasher,) " should have been *antecedent* to the prose record ;" (the record made by Joshua.) He even claims "that it is more reasonable to suppose, that the flight of the winged Pegasus should have outstripped the tardier movements of the pedestrian muse !" We profess to know a little of almost every thing ; but we have no knowledge of his meaning here. He has evidently had the good fortune to dive so deep into the merits of his own cause, as to bring back proofs with him that he has been to the bottom. Well, perhaps the sentence which immediately succeeds is epexigetical, and will throw some light on its predecessor. He adds, " the shout of victory and the telegraphic announcement frequently find utterance in poetic numbers, while history, with a graver dignity, enacts the imperishable record, when the tide of excitement shall have given place to the calmer flow of unexaggerated truth." This is somewhat more lucid and intelligible ; a plain English translation of which is, " The book of Joshua was evidently not written till abundant time had been given for the flight of the winged Pegasus." The man whose credulity can overcome such obstacles as these, will never find any in the way of a position which he wishes to establish. Our Reviewer may rest easy, too, we think, as to another point : admitting his position as absurd as we regard it, he has reached his ultimatum in absurdity. He cannot be more so, for the reason assigned by a recent writer, that the weather could not be any colder—the thermometer was not long enough. The mercury was in the bulb ; how could it go lower? So with him, who in the face of such time defying proofs of the utter hopelessness of his cause, still persists in endeavoring to defend it ; he has sunk himself in the scale of a generous and accurate estimation of these things so low, there is no room to go lower. He is in the very bulb of congealed credulity.

We say, then, in his own language, " when no other object in the universe is proposed, but to support a favorite theory, we do, in the name of Christianity, in the name of candid criticism, and in the name of the sacred regard we have for the integrity of that book which contains the principles of our cherished religion, most earnestly and most solemnly protest against such trifling with the word of God as this." Physician, take your own pill.

But when was the book of Joshua written? The Reviewer thinks that many things therein found did not occur till after Joshua's death ; so that *they* certainly could not have been recorded by his pen. To this position he is driven, that he may find time for his " winged Pegasus" and his " pedestrian muse" to go forth proclaiming the victories of Joshua, and the miracles he wrought by a " poetic effusion,"—ere "history, with a graver dignity, shall enact the imperishable record." When, wherefore, was this record made? And by whom? .Was he a man whose testimony we are to receive, as one of those "holy men of old who spake as they were moved by the Holy Ghost?" Most certainly, if the book be any part of the Bible. And this man, whether Joshua or somebody else, inspired of God to record that and only that which is truth, finds it necessary, in order to command belief, to appeal to a piece of fugitive poetry which had been dropped in the flight of a "winged Pegasus!" Nothing of German Rationalism in this!

But the Professor, somewhere along here, sees so many and serious difficulties gather thick and dark around his cause, that he expresses a willingness to give up *all after the appeal in verse* 13. (Review, p. 508, bottom.) But we cannot concur: there is such a marked family likeness in all its parts, that we are disposed still to maintain for them a common parentage. Our extract from the book of Jasher shows, with great plainness, that this strong resemblance is caused by a common origin, and a common character. We shall endeavor to see that all, both before and after the appeal, share one, common fate.

Let the supposition, then, be made, that Josh. x. 12 –15 is to be retained, because the thing it states is true. Wherefore this citation then of another writer? Is it to command belief? Where, in all the word of God, do we find another case like it? Inspired men, in every part of the Bible, are remarkable for moving directly along in their narrative, as if the thought not once occurs to them that their testimony will not be received. Why this trembling, this apparent misgiving as to the reception which their testimony will meet with? They could record the history of every other miracle in the

Bible down to the resurrection and ascension of Christ;
and make use of no long preface to prepare the mind of
the reader for something strange and unaccountable;
and when announced, they do not pause and appeal to
the book of Jasher or to anything else, with a view to
sustain themselves and command belief. Every record
is made with a coolness and a deliberation which look
like anything rather than the fear of not being credited.
And we love the Bible for this very thing; it looks like
the book of God, instead of "the book of Jasher." There
is something here which carries great weight with it.

Our Reviewer appears to have had some knowledge
of the arts of controversy, and to have availed himself
of that knowledge, on several occasions: sometimes he
has found it convenient to act upon the principle, that
" the better part of valor is discretion." We have an
example of this in his passing by, without noticing, a
single consideration found on pages 110, 111 of the
Examination. The book of Jasher is referred to once
more in the Bible, viz: in 2 Samuel i. 18. There, on
the occasion of the death of Saul and Jonathan, David
composed an Elegy; at the commencement of which, we
are told, as in the passage in dispute, " this is written in
the book of Jasher." *What* is written there? The
Elegy of course.* Well, then, here is an event recorded
in this book, at least four hundred and thirty years later
than that referred to in the passage of Joshua! Did the
learned Professor's " winged Pegasus" continue his flight
for so long a period as this? How shall this difficulty
be disposed of? On the supposition that a poem was
written announcing the event, as the Reviewer himself

* The passage referred to in the book of Jasher, ch. lvi. 9, is represented as
being Jacob's dying address to his son Judah!

maintains, immediatly after the miracle and before the sacred penman had had time to record it, how shall we account for the fact, that another event, which did not transpire till *four hundred and thirty years afterwards*, is written in the same book and said to have been recorded by the same writer? Must we regard Jasher, or the author of that book, a prophet? Why did not the Reviewer think of this difficulty; or knowing it, why did he not look out a way around it? It would have enabled us to understand far better than we now do, the extent of the flight of his famous "Pegasus." Perhaps he would escape from this dilemma as a certain Mormon did from one not less fatal to the claims of *his* book. He had been asked to account for the fact, that in the book of Mormon there were several literal quotations from Shakspeare. "Now," said the inquirer, "your book claims to have been written some seven or eight hundred years before the Christian era; how is it, that your author quotes from Shakspeare?" "He does not," replied the confused Mormon, "Shakspeare qotes from him."!

In the same way the ground of the Review may be defended, and in no other; you must admit that a book has been twice quoted by inspired men, while the book itself is not in existence till a thousand years or more afterwards! A piece of fugitive poetry, by a profane author, a flying scroll dropped from the pocket of a "pedestrian muse," a record made by the genius of a "winged Pegasus," and thrown upon the winds, in his flight hap-hazard through the heavens quoted by inspired men, in order to gain for themselves a credibility in the subject matter of their own testimony in respect to a transaction which thousands and tens of thousands could testify to as well as themselves!   Surely, a faith that can bridge such a gulf of difficulties as this, is not to be despised!

Our Reviewer has succeeded, as he thinks, in convicting the author of the Examination of a great mistake in supposing that Josephus had noticed the book of Jasher. After quoting our reference, he says, " But to those of our readers whose memories may not be so fresh in this author, (Josephus) what will be their surprise to be told that Josephus, so far from giving an opinion at full as quoted above, concerning the book of Jasher, has never once named the name of Jasher, throughout the whole of his histories, nor even so much as intimated that he ever heard of such a book !"   (Review, p. 511.)   On p. 512 of the same, he gives us the words of Josephus, which have been *believed* to refer to the book of Jasher, "Now, that the day was lengthened at this time, and was longer than ordinary, *is expressed in the books laid up in the Temple.*"   " We can easily see," adds this Reviewer, " that it is not among the wildest of conjectures to suppose that the book of Jasher was intended."   Nay ; he admits that " this opinion gains a strength of probability amounting, *perhaps*, to inference."

It is no uncommon thing for a certain class of writers to attempt to argue both sides of a question.   Either from excessive vanity in supposing that they could make out a much stronger case than their antagonists, they step over to the other side of the controversy ; or they have not the penetration to perceive, that their arguments prove exactly the opposite of what they had supposed.   We do not pretend to say which is the case before us ; but feel disposed to give the Reviewer all the advantage he may reap from a choice between evils.

We can conceive of no higher motive that could have governed *him*, than a willingness to trifle with the good sense of his readers ; at first to deny utterly that Josephus had said anything that could be fairly construed into a reference to the book in question ; then proceed directly to quote what has been by every one regarded as a reference to the book and its author, and afterwards admit that it is altogether probable Josephus *did* refer to the said book !

If however we have erred in this, we are not alone in our error, as is abundantly evident to every one who knows anything about the matter. The learned editor of the book, now lying before us, expresses himself of the same opinion. Mr. Horne, Bp. Lowth, and others without number, think with him. Nevertheless we are not unwilling it should pass without amendment, that Josephus *was* most profoundly ignorant of any such book, for the very grave and sufficient reason, *there was none.* Neither Greek nor Roman historians know anything about it ; which abundantly accounts for the fact, that the older MSS. of the Septuagint (the Vatican, and the Alexandrine) have not the passage in dispute. All which goes to confirm us in the opinion we have long cherished, and many times expressed, that the book in question, at least in its present form, is not very ancient

Is it not somewhat amusing and instructive to see our antagonist taking refuge, at this stage of the discussion, in the obscurity which he says hangs over the whole subject of said book ?—after valorously meeting the argument of the examination drawn from the absurdity of supposing that a record of the event could have been extant so as to have been quoted by Joshua ; and having glanced, too, at the hopeless dilemma in which the other reference to this book places him, the Reviewer gravely entrenches himself behind these difficulties !   An easy way truly, of getting out of trouble !   And must he not be favored with an unusual amount of self-esteem, who can keep his countenance when he asks a generous reader to give any weight to his arguments or conclusions?   Having fought and retreated inch by inch over the whole territory, he gravely assures his reader that nobody knows anything about the book !

He evidently shows an anxiety to close up the discussion on this part of the subject.   He remarks, " if it character could be determined to be such as is supposed ; if the little volume of miscellaneous forms" (*poems?*) " should be brought forth from the dust of slumbering ages " entire and perfect, it yet has no further bearing on the subject or argument, than to indicate the probable actuality of the event disputed."

· "The little volume," as we have already said, is before us.   We perceive not the faintest traces of the " dust of slumbering ages" upon it ; on the contrary, it is quite a new book, divided up into chapters and verses like all that class of books, and bearing a marked resemblance to that whole family of Apocryphal writings which first saw the light about the commencement of the dark ages, and which contributed, more than any other cause, to form that darkness. The ascension of Isaiah, the book of Enoch, the Apocalypse of Elijah, that of Zephaniah and of Zecharia, nay, even of Adam, Abraham, Moses, Hystaspes, Peter, Paul, Cerinthus, St. Thomas, and of Stephen, together with a multitude which cannot even be named, all come before us claiming a very high antiquity, of course, but unfortunately, like " the little volume" in hand, bringing with them statements which point with

unerring aim to the days of monkish sway, when superstition and bigotry were the winding sheet of the church.
Not only the theology of that age, but its literature, so
far as it had any, was in most perfect harmony with the
labors of our Reviewer, in that it was glad, at all times,
to wrap itself in a mantle of marvellous obscurity.

Having overthrown, as he thinks, the first three arguments of the examination, the Reviewer is brought to
that which regards the poetic character of the disputed
passage. "While the surrounding text is for the best
of reasons the gravest prose, the passage itself is poetry."
This remark is expressly limited to that part of verses
12–15 which refers to the questioned miracle; the rest we
admit is prose. See Bib. Rep. for Jan. 1845, p. 113.
We shall endeavor to be present, while this argument,
like its unfortunate predecessors, is slain.

He commences the attack by assuring the reader, that
" neither himself nor Mr. Hopkins knows enough of
Hebrew *prosody*, to be able to affirm that this passage is
poetry." It was not of prosody, directly, that we affirmed,
but of poetry. We said then, and now repeat it, " accompanied with the necessary argumental investments," *this
passage is poetry*, while all the surrounding text, or in
other words, the *true* record, is prose. That, and the
whole of that which relates to the point in debate, *is
poetry*. The Reviewer denies this, declaring that neither
of us knows any thing about it. There are some reasons
to doubt whether the Profr. knows enough to enable him
to say this of himself or any body else.

But if he is so profoundly ignorant of the distinguishing qualities of poetry in general and of Hebrew poetry
in particular, as not to see them in verses 12, 13, how is
he prepared to say whether Mr. Hopkins understands

the matter or not? We shall be sorry, indeed, to learn that *his* ignorance on a given subject is proof that nobody understands it. The flight of his famous Pegasus, according to his own showing, is not likely to prove intelligible to him. That he does *not* understand the matter at all, he seems determined to place beyond dispute. "The characteristics," he says, "by which we are accustomed to distinguish poetry, are these, to wit, the determination of the verse by a certain number and quantity of the syllables in each." Will the learned Professor deny that the book of Job (excepting chaps. 1, 2, and a verse or two at the close) is poetry? And can he find here his "determination of the verse?" etc. etc. Let him look also at the book of Psalms and that of Proverbs; then let him stretch his line upon the Prophets, and upon many other passages of Scripture, which are as clearly poetry as is Milton's Paradise Lost, and are as easily distinguished from prose as Exodus xv. 1–21 is from what precedes or follows it.

But, we will leave the question of our own, and that of the Professor's, knowledge of Hebrew poetry to be settled by an appeal to witnesses that are not only indisputably competent, but disinterested and impartial. Let it be remembered, we have asserted in the examination, and repeated here, that the passage in dispute is poetry, while all that precedes or follows is prose; and on this circumstance have maintained that the whole is *an interpolation.* But Mr. J., our learned Professor, *denies it;* yet on page 508, he says, that which follows the question in v. 13, ("Is not this written," etc.) "is a little *more* poetical than that which precedes it." There are degrees then, it seems, in poetry, according to his own standard, and that too, when there is no poetry at all! But not to dwell here, Professor Hengstenberg of Berlin, in support of the point now under consideration, remarks, " the book of Jasher was undoubtedly *a poetical book*, this is evident both from the poetical character of the words, (referring to the passage in Joshua,) HERE ALLOWEDLY BORROWED FROM IT, *in which the parallelism of members cannot be mistaken.*" *He* can determine whether the passage be poetic or not, by another and very different consideration from that which regards " the number and quantity of syllables in each verse ;" viz. " the parallelism of members." And the Prof. adds the testimony of Masius in support of the poetic character of the passage. " There can be no doubt," says M., " that the words, 'the sun stood still in the midst of Heaven, and hasted not to go down about a whole day,' *are rythmical*, and are borrowed from the book of Jasher." M. Dupin regards the book of Jasher a collection of poems, " BECAUSE THE WORDS *cited by Joshua are poetical expressions, not very proper for historical memoirs.*" And Dr. Clark (see com. in loco,) not only admits the poetic character of the passage, but maintains that it is even *rythmical.* Will the professor make war with his theological godfather ?

The inconsistency, if not even folly, of the Reviewer's position here, is the more remarkable when we call to mind the circumstances which created a necessity for his " winged Pegasus." It will be remembered, that the ground taken in the Examination, is, that it is absurd to suppose that a poem should have been written by Jasher or any body else, commemorative of the miracle, before a record of it was made, or would have been made, by the sacred historians, had it ever occurred. In answer the professor stoutly maintains, " that it is not only in accordance with nature, but it is also *more reasonable* to suppose that *the poetic effusion should be antecedent to a prose record*, and that the winged animal should have outstripped the tardier movements of the pedestrian muse." (Rev. p. 509.) Here it will be observed, the question of poetry is not only maintained, but the writer becomes so exceedingly anxious to get out a version of the whole matter in the form of a poem, "*before htstory*, with a graver dignity shall have had time to enact the imperishable record," that he even makes his "winged creature" outstrip the "pedestrian muse." A plain English translation of which is, if I understand it, "one poetic courier outstrips another," instead of outrunning a herald of prose. All which is bombastic sublimity, and withal very pertinent to the Reviewer's great object no doubt.

But when he arrives at the argument in the Examination, which is based on the very thing here contended for, that is, so far as the question of *poetic character* is concerned, then forsooth, neither Mr. Hopkins, nor Professor Johnson, with all our critical acumen, our knowledge of Hebrew, (after it 's translated into English,) and of Josephus and the Rabbins, "knows enough of Hebrew *prosody*, to be able to affirm that this passage *is poetry*."

If then, kind reader, in our further humble endeavors to follow the Professor, we shall in some instances fairly lose our way, we must not be regarded as worthy of stripes and imprisonment. It is not, in fact, always easy to look after a writer who is bent on maintaining all sides of the question.

We come, then, to the annihilation of the sixth argument of the Examination. This, as the reader will find, (see Bib. Rep. p. 117,) is, " the absence of all knowledge of any such event, preserved either by history or tradition, in any part of the world, the utter silence of the whole human race in respect to any such day since time began." This, as it is thought, is impossible, if such a day had ever been. The Noachian Deluge, which destroyed the whole world, is everywhere remembered in the new; but here an event every way as miraculous and as grand, occurring much later and destroying *nobody*, is unknown to *everybody !*

The Reviewer attempts to account for this, by supposing that " the flood left some natural monuments in all parts of the earth, to declare its existence, while the stopping of the sun and moon and the consequent prolongation of the day would leave none." Does this gentleman ask us to believe that the *cause or causes* of this universal knowledge of a flood is the existence of certain marks or effects which it produced in the surface of the globe? Does he gravely assert that the North American Indian, the ancient inhabitants of Mexico, to say nothing of still more barbarous tribes, have had the penetration to spell out the history of the flood, just as the geologist does, from the traces which remain in the rocks, and hills, or in the piles of water-washed pebbles which lie heaped upon the earth's surface? Is he ignorant, that among those nations and tribes which had scarcely the penetration to know any thing of a cause from seeing only the effect, *the fact* of a remembrance of the flood is proof of its existence next to that of sacred writ!

Perhaps we may as well leave this subject here, since, after having showed us how to account for the silence of the world in regard to that event, without being compelled to admit that it never took place, our Professor makes out to fish up a tradition from the profound depths of the past, which he thinks worthy of all acceptation : and shaking the scourge at us for having maintained, as we did in the Examination, that earth was as silent as the grave respecting any such event, he proceeds to bring forth the tradition. This we shall be disposed to regard " a timely delivery ;" the reader shall have it at full length.

" It was fabled that in the far time the chariot of Phœbus was committed for a day to the guidance of his youthful son. The fiery coursers mount the skies with their wonted ardor. Soon aware of the absence of their rightful master, and spurning the authority of puerile ambition, they became more than ever impatient of control. Lifted to so dizzy a height, the untried charioteer becomes weak and at length stiff with fear. The reins slacken upon the backs of the celestial steeds, now full heated by the arduous labors of the morning. At the touch they dash wildly away from the accustomed track, and wander at large over the wide scope of heaven. After coursing through all the region of the fixed stars, thawing from the torpidity of his eternal winter, the serpent that surrounds the pole, frightening the solemn Boötes with the lumber of his huge wagon to an undignified attempt to run, and spreading consternation through all the upper air, they at length come plunging precipitately earthward, and the moon sees with astonishment the horses of her brother taking their diurnal course beneath her own. Earth now becomes sensible of the disorder of heaven. Her clouds first are dissolved in vapor, the mountain tops begin to burn ; the surface every where is dry and cracked; the herbage is withered and parched; the forests, instead of a protecting shade, afford material to the conflagration; cities and nations seem devoted with the general ruin; the fountains are slaked; the rivers decrease; old ocean is contracted in his bed beyond the power of the sea-god to resist, and through the yawning caverns the upper light surprises the gloomy sovereign of the shades and his dusky mate in the abodes of Tartarus. The omnipotent Jupiter now from his lofty throne, consulting the sum of things, sends forth the winged thunderbolt, and strikes the hapless youth at the same time from the chariot and life."

"Here then," adds the Professor, "is a tradition, in which, when we have made due allowance for the exaggerations of licensed antiquity, for the factitious ornaments of poetic imagining," etc., "we shall recognize all the principal features which a tradition of this miracle, (the stopping of the sun and moon,) could be expected to contain. Even for the Deluge, a retributive judgment of heaven so stupendous and awful, even for this we challenge the production of a traditional testimony more clear and satisfactory."

Verily, here is something remarkable. In a tradition, or something else, we scarcely know what to call it, in which the fiery coursers harnessed to the sun are represented as running away with it and dragging it all over the universe of God, the learned Professor can discover the remembrance of the *sun and moon standing still about a whole day!* No marvel that he should put in for " a due allowance for the exaggerations of a licensed antiquity ;" it were well, at the same time, to stipulate for a little allowance for a few things this side of an tiquity.

Well, he evidently thinks much of it; perhaps we do him injustice that we think so little. He can get along by means of it somewhat smoothly with an argument which piled a mountain in his path, around which he saw no way either for himself or any body else. The profound ignorance of a world with respect to any such day since time was, is of itself sufficient to grind an opposite opinion to powder.

Without controversy, there was an imperious demand for something of the kind. Mr. Horne felt this, and therefore it was that he introduced the passage from Herodotus. In the absence of a better he is obliged to rest satisfied with that. But our Reviewer would have us estimate *his* as highly as *he* does. It is no new thing, however, that extreme want should create a value where it would not otherwise have existed. The Bible refers us somewhat particularly to a period where *sheer want* brought an ass's head into market.

The next argument in the Examination our Professor thinks as little of as we do of his tradition, if we may judge from the manner in which he has treated it. He has read, as he informs us, somewhere in the course of his researches after wisdom and knowledge, "that the preposition *'upon'* once gave rise to an elaborate discussion in the British Parliament, to determine whether it meant *before* or *after*." This, as it would seem, is sufficient to satisfy him, that when Joshua, standing at Makkedah, near the close of the day, gave command that the sun and moon should halt "upon Gibeon," *a city lying directly east of him,* he meant only that the sun should stand still either "before" or "after" Gibeon. This does not indeed, "out Strauss Strauss;" for however strange may have been his conceptions in the paroxysms of his folly, he never thought to treat a serious matter with such unblushing levity as is here. However, it was the best disposal of that matter that the nature of the case and the cause to be maintained admitted. The passage which the Professor endeavors to defend, as any one may see, represents Joshua as standing at Makkedah, near the hour of sunset; giving command that the sun should pause upon or over Gibeon, and the moon in the Valley of Ajalon. But Gibeon is east of Makkedah some eighteen or twenty miles; and Ajalon *southeast* nearly the same distance. The *sun* at the hour of the day required by the conditions of the question, must have been northwest from the locality which Joshua is occupying; and the moon, to have been seen at all, must have been just rising over Gibeon. Why did not the Reviewer, at this point, settle the whole difficulty, as he did in his last struggle with v. xv, (to which we shall attend soon,) by picking a flaw in the translation? He might have proved, at least to his *own* mind, if not to his reader's, that the *east* meant *west*, and by *the sun* we should understand *the moon*. We shall find ere we close, as I have just intimated, that he has actually undertaken about as much as this, in the way of Biblical criticism or philological disquisition.

The eighth argument of the Examination was, "This so called miracle, (the stopping of the sun and moon,) is not once referred to in the Scriptures, not once cited by Prophets, Apostles, or any of the sacred penmen. This is incredible on the supposition that such an event actually occurred. Throughout the entire volume of Inspiration, there is a constant recurrence to the recorded events of Scripture—those which were the unquestionable displays of Divine and miraculous power—every historian referring back to manifestations of God's parental care of his people, or to the retributive chastisements of his enemies. But not once is this miracle referred to; not a solitary allusion to the arresting of the luminaries of heaven, that Joshua might have light to make a full end of the enemies of the King."

The reader must not forget, that this miracle, if it ever took place, was second to none recorded in the Bible. A more magnificent display of Divine power, a more grand and sublime example of the power of faith, is not on record anywhere: and yet the Psalmist, in his enumerations of God's miraculous works, (see Ps. 106-107,) not once thought of the event in question. He could sing, "Thou hast brought a vine out of Egypt, Thou hast cast out the heathen and planted it," etc., (see also Ps. 78, passim et per totum,) and not once mention this great work by Joshua. Paul, in his Epistle to the Hebrews, when recounting the triumphs of faith, refers to that of Rahab, and Gideon, and Sampson, and Jephtha; but of Joshua arresting the sun and moon in the heavens, not a word is said! It is not enough to say of this, "it is incredible;" it is altogether improbable, if not impossible.

The only passage in the Bible which can be thought to be a reference to the event in question, is Hab. iii. 11. —"The sun and moon stood still in their habitation." But if this was *literally* so, how shall we understand v. 6 of the same chapter? "He stood and measured the earth; he beheld and drove asunder the nations; and the everlasting mountains were scattered, the perpetua. hills did bow." Did any thing take place *literally* as is represented here? Are there any records found of scattered mountains, nodding hills, etc., etc.? Where shall we look for an event which shall correspond *literally* with the declaration, " he had horns coming out of his hands;" or this, " Thou didst walk through the sea with thine horses?" The fact is, as every reader with plain good sense knows, the whole passage is to be understood as highly figurative and poetic ; and that if we must understand v. 11 as referring to an event which occurred according to *the letter*, then we must look for the time and place where the Almighty was seen walking on glowing coals of fire, carrying a bow and arrows, riding on horses and guiding the prancing chariot. We must use one and the same rule for intepreting v. 6 as v. 11, or any other part of the chapter. No man, in the exercise of his reason, will stretch the line of a literal interpretation on v. 11, then lay it aside and take that which he would apply to metaphor, hyperbole, or some other figure of speech : he must measure all by one rule. Verse 11 is found, as the reader will see by recurring to " the song " which we have taken from the book of Jasher, letter for letter as it stands in Habakkuk. The supposition, then, which we regard as worthy of all acceptation is, that Hab. iii. 11 is not a reference to Joshua x. 12–15, but on the contrary, *is the passage which has been taken up and amplified and magnetized by the author of the book of Jasher, just as we find there*. It is admitted in the Examination, that a single case of clear and indisputable reference in the Bible, to any such event, would settle the question forever; then it is fairly shown that Hab. iii. 11 is *not* a reference, but is the original of the passage in dispute. The Reviewer, at this point of discussion, evidently betrays the feeling, that " dissection " seems likely to happen to *his* cause instead of mine. His irony combined with one or two

awkward attempts at wit, and these set in a frame-work
of misrepresentation, help him over a difficulty of which
he evidently knows not how else to dispose. It is far
easier, he finds, to turn the arguments of his " modern
Daniel " into ridicule, and blow the snuff of suspicion
into the eyes of his reader, than to answer these arguments fairly and manlike.

Let us look at a single instance of misrepresentation.
He endeavors to inspire the posthumous remains of his
cause with something of life and interest, by representing the writer to have said, that " not a single expression in Hab. iii. can be for a moment supposed to have
had reference to an act that ever transpired." By omit-
ting the word " *literally* " in this sentence, he has put
into the writer's mouth what the writer never said, as
any one will see by turning to the passage in question,
where he will find it repeatedly explained, by being
varied several ways in order to prevent being misunderstood. He that can defend his cause only by misrepresentation, has a bad cause to defend.

We do not know who are the readers of the Methodist
Quarterly Review; and consequently cannot tell who
may have read the statement just quoted. We suppose
they are men in search of truth. If so, we are compelled to say, their prospects for finding it in the writings or essays of our Reviewer, are not the brightest,
if we may judge from the specimen of his veracity now
before us. Any man who will take the trouble to inquire
into this matter, who will read carefully the remarks on
this subject found in the January No. of Biblical Repository, 1845, pp. 123–127, will certainly see that we have
said no such thing. The death of utter annihilation had
already settled under the nails of his gasping cause, and
neither stimulants nor galvanism could save it from the

grave, but misrepresentation would prolong its existence a day or two ; and accordingly we have it. This is the whole explanation.

We do most firmly believe and have ever maintained, that all the statements of this chapter, like every thing else, which is truly the word of God, are true ; having fact for their basis, but poetry for their dress. They all refer to, and, in the high colored language of oriental poetry, *describe events which actually took place.* But what were the events ? . This is the question. To what does the sacred penman refer, when he represents the Almighty as walking upon glowing coals of fire ? He did something which the Prophet referred to ; but what was that something ? In like manner, something grand, magnificent and probably miraculous, is referred to in v. 11. "The sun and moon stood still," etc., but what was it ? The Reviewer may say it was one thing ; the author of the Examination may think it was something else ; both admit and both maintain it was *something.* The one contends it was *literally* so ;—the other that if you say this of verse 11, you must say it of the whole poem ; the nodding hills, the trembling mountains, the Lord with bow and arrows, etc., etc. But this would be most absurd. There is therefore not a solitary reference, not an allusion in all the Scripture to any such event as that which the passage from Jasher describes ; wherefore we conclude, for the best of reasons, that no such event occurred.

But the Professor, having vanquished his antagonist, as he thinks, and given a very satisfactory account, at least to himself, of all the arguments with which the passage in Joshua had been assailed, excepting *two*, concludes that even these do not amount to much. After which, and just as he is retiring from the field so man-

fully defended, he brings forward the long promised
" *conjecture.*" It is, that v. 15 should read, " And
Joshua returned and all Israel with him unto the camp
at *Makkedah,*" instead of Gilgal. The Hebrew letters
in " Hagilgallah," he thinks are so nearly like those
which are combined to form the name " Makkedah,"
that some early, careless transcriber mistook the one for
the other. " Alas, master ; for it was borrowed, and is
good for nothing at that !" The reader will find it duly
drawn out in Dr. Clark's commentary upon the passage,
and what will be particularly interesting too, will be the
discovery, that *the tradition* which the Reviewer thinks so
much of was referred to by the Dr. He thought little
of both, however ; he did but name them. It seems to us
not a little remarkable, that he who was so fearfully
alive to everything like speculation or theory, as to be
able to smell the " abstractional intellectualities of
Kant " in all parts of the Examination, and detect, as by
a kind of theological instinct, " Rationalism, skepticism,"
(and what not?) in everything of the kind, *he* it is who
can furnish us with such a " suggestion " as we have
above ! " Hagilgallah," in the Hebrew character, " is
formed of letters so nearly resembling those which are
combined in Makkedah, as to be easily mistaken the one
for the other !"* And the man who says this professes
to understand Hebrew ! He professes, also, a most profound regard for the sacred record, is alive to everything
which shall combine for its defense, and opposed to that
which may serve to shake our confidence in it ! Verily,
the Bible in passing from the hands even of a Strauss,
to those which deal thus freely in " suggestions," made

*The reader may have the benefit of his own eyes on this subject, whether he under-
stand Hebrew or not.   הַגִּלְגָּלָה Haggilgallah for בְּמַקֵּדָה Be-mak-ke-dah !   Marked resemblance, indeed !

up of proposed alterations, is sent in effect, from Herod to Pilate.

We deem it proper here to say, that we have been pained and disgusted with the bombast which everywhere appears in the Review. Could we have persuaded ourselves, that the merits of the question would have been clearly seen by every reader, and that the cause of truth would not in any measure have suffered from our silence, we should not have replied. If we have taken ground which can be maintained, it is *important* ground; if otherwise, the only favor we ask, is, that our position be overthrown by *argument*. We count him a friend and an honorable man, who, with his literary, theological or philological claymore, shall cleave our theory and its arguments from head to heel. But let no one who wishes to be respected, as a scholar, or a gentleman attempt to settle a grave point like that we have now disposed of, by the potent energies of a " WINGED PEGASUS."

The Reviewer, then, is welcome to the unenvied reputation which he may derive from the flippant assurances with which he has closed his labors, viz., that *he* has not " spent ten years of study " on the subject under debate; assurances, gathered, we admit, by implication, but wholly unnecessary. No one who shall read *this* article, will need to be informed of it. He appears already to have reached that round in the ladder of self-exaltation which leads him to infer the success of an enterprise, from the single fact, that he had had the temerity to undertake it. An elevation to which we hope never to attain. And thus we take leave of what is left of the Reviewer.

* 9 7 8 3 3 3 7 8 1 5 4 3 1 *